NUCLEAR RIGHTS/
NUCLEAR WRONGS

NUCLEAR RIGHTS/
NUCLEAR WRONGS

Edited by

Ellen Frankel Paul

Fred D Miller Jr

Jeffrey Paul

and

John Ahrens

BASIL BLACKWELL
for the
Social Philosophy and Policy Center
Bowling Green State University

First Published 1986
Basil Blackwell Limited
108 Cowley Road, Oxford OX4 1JF, England

British Library Cataloguing in Publication Data
Nuclear rights/nuclear wrongs.
  1. Military policy——Moral and ethical aspects
  I. Paul, Ellen Frankel   II. Miller, Fred D.
  III. Paul, Jeffrey   IV. Bowling Green State University.
  Social Philosophy and Policy Center
  172'.42   U22

  ISBN 0-631-14964-3

Library of Congress Cataloging-in-Publication Data
Nuclear rights/nuclear wrongs.

  1. Nuclear warfare——Moral and ethical aspects——
Addresses, essays, lectures.   2. Military policy——Moral
and ethical aspects——Addresses, essays, lectures.
I. Paul, Ellen Frankel.
U263.N759 1986   172'.42   85-26711
ISBN 0-631-14964-3

Typesetting by Katerprint Co. Ltd, Oxford
Printed in Great Britain by Whitstable Litho, Kent

3086 26

CONTENTS

INTRODUCTION

Nuclear warfare is the most terrifying prospect facing the human race today. For the past forty years, the existence of The Bomb has haunted us and confronted us with many questions. What chain of events might unleash a nuclear holocaust? What would be the consequences of a nuclear exchange in terms of suffering, death, destruction, and even climatic catastrophes such as nuclear winter? What does the acronym for our prevailing defense policy, "MAD," stand for: mutually assured deterrence or mutually assured destruction? Even granted that MAD is a bankrupt policy, which alternative policy would prove more effective? Would it be the nuclear freeze or would it be the Strategic Defense Initiative (called the "Star Wars" defense by skeptics)? The exploration of these questions in the news media, television docudramas, public debates, and classroom discussions often combines mindboggling statistics and facts about military hardware with grizzly visions of nuclear nightmare.

This volume adds much needed perspective to the nuclear controversy by examining in a rational and reflective way the basic *moral* questions. As the title NUCLEAR RIGHTS/NUCLEAR WRONGS suggests, there are basically two questions to be asked about modern warfare:

Which defense policies are right, i.e., which uses or threats to use nuclear weapons and other military means are justified on the basis of moral, philosophical reasoning?

Which defense policies are wrong, i.e., prohibited by considerations of moral philosophy?

This collection of essays approaches these questions on several different levels and from different political points of view. It places the questions of nuclear deterrence in the broader framework of the philosophy of defense, examining the morality both of self-defense and of the defense of others. The book as a whole provides a critical overview of all of the important defense options currently under discussion: mutually assured destruction, optimal deterrence, countervalue and counterforce strategies, unilateral arms reduction and disarmament, and the Strategic Defense Initiative. Some of the essays also examine the role of ideology in provoking and perpetuating the arms race, while others examine revolution, terrorism, and popular political movements concerned with defense and arms reduction. Finally, one historical essay explores a question which has continued to haunt the West: do democratic, liberal societies have the moral and cultural resources to defend themselves?

This book is a contribution to the ethical and philosophical dialogue about nuclear warfare. Rather than dogmatically agreeing upon a single approach to the difficult issues of defense policy, the authors represent the entire spectrum of opinion. The authors arrive at quite different conclusions and often argue from divergent moral assumptions. Because all of the essays are persuasively argued by leading scholars in the field, readers will be challenged to reexamine their own assumptions and positions and will gain a fuller appreciation of the rights and wrongs of nuclear warfare.

The Morality of Defense

The first two essays set the stage by addressing fundamental questions about the morality of war.

Eric Mack's piece, "Three Ways to Kill Innocent Bystanders: Some Conundrums Concerning the Morality of War," treats the fundamental moral question, "When is it permissible to kill innocent bystanders?" This question is fundamental for the obvious reason that even the most surgically precise Western nuclear counterattack against Soviet military targets would unavoidably kill many civilians who were in no way responsible for the decisions of their leaders which precipitated the war. Indeed, unless the killing of innocents can be morally justified under certain circumstances, all warfare, even the most defensive in nature, would be indefensible. Mack tackles his task by developing a series of scenarios in which a person can save himself only by taking an action which will result in the death of an innocent bystander. As the plot thickens, it becomes clear that it makes a difference whether the killing of the bystander is intended or merely foreseen, and so Mack makes great use of what is called the Doctrine of Double Effect. But this doctrine will not solve the whole problem, and Mack supplements and modifies it with the Doctrine of Counterforce Defense and the Doctrine of Antecedent Causation. The latter doctrine provides Mack with the key to his solution: that when an agent is presented with an inescapably perilous condition which will inevitably result in a fatal outcome to someone, he should not be held culpable for a choice that in effect selects the victims, as long as their deaths are not his aim. The moral responsibility lies, rather, with the person who created the perilous situation in the first place.

Baruch Brody's essay, "The International Defense of Liberty," is also concerned with a broad theoretical issue. When should a state come to the aid of citizens of another state in order to help the latter defend their liberties against an aggressor? Does a state have obligations to another state when no treaties or obligations of gratitude bind the two states together? Brody proceeds to examine this issue by first looking at instances in which the use of force would be justified on the individual level. He argues that the use of force is always problematical because it seems to violate a right of the person against whom it is used. Thus, a special justification is necessary for the use of force in any particular case: that the person has waived his right to life or bodily integrity; that he has lost his right; that other rights and/or the rights of others take precedence; or that violation of the right is a lesser evil. Upon this base, Brody builds an intricate argument to determine when states are justified in authorizing individuals to use force against others, and when they are obliged to aid in the preservation of the liberties of citizens of other states. He concludes that there are, indeed, cases in which it is legitimate for a state to use force to defend the liberties of others, even if this requires the state to coerce its citizens to some degree by conscription and taxation to pay for the army. Of course, at some point the obligation would break down, as the burden of fighting the other people's war became too onerous.

Defense Policies: Their Morality and Efficacy

The essays in this section of the book are more policy-oriented than those in the first section, but they are also devoted to analyzing policy choices from a moral perspective.

"Nuclear Deterrence and Arms Control: Ethical Issues for the 1980s," by Robert Pfaltzgraff, asks what our defense posture ought to be in an era when the Soviet Union has attained superiority not only in conventional forces (as it did some time ago in the European theater), but also in nuclear force levels. This new reality poses both strategic and ethical problems for the United States and its allies. Pfaltzgraff views the West as torn between the strategic necessity to preserve our offensive nuclear weapons as a deterrent to the Soviets, and the ethical compunctions most Westerners have against ever using such weapons should deterrence fail. Unlike several of our authors, Pfaltzgraff is not unduly pessimistic about the continued success of deterrence. He points out that, forty years after the end of the Second World War, the two superpowers have not gone to war with each other. Also, he fears the United States' deterrent capacity far less than the Soviet strategic buildup that has been going on for the last decade; in this, too, his moral sensibilities differ dramatically from those of some of the other authors in this section. In short, he holds no truck either with the advocates of mutually assured destruction (MAD) or with those who prefer minimal deterrence. The former are too ready to hold Western lives hostage to the mercies of the Soviets, while the latter ignore the emphasis on military superiority in Soviet military doctrine. Pfaltzgraff's preferred course for United States defense policy includes force modernization, arms control as a means to build support for modernization, and deterrence based on enhanced survival rather than mutual destruction. Thus, he looks approvingly on the Reagan Administration's Strategic Defense Initiative.

"Optimal Deterrence" is the title of a piece by Steven Brams and Marc Kilgour, who employ game theory to discover how the West ought to defend itself. The authors start by highlighting the supposed absurdity which underlies the policy of deterrence by the superpowers. Deterrence is controversial because many people fail to see why a country that was attacked would carry out its threat to visit destruction on its attacker: they argue that it would be irrational to do so because this would precipitate another round of attack and counterattack. Many people wonder why it wouldn't be more rational for the aggrieved party simply to absorb the blow and refuse to escalate the conflict. From an analysis which starts out deceptively simply – with a discussion of the game of Chicken – Brams and Kilgour conclude that making threats is the optimal way of playing the superpower game. "Coupling a no-first-use policy with robust threats, appears to us the best one can do in a world that seems to make superpower confrontations unavoidable." Mutual deterrence by the superpowers is the policy most invulnerable to misperceptions or miscalculations by the players. The authors prefer to read the acronym MAD as mutually assured *deterrence*, rather than *destruction*.

David Hoekema's "The Moral Status of Nuclear Deterrent Threats" is concerned with the same paradox that puzzles Brams and Kilgour, but his conclusion differs radically from theirs. What makes a policy of deterrence so horrifying, and so philosophically interesting is that, in order to achieve an inestimable good (the avoidance of a nuclear war that could destroy mankind), we must threaten to do incalculable harm (visit destruction on any adversary who attacks us with nuclear weapons). Hoekema proceeds by examining some general principles concerning the morality of threats. He concludes that the moral case for threatening a nuclear attack – whether as a first-strike or in retaliation – must inevitably fail. While the threat to use conventional weapons of war in retaliation for an attack may be justified, nuclear weapons possess such an awesome capacity for destruction that the threat to use them cannot be justified. The implication of Hoekema's reasoning is that our nuclear weapons should be dismantled and that we should rely on several thousand highly accurate conventional weapons which we could threaten to use against an enemy's cities and military bases.

Steven Lee is also concerned with the paradoxical features of nuclear deterrence. In his piece, "Morality and Paradoxical Deterrence," he scrutinizes some of these paradoxes, and principally one that he calls the "rationality paradox": while it is rational to threaten nuclear retaliation, it would not be rational to carry out the threat; but what would not be rational to do is not rational to threaten to do. Nuclear warfare also generates *moral* paradoxes in addition to this *prudential* paradox. The only real way out of these paradoxes, Lee thinks, is nuclear disarmament. He fears that the new trend towards counterforce targeting (i.e., the targeting of an enemy's military and command structures), because it makes nuclear war more thinkable, is even worse than the old deterrence based on mutual destruction (or countervalue targeting, the targeting of an enemy's cities). The latter at least had the curious virtue of making war so horrific that it no longer seemed a rational means of pursuing national advantage.

In "Conflicting Conceptions of Deterrence," Henry Shue reflects upon and finds wanting the position of those who, like Albert Wohlstetter and Robert Pfaltzgraff, argue for a modernization of our offensive nuclear weapons to enhance their accuracy and the erection of a defensive "shield" of the Star Wars variety. Shue fears that this policy would destroy any hope there still might be of avoiding nuclear war. The Wohlstetter position favors counterforce targeting, on the assumption that such a policy of aiming at military and command structures of the enemy would minimize casualities, especially when compared to countervalue targeting. Shue doubts that this view is based on solid evidence; even in counterforce targeting, he contends, enormous numbers of innocents will be slaughtered. In fact, he seems highly skeptical about whether any deterrence strategy can ever be morally accept-able. Perhaps a counterforce capability with a low ceiling on quantity might just barely squeak through. This would avoid an endless arms buildup because each country would not feel that it had to match an increase by the other. Thus, the relentless competition endemic to a counterforce posture like Wohlstetter's could be avoided. Under such a limited counterforce doctrine, America's nuclear arsenal might be safely reduced by 90 per cent. Thus, Shue sees himself in something of a compromise position between those who argue that a limited force of perhaps two thousand warheads is not enough militarily and those who contend that it is too much morally.

Douglas Lackey's "Immoral Risks: A Deontological Critique of Nuclear Deterrence," is another critique of nuclear deterrence which finds the posture generally indefensible. Instead of employing a utilitarian moral principle to examine the morality of nuclear deterrence (i.e., a principle that looks to the outcome of actions and judges them moral if the good produced outweighs the bad), Lackey takes a deontological perspective (i.e., he examines the rightfulness of the actions themselves). In an earlier piece Lackey took the utilitarian tack, and he now laments the fact that so few of his critics were convinced by his argument that a nuclear war which might arise under an American nuclear deterrence policy would be at least fifteen times more deadly than one which might occur under an American policy of unilateral disarmament. Given the recent evidence on nuclear winter – the phenomenon of a large-scale nuclear war producing so much soot in the atmosphere that the sun's rays would be blocked out sufficiently to devastate the planet – Lackey feels that his old argument is even stronger today. In this essay, Lackey proceeds to examine nuclear deterrence as a risk management procedure in which the United States attempts to reduce the risk of a nuclear attack to itself by increasing the risk of an American attack on others. Construed in this way, America's deterrent posture appears morally dubious: Americans have inflicted risks on others who have in no way consented to them. In contrast to Pfaltzgraff, Lackey is much concerned about the risks of deterrence, and finds myopic the typical American's exclusive focus on the risk from Soviet missiles should deterrence fail.

Democracy, Dictatorship, and War

The essays in this section try to place the issues of defense policy in a broader perspective, relating them to the values and beliefs of democracy and Marxism–Leninism.

Aaron Wildavsky, in "No War without Dictatorship, No Peace without Democracy: Foreign Policy as Domestic Politics," begins by exploring the connection between opposition to American foreign policy and opposition to the political and economic system of the United States. In the earlier post-War years, America was not faced with substantial numbers of internal critics who felt alienated from its democratic system; but today it is. And this fact makes it enormously difficult to arrive at any consensus about how American foreign policy should proceed. If the American system is so morally defective, why defend it? And so America's critics are perpetually suspicious of the motives of its leaders in the foreign arena. Those who feel alienated from American society also tend to attribute benign intent to the Soviet Union, and this too makes the policy maker's task more difficult than it used to be. Wildavsky holds a position antithetical to the dissidents. He believes that there is an ineluctable connection between Marxist–Leninist regimes and warlike behavior and intentions. Marxism and militarism, he claims, go hand in hand. In contrast, democratic regimes do not make war on each other. Wherein, then, lies mankind's hope for avoiding a nuclear war? Principally, Wildavsky thinks, in a moral vision which looks to the pluralization of the Soviet Union, not to the weakening of the defense postures of the democracies. He concludes with two aphorisms: without dictatorship there is no war; without democracy there is no peace.

Paul Seabury's paper, "Marxism–Leninism and its Strategic Implications for the United States," is in many ways complementary to Wildavsky's. Seabury explores the implications of Marxist–Leninist ideology for Western defense policy and for United States strategic policy in particular. He begins by bemoaning the fact that Americans have not taken Marxism–Leninism seriously as an ideology. Ideas do have consequences, Seabury argues, and we ignore the connection between Marxist ideology and practice at our peril. The Soviets still adhere to Lenin's adaptation of the German military theorist Karl Von Clausewitz's dictum that war is a continuation of politics by the addition of other means. Lenin reversed the dictum: politics is a continuation of war by other means. In times of war as well as in times of peace, the Soviet Union operates on a war footing. Thus, Marxist–Leninist regimes throughout the world are great garrison states. Also, they are expansionist states which constantly seek to spread their ideology to other countries, particularly to Third World nations.

"Tocqueville on War" is Eliot Cohen's attempt to take a giant step back from the fray and gain some perspective on warfare and democracy by examining the thoughts of Alexis de Tocqueville, the nineteenth-century French political theorist and observer of the American scene. In his *Democracy in America* (1835–1840), Tocqueville had some important insights into the relationship between democracy and defense that have too often, Cohen believes, escaped the attention of contemporary writers on the subject. A Tocquevillian approach to problems of contemporary military strategy would point us in new directions. It might suggest institutional reforms that would lead to the creation of a more coherent strategic culture. Rather than searching for narrow, technological solutions to the problem of limited war such as Vietnam, it might suggest that we first must understand the relationship between civil and military cultures; it would emphasize the intimate link between strategic difficulties and institutional pressures.

The essays in this book should provide some needed perspective on the issues of the defense of the Western democracies in general and nuclear defense in particular. A fuller appreciation of the moral rights and wrongs of alternative defense policies will, we hope, lead to wiser decision making in the future.

CONTRIBUTORS

Eric Mack is Associate Professor of Philosophy at Tulane University. His research interests involve topics in moral, political, and legal philosophy. Among his recent articles are: "In Defence of Blackmail," in *Philosophical Studies*; "The Moral Basis of National Defense," in *Defending a Free Society*, ed. R. Poole; "Deontologism, Negative Causation and the Duty to Rescue," in Gewirth's *Ethical Rationalism*, ed. E. Regis; and "The Ethics of Taxation: Rights versus Public Goods?" forthcoming in *Taxation and Capital Formation*, ed. D. Lee.

Baruch A. Brody is the Leon Jaworski Professor of Biomedical Ethics at Baylor College of Medicine and Professor of Philosophy at Rice University. His most recent books include *Identity and Essense* (Princeton University Press: 1981) and *Ethics and Its Applications* (Harcourt Brace Jovanovich: 1983). He is currently working on a book entitled *Beyond Paternalism and Autonomy*.

Robert L. Pfaltzgraff, Jr., is Shelby Cullom Davis Professor of International Security Studies at the Fletcher School of Law and Diplomacy, Tufts University, and President of the Institute for Foreign Policy Analysis, Inc., Cambridge, MA., and Washington, DC. His most recent publications include *International Security Dimensions of Space* (1983), and *National Security: The Decision-Making Process* (1984).

Steven J. Brams is Professor of Politics at New York University. His recent books include *Superpower Games: Applying Game Theory to Superpower Conflict* (1985), *Superior Beings: If They Exist, How Would we Know? Game-Theoretic Implications of Omniscience, Omnipotence, Immortality, and Incomprehensibility* (1983), and, with Peter C. Fishburn, *Approval Voting* (1983).

D. Marc Kilgour is Associate Professor of Mathematics and Chairman of the Department of Mathematics at Wilfrid Laurier University (Canada). His research interests include mathematical modeling, especially using game theory, and his recent articles have appeared in *Canadian Journal of Political Science*, *Public Choice*, and *Theory and Decision*. Research on his article with Steven J. Brams in this volume was done while he was Visiting Associate Professor in the Department of Systems Design, University of Waterloo, during 1984–85.

David Hoekema is the Executive Secretary of the American Philosophical Association and Assistant Professor of Philosophy at the University of Maryland. His publications in this area include "Intentions, Threats and Nuclear Deterence" in *The Applied Turn in Contemporary Philosophy* (Bowling Green State University 1983).

Steven Lee is an Associate Professor of Philosophy at Hobart and William Smith Colleges. He is co-editor (with Avner Cohen) of *Nuclear Weapons and the Future of Humanity: The Fundamental Questions* (Totowa, NJ: Rowman and Allanheld, 1985) and author of "The Morality of Nuclear Deterrence: Hostage Holding and Consequences" in *Ethics* 95. In addition, he has published in the areas of philosophy of law, social philosophy, and action theory.

Henry Shue is Senior Research Associate at the Center for Philosophy and Public Policy at the University of Maryland at College Park where he is the principal investigator examining the moral aspects of three proposed departures from the continuing counterforce buildup: the defensive transition, finite deterrence, and prompt rejection of nuclear forces. He is in the early stages of a monograph with the working title, *The World's Last Night*. Best known for his defense of core economic rights in *Basic Rights: Subsistence, Affluence, and U.S. Foreign Policy* (Princeton, 1980), he has recently published articles including "The Burdens of Justice" and "Subsistence Rights."

Douglas P. Lackey was a student of J. N. Findly at Yale and is currently Professor of Philosophy at Baruch College and the Graduate Center, City University of New York. His publication in this area include the articles, "Ethics and Nuclear Deterrence" (1975), "Missiles and Morals" (1982), and "Disarmament Revisited" (1983). His book, *Moral Principles and Nuclear Weapons* was published by Rowman and Allanheld in 1984.

Aaron Wildavsky is Professor of Political Science and Public Policy at the University of California, Berkeley. He is the author of *The Nursing Father: Moses as a Political Leader* and (with Mary Douglas) *Risk and Culture*. He has edited and contributed to *Beyond Containment: Alternative American Policies Toward the Soviet Union*.

Paul Seabury is currently Professor of Political Science, University of California, Berkeley, specializing in U.S. foreign policy problems. He is co-author, with Professor Walter McDugal, of the *Grenada Papers* published by the Institute for Contemporary Studies in 1984.

Eliot A. Cohen is an Assistant Professor of Government at Harvard University, from which he received his B.A. and Ph.D. degrees. Next year he will be a Visiting Associate Professor of Strategy at the U.S. Naval War College in Newport, Rhode Island. His most recent book is *Citizens and Soldiers: The Dilemmas of Military Service* (Ithica: Cornell University Press, 1985), and he has published numerous articles on defense issues in *inter alia, International Security, Foreign Affairs, Commentary*, and *The Public Interest*.

Social Philosophy & Policy 3:1 Autumn 1985 ISSN 0265-0525 $2.00

THREE WAYS TO KILL INNOCENT BYSTANDERS: SOME CONUNDRUMS CONCERNING THE MORALITY OF WAR

Eric Mack

I. INTRODUCTION

This essay deals with the hard topic of the permissible killing of the innocent. The relevance of this topic to the morality of war is obvious. For even the most defensive and just wars, i.e., the most defensive and just responses to existing or imminent large-scale aggression, will inflict harm upon – in particular, cause the deaths of – innocent bystanders.[1] The most obvious and relevant example is that of innocent Soviet noncombatants who would be killed by even the most precise defensive strike against Soviet strategic weapons or troop formations that is now possible. Should there be no vindication or, at least, no excuse for some killings of such innocent bystanders, morality would dictate that even defensive counterforce measures against largescale attacks should be renounced.

This conclusion holds even if one accepts a moderately permissive right of self-defense. A narrow right of self-defense would allow the defender to use harmful force only against a *guilty* aggressor. Such a legitimate target would be a person who intentionally or recklessly initiates (or aids in the initiation of) a threat against the defender. A moderately permissive right of self-defense would also allow the defender to use harmful force against an *innocent* aggressor. Thus, on this slightly more expansive view, a defender could use force against a person who under duress or under the influence of a delusion initiates (or aids in the initiation of) a threat against the defender. Indeed, this moderately permissive right seems as permissive as any coherent right of self-defense can be. For insofar as an act is *an act of defense*, it must be directed at an aggressive threat. Insofar as an act strikes out at nonaggressors, its status as a defensive act is at least questionable. So, it seems that the

---

* For their listening, criticisms, and suggestions, I am indebted to Mary Sirridge, the participants in the Tulane Philosophy Department research seminar, and the editors of *Social Philosophy and Policy*.

[1] Of course, not all bystanders are innocent – just as not all innocents are bystanders. This is so obvious that I shall permit myself to speak of killing bystanders and killing innocents and allow the context to reaffirm that what is always meant is killing innocent bystanders (or bystanders whose guilt does not render it permissible to kill them). For a vindication of grouping innocent aggressors, but not guilty bystanders, with guilty aggressors, see Jeffrie Murphy, "The Killing of the Innocent," *The Monist*, vol. 57 (Spring 1973).

most one could expect from the right to self-defense in itself would be a vindication of the defensive harming or killing of aggressors. By itself, this right of self-defense does not speak to the morality or permissibility of killing innocent bystanders. Something beyond the invocation of this right is needed to vindicate actions which kill such bystanders and, thus, to support any likely real-world defense against large-scale attacks.

In the absence of such a further justification, we would have to adopt the quasi-pacifism of allowing very small-scale defense but no large-scale defense. This quasi-pacifism, which will be required of us if no killings of innocents are permissible, i.e., if one cannot supplement the moderately permissive right of self-defense, constitutes only one horn of the intellectual dilemma. The other horn is a commitment to the permissibility of the direct and intentional sacrifice of some people's lives for the sake of the lives or liberties of others. In searching for some principle which permits the killing of bystanders, we may find ourselves driven onto this second horn. The problem is to find a coherent and principled path between the over-restriction of the first horn and the moral license of the second.

To get a preliminary fix on the philosophical task at hand and on the character and appeal of a couple of proposed solutions, I will consider a series of cases in which the only action by which a person facing attack or other grievous danger may save herself will itself cause the death of an innocent. (For each case it is assumed that the individuals are "strangers" to one another, i.e., have no special ties or responsibilities, and that Alice, our recurring agent, knows the specified facts of the case.)

Case 1 Alfred is about to dislodge a boulder. Despite Alfred's careful inspection of the hillside below, he does not realize that the rapidly accelerating boulder will kill Alice unless she takes action. But Alice is well-camouflaged and immobilized, and she can prevent this catastrophe only by firing her bazooka at Alfred.

Case 2 Alfred is about to dislodge a boulder which will accelerate down the hillside and kill Alice unless she fires her bazooka at Alfred. Unfortunately, if the bazooka is fired at Alfred, the explosion will also kill Auberon, who happens to be walking just behind Alfred.

Case 3 Alfred is about to dislodge a boulder, etc. Unfortunately, Alfred himself is out of the line of fire of Alice's bazooka. However, Alice can use her bazooka to kill Alyosha, Alfred's beloved son, who is not participating in anyway in the dislodging of the boulder. Killing Alyosha will distract Alfred from dislodging the boulder, and only in this way can Alice thwart Alfred's "attack."

Case 4 Alice and Allen are victims of a dreadful kidney infection. The only way for them to survive is for each to receive a transplant of one of Alyosha's kidneys. Unfortunately, removing both healthy kidneys from Alyosha will kill him.

In Case 1, the person whom Alice must kill in order to eliminate the threat to her life is not an innocent *bystander*. Although innocent, Alfred is nevertheless the source of the danger to Alice. It is his activity which threatens Alice's life. It is a presumption of this paper that the right to self-defense is at least moderately permissive. It encompasses a right to defend oneself against others even when their threatening activity is innocent, i.e., not intentional or culpably reckless or negligent. Part of the reason for including Case 1 is to remind us of this presumption.

In Case 2, Alice's action (Act 2, the incidental killing of Auberon) does involve the killing of a bystander. I begin this essay with the sense that, tragic as such an action would be, Alice's self-defensive action against Alfred remains permissible even though this action also (incidentally) yields the death of a bystander. I also take it that most observers – especially most nonpacifists – share this sense of the permissibility of Act 2. In contrast, I begin this essay with the sense that Act 3 (wherein Alice thwarts Alfred's "attack" by killing Alyosha) is much harder to accept as morally permissible. I take it that many observers – including many, if not most, who have the sense that Act 2 is permissible – would like to be able to judge it ethically impermissible to thwart Alfred's "attack" by means of killing Alyosha.

Case 4 is presented at this early point to counteract any temptation which the reader might feel to move from the acceptance of Act 2 to the acceptance of Act 3. For it seems that if it is permissible for Alice to kill Alyosha in order to distract Alfred (Act 3), it is also permissible for Alice (or Allen) to kill Alyosha in order to get hold of his kidneys (Act 4). A major part of the motivation for drawing the moral line between actions like 2 and actions like 3 lies in the difficulty of accepting as morally permissible actions like 3 without also accepting actions like 4. One wants to draw the crucial moral line between, on the one hand, defensive acts which incidentally kill bystanders (Act 2) and, on the other hand, responses to danger which proceed by intentionally killing innocents. For only this distinction will allow us an escape from quasi-pacifism while not carrying us over into the moral cannibalism exemplified by the expropriation of Alyosha's bodily organs.

The goal of this essay is to provide a theoretical justification for this intuitive sense of a crucial moral difference between Act 2 and Act 3.[2]

What implication does this distinction have for warfare between nations? If the sort of incidental killing in the course of self-defense which is exemplified in Act 2 is permissible, this strongly suggests the permissibility of defensive counterforce strikes. Admittedly, these strikes will be deadly to many innocent bystanders, especially the most innocent bystanders of all: children with the misfortune of residing in the Soviet Union. In contrast, if the sort of killing of bystandes exemplified in Act 3 is impermissible, this strongly suggests the impermissibility of defensive countervalue strikes of the sort represented by a Mutual Assured Destruction strategy.

The structure of this essay is essentially dialectical. In Part II, I focus on the Doctrine of Double Effect. I defend the coherence and moral significance of that doctrine's distinction between intended and (merely) foreseen consequences. But I also point to probiems stemming from the unrestricted application of this distinction – in particular, from its application outside the context of defensive action. In response to these problems, I examine, in Part III, a doctrine that centers on the right to self-defense, *viz.*, the Doctrine of Counterforce Defense. Counterforce Defense employs the intended vs. foreseen distinction from the Doctrine of Double Effect only for the limited purpose of vindicating defensive activities which have the deaths of bystanders among their foreseen, but not intended, consequences.

The range of permissible killings of bystanders generated by this Doctrine of Counterforce Defense will turn out to be too narrow. There are some cases of the permissible (forseen, but unintended) killing of bystanders which cannot be construed as exercises of a right of defense. This defect with Counterforce Defense, which makes it less than a full account of the permissible killing of innocents, will lead to the position developed in Part IV: the Doctrine of Antecedent Causation. Like Counterforce Defense, but unlike Double Effect, Antecedent Causation insists that it is only within some special context of action that some unintended (but foreseen) killings of bystanders are permissible. However, this special context of action extends beyond cases of attack by other persons.

The body of this paper will, I hope, give substance and meaning to this introductory indication of its structure.

---

[2] As such an account develops and illuminates the specific judgments which it takes as its preliminary data, we can be more secure in those initial judgments and more confident about extending those judgments to initially more puzzling cases (or pairs of cases). (It is because the development of such a justifying account is already in progress that, later in this paper, I permit myself less guarded judgments about particular cases.) And these more extensive judgments themselves can credibly guide refinements in the theoretical account. The hope, of course, is that the judgments and the justifying account will enjoy sufficient independent plausibility that they will reinforce one another, and not just be two ways of proclaiming the same prejudices.

II. THE DOCTRINE OF DOUBLE EFFECT

The moral line which I have drawn between Case 2 (in which bystanders are incidentally killed) and Case 3 (in which the killing of bystanders is essential to the defense's strategy) is the very line endorsed by adherents of Double Effect (DE) and of its instantiation in Just War Theory. Perhaps, then, DE is the correct *basis* for this distinction. A crucial component in DE is, of course, the claim that an effect of an action which would render an action morally impermissible were it intended may leave the action permissible if that effect is foreseen but not intended.

In Case 2, for instance, the intended effect of Alice's firing her bazooka is the incapacitation of Alfred (or the death of Alfred or the saving of her life or the protection of her life against Alfred's "aggression." The second (hence, "double") and foreseen but not intended effect is the death of Auberon. According to a standard application of DE, Alice's action would be impermissible if this second effect were intended. This is precisely the situation in Case 3: the second effect, Alyosha's death, is intended, if not as an end-in-itself, at least as a means to Alice's end of incapacitating Alfred. And, precisely because it is intended, the resulting death of an innocent bystander renders Act 3 impermissible. In Case 2, Alice does not do something to Auberon *in order to* prevent her own death. But in Case 3 she does something to Alyosha precisely in order to prevent her own death. And similarly, in Case 4, Alyosha's death would be a result of something that is done to him in order to save the lives of Alice and Allen.

It is not an easy matter to say what lies behind the plausibility of DE. The key idea is that what one is doing (or what one is characterized as doing for the purpose of moral evaluation) is crucially determined by what one's intention is. So, in firing her bazooka at Alyosha (in Act 3) Alice would be engaged in killing an innocent bystander, bringing about an innocent bystander's death, in a way in which she is not engaged when she fires her bazooka at Alfred (Act 2). The two killings are different in kind because their intended effects are different in kind. The intended effect of an action is not what the agent happens to envisage at the moment of action. Rather, it is the goal which calls forth and contours the agent's action. Thus, it is characterized as a "direct" effect of the action: it is that toward which the act is directed. In contrast, the "second" effect is incidental to the action, in that it plays no role in calling it forth or guiding its structure. The agent would act in precisely the same way even if the second effect were not an upshot of her activity. Incidental as it is to the action and its structure, the unintended effect is merely an "indirect" effect of that action.

For instance, Alice's firing at Alfred (Act 2) is not done at all in response to the presence of Auberon. But quite the contrary is true vis-à-vis Alyosha if

Alice chooses to save her life in the circumstances described in Case 3. In Case 2, Alice faces the prospect of indirectly killing Auberon, while in Case 3, she faces the prospect of directly killing Alyosha. Further, advocates of DE will often distinguish cases in terms of whether or not an agent's action would involve the death of the bystander as either a means or an end. Alyosha's death would be the means by which Alice saves herself from being killed (Case 3) and the means by which Alice and Allen are saved (Case 4), while it seems natural to say that Auberon's death would not be a means by which Alice saves herself (Case 2).

DE has been subject to a number of well-known criticisms. One crucial family of criticisms centers on the question of what the criteria are for an effect to be intended rather than merely foreseen. Suppose that, in defense of Alice's firing the bazooka in Case 3, it is suggested that all that Alice intends is that Alfred be distracted. At most, she intends to accomplish this by confronting Alfred with a vivid presentation of Alyosha being exploded. She by no means intends, according to this suggestion, that Alyosha *be* exploded. She fires the bazooka, not to explode Alyosha, but to traumatize Alfred from the experience of seeing Alyosha being exploded – an experience which Alice would prefer to be non veritable. Similarly, it might be argued that, in Case 4, the intended means is simply the removal of Alyosha's kidneys. Alice and Allen would certainly prefer that Alyosha not die as a result.[3] Clearly, if DE permits such defenses for killing Alyosha, it is useless for drawing the moral lines which its advocates endorse.

Now, perhaps there is something fishy about this defense of Act 3 which has been attributed to the advocate of DE. For the fact of the matter in Case 3 is that Alice can only create the impression of Alyosha's being exploded *by exploding him*. So her means to the intermediate end of creating this impression is to explode Alyosha. She will aim at Alyosha, making sure that the explosive shell really enters his body. If so, the friend of DE can reject the imputation that he must allow Act 3. But the critic of DE may fall back to a more general argument. This critic may begin by proposing that, in the spirit of DE, we distinguish between intending to blow up Alyosha and intending to kill him and between intending to remove Alyosha's kidneys

---

[3] In seeking to allow certain abortions traditionally disallowed under DE, Germain Grisez has argued that an effect is not intended as long as an alternative course of action which had the same acknowledged effect and lacked the putatively merely foreseen effect would have been pursued, if it had been available. For instance, if a woman having an abortion would have placed the fetus in an artificial womb were one available, then the death of the fetus from the actual abortion is not intended. (Grisez means to imply – probably correctly – that for most actual abortions the artificial womb would not be exploited. Thus, for Grisez, most fetal deaths remain intended.) But this criterion surely seems to imply that the death of Alyosha in Cases 3 and 4 is unintended. And these implications cannot be welcomed by Grisez or any advocate of DE. See his "Toward a Consistent Natural-Law Ethics of Killing," *American Journal of Jurisprudence*, vol. 15 (1970).

and intending to kill him. The critic then points out that, if we make these distinctions, the advocate of DE should allow Acts 3 and 4 as much as he allows Act 2. Now the critic does not expect his proposal to be accepted. Rather, he expects that, in seeking to reject it, the advocate of DE will blunder. Specifically, he expects that in insisting that Alyosha's death in Cases 3 and 4 is really intended the advocate of DE will (unintentionally) commit himself to the intentional status of Auberon's death in Case 2. For it is anticipated that the advocate of DE will assert something like the following: An upshot is intended by Alice if it is caused by, and closely causally connected to, something which Alice brings about as a means or an end, and Alice is (reasonably ?) aware of this connection.[4] On the basis of such a proposal, the advocate of DE could classify Alyosha's death (in Case 3 and 4) as intended and, thus, as impermissible. But, the critic is ready to point out that, on the same basis, Auberon's death in Case 2 would count as intended and impermissible. Thus, the critic hopes to conclude, DE does not succeed at allowing us to escape the moral cannibalism of Act 4 without embracing the quasi-pacifism entailed by condemning Act 2.

Let us assess this critical move. The advocate of DE must acknowledge that the anticipated objective which guides and structures Act 4 is not Alyosha's death but, rather, the removal of his kidneys. Must the advocate of DE maintain, then, that what differentiates Act 4 from Act 2 is that there is greater causal proximity between the removal of Alyosha's kidneys and Alyosha's death than there is between the destruction of aggressor Alfred and the death of bystander Auberon? If degree of causal proximity is the crucial variable for the advocate of DE, the DE is in big trouble. For it is difficult to imagine how degrees of causal proximity can be measured, and it is equally difficult to see how this mere difference in degree should yield such a dramatic difference in kind between permissible and impermissible killings.

I believe, however, that the friend of DE can avoid this precarious reliance upon claims about relative causal closeness. Consider the following two cases:

> Case 3' This case is the same as Case 3, except that Alice's bazooka fires a shell which creates the visual image of Alyosha being blown to bits. This will distract Alfred. Unfortunately, the burst of the shell (which will occur x yards from Alyosha) will knock Alyosha down and, thereby, cause his death.

[4] See Philippa Foot, "The Problem of Abortion and the Doctrine of Double Effect," J. Rachels, ed., *Moral Problems*, 2nd ed., (New York: Harper and Row, 1975) pp. 61–62.

Case 3* This case is the same as 3′, except that Alice's shell will only produce a convincing image of Alyosha's being blown to bits if it explodes within x yards of Alyosha, and an explosion of that proximity is sure to knock Alyosha down and, thereby, cause his death. Thus, Alice's aim must track Alyosha's movements.

Case 3′ is awfully close to Case 2, for it is designed to make Alyosha's death incidental to Alice's action in the same way that Auberon's death is in Case 2. The friend of DE should allow action 3′. Case 3*, in turn, is awfully close to 3′. In particular, the causal distance between the (tactical) end which guides Act 3′ and Alyosha's death is precisely the same as the causal distance between the (tactical) end which guides Act 3* and Alyosha's death. Morally it seems correct to assimilate 3′, in which Alyosha's death is incidental to creating the impression of his death, to Act 2. However, morally it seems correct to assimilate 3*, in which Alyosha's death is the means by which the action proceeds, to Act 3. If this is correct, a moral difference exists which is associated with the incidental vs. intended death distinction, and which does *not* depend upon differences in causal proximity.

Accounting for this moral difference between 3′ and 3* requires a restatement of certain of the notions which underlie DE. In 3′, Alice's intended means is the explosion of a bazooka shell which, because of the image thereby projected, will distract Alfred. Her intended means, her (tactical) end, does not require her to do anything to Alyosha. Certainly, what she intends is not a violation of Alyosha's rights. (This is to say more than that she does not intend to violate Alyosha's rights. Presumably, even the most bloodthirsty murderers do not usually have the violation of rights as their guiding purpose.) But in 3*, Alice's intended means is the explosion of the bazooka shell within x yards of Alyosha. It is this (intermediate) goal which structures her action. Alice makes use of Alyosha's presence, and his endangerment is encompassed within Alice's plan of action. Exploding a bazooka shell within x yards of someone (when x is small), is doing something to that person. Indeed, it is doing something which violates that person's rights. Similarly, the physician in Case 4 intentionally does something to Alyosha – something which violates Alyosha's right to, let us call it, his bodily integrity.[5] The advocate of DE seems to be in pretty good

---

[5] The language of doing something to a person in order to deal with a threat versus doing something to (or with) the threat follows Judith Thomson in her wonderfully provocative "Killing, Letting Die and The Trolley Problem," *The Monist*, vol. 59 (Spring, 1976). One of the most suggestive points in favour of DE is how philosophers who do not want to be advocates of it, such as Thomson (and myself), find themselves returning to pronouncements which look to all the world like formulations of DE. (For Thomson's rejection of DE, see her "Rights and Deaths," *Philosophy and Public Affairs*, vol. 2 (Winter 1973).

shape if he holds that something that person A undergoes counts as an evil intended effect of person B's action if and only if: (i) under a description which explains the timing and structure of B's activity, that activity is a violation of A's rights; and (ii) what A undergoes is a violation of his rights or is a standard result of that violation of rights.[6]

A further pair of examples may be helpful both to clarify further the moral difference between intended and (merely) foreseen consequences and to emphasize that the question of whether or not an untoward effect is intended is not a matter of its causal proximity to what clearly is intended. Consider one sort of deflection case discussed by Phillipa Foot and Judith Thomson.[7] A passenger on a runaway trolley with a dead driver must decide whether to allow the trolley to continue on its present track and, thereby, strike and kill five innocent people stuck on that track, or to turn the trolley onto another track and, thereby, have it strike one innocent person stuck on that track. Thomson, and advocates of DE (and possibly, Foot), allow the passenger to turn the trolley. And advocates of DE, at least, assert that the death of the one person would be unintended, albeit foreseen. Now, the critic of DE might argue that all that lies behind this assertion is the causal distance between the (unproblematically intended) turning of the trolley's wheel (or the trolley's actual movement onto the alternative track) and the death of the one individual. This causal distance is indicated by the fact that it would not be causally fantastic for the trolley to be turned and yet, due to unusual circumstances, the death of that innocent person not occur.

But, against this critic, it is easy to imagine other examples in which: (i) there is much more causal distance (as this is intuitively sensed) between what is unproblematically intended and an untoward effect; and yet, (ii) *this* more distant effect is intended while, and in a way in which, the causally closer untoward effect in the trolley case is not. Consider a variant on the usual organ transplant cases. Person A's vital organs are needed in order to save the lives of B, C, D, E, and F. But A's organs need not, indeed, let us suppose, cannot be personally removed by the attending physician. Rather, the physician needs to press a button to set in motion an assembly line which will create a robot to harvest the vital organs from A. There is more causal distance (as this is intuitively sensed) between the physician's pressing that button and A's loss of his vital organs than there is between the passenger's turning the

<hr>

[6] Any theory of responsibility for harm that does not have bizarre implications needs something like a distinction between standard and non-standard (or proximate and non-proximate) results. If Alice can distract Alfred only by chopping off Alyosha's finger and proceeds to do so for that reason, then Alyosha's loss of his (rightfully held) finger is intended. But if this loss leads to Alyosha's death only through a highly circuitous, non-standard, and lengthy causal route, then Alice cannot be said to have violated Alyosha's right to life.

[7] These cases are discussed throughout "The Problem of Abortion and the Doctrine of Double Effect" and "Killing, Letting Die and the Trolley Problem."

trolley and the death of the innocent person stuck on the track. But it remains true that A's loss of his vital organs is the physician's intended means, while neither the immobilized person's death nor his being struck by the trolley is the trolley passenger's intended means. At issue here is the question of whether or not the effect of an action, construed as a goal of the agent, explains that agent's course of action. Neither the prospect of the death of the innocent nor the prospect of his being struck down explains the action of the trolley passenger. But it is precisely the removal of A's organs (which violates A's rights and causes his death) which explains the physician's behavior.

Thus, an examination of the problems for DE that have to do with the criteria for an effect being (merely) foreseen and not intended leaves the friend of DE unembarrassed. With respect to the range of cases presented thus far, the advocate of DE can explain why he draws the moral line where he does. And that moral line turns out to be drawn where he wants it. But there are other cases of killing innocent bystanders in which the apparent implications of DE run counter not only to most people's moral intuitions, but also to what I expect are the settled judgments of most advocates of DE. Consider, then, Case 5:

> Case 5 Alice and Allen are critically ill roommates in a hospital. They can be saved only by the release into their room (by a currently unspecified agent) of a gas which is fatal to anyone not suffering from their particular disease. Unfortunately, Alyosha also occupies their room. He has recently returned to health and is about to be discharged. But the gas must be released immediately, before Alyosha can leave the room, if it is to save Alice and Allen.[8]

If any evil effect is foreseen but not intended, in the general spirit of DE, it is the death of Alyosha in Case 5. But I take it that the killing involved in Act 5 is *not* permissible and that this judgment would be made by anyone who rejects the useful killings involved in Acts 3, 3*, and 4.

It is, of course, true of Act 4 (the organ expropriation) and of Act 5 that if the act is not performed, two lives are *not saved*, whereas if the act is performed, a life is *taken*. Defenders of a morally significant distinction between killing and (merely) not saving can invoke this distinction to account for the impermissibility of Acts 4 and 5. In these cases, to act is to kill, whereas not to act is (merely) not to save. And advocates of the killing/not saving distinction and its moral significance will hold that it is much more

[8] Cf., with the case in Foot, p.68. The specification of the releasing agent plays a crucial role in the further discussion of this case in Part IV.

important to abide by one's duty not to kill than to abide by whatever duty one might have to save. Thus, a distinction quite different from DE's contrast between intended and (merely) foreseen deaths may handle cases like 4 and 5 quite well.[9]

But this point cannot be too comforting to the advocate of DE who after all, sets out to argue that some killings of bystanders (and not merely the failure to save them) are permissible. And the DE argument for the permissibility of killing Auberon in Case 2 seems to work just as well for the permissibility of fatally gassing Alyosha in Case 5. Indeed, the same argument allows the killing of bystander Alyosha in the following variation on Case 5:

> Case 6 Alice is pregnant with little fetus Alyosha (who we assume to have the full moral status of a person). She also happens to be critically ill, and her life can only be saved by ingesting some chemical which is fatal to anyone, including fetuses, not suffering from her particular disease. If the drug is to save her, she must take it immediately. (But if Alice does not take the drug, her death will be delayed long enough for Alyosha to be born in good health.)

Case 6 represents exactly the special sort of abortion which traditional defenders of DE *have allowed*.[10] It should be no surprise therefore, that the friend of DE is committed to allowing Act 5.

The advocate of DE might argue that he also believes in the killing/not saving distinction. He might, then, acknowledge that these two doctrines will sometimes clash. When one can intentionally accomplish the saving of lives only by incidentally taking lives, DE will approve this tradeoff, whereas the doctrine that taking lives is much worse than not saving them will disapprove. Precisely this conflict of principles exists in Cases 5 and 6. If the advocate of DE wants to deny that it is permissible to gas Alyosha, he must hold that, when this clash of principles occurs, DE gives way before the rule that taking a life is much worse than not saving a life.

---

[9] For part of such a defense, see my "Bad Samaritanism and The Causation of Harm," *Philosophy and Public Affairs*, vol. 9 (Summer 1980), and "Deontologism, Negative Causation and the Duty to Rescue," E. Regis, ed., *Gewirth's Ethical Rationalism* (Chicago: University of Chicago Press, 1984).

[10] When Foot proposes that the killing/letting die distinction (and the associated greater stringency of negative duties over positive duties) do the work that some have assigned to DE, she does not clearly acknowledge that, *ceteris paribus*, this substitution leads (again, on the assumption of fetal personhood) to an even stronger anti-abortion stance than that adopted by the advocate of DE. Foot seems to be distracted by her concern with the even more special class of cases in which *both* parties will die unless one of them (e.g., the fetus) is killed, and the special reason why, in these cases, killing the fetus is permissible. Cf., Foot, pp.69–70.

But the standard advocate of DE may not be willing to make this move. For it requires that he give up the permissibility of Act 6. Moreover, as it stands, this retrenchment by the advocate of DE is too *ad hoc*. There is no explanation of why DE *should* retreat before the killing/not saving doctrine whenever these two principles yield conflicting conclusions. Note, however, that this retrenchment is equivalent to the view that only when a killing would be prevented (and not merely when a life would be saved) is the incidental killing of bystanders permissible. This is essentially the Doctrine of Counterforce Defense, the basis and plausibility of which I turn to in the next section.

Finally, we should consider another argument against the proposition that the advocate of DE must endorse Act 5. This argument also contains intimations of the Doctrine of Counterforce Defense. The traditional advocate of DE always maintains (often without clear theoretical motivation) that not just any combination of intended good effects and foreseen evil effects will yield the permissibility of an action. He does not want to say that if my intention is to provide spectacularly pleasing fireworks to the folks in New Jersey, it is permissible for me to blow up New York. Here, the foreseen evil is disproportionate to the intended good. The problem for the advocate of DE has always been to spell out what constitutes an acceptable balance between intended good and foreseen evil and to avoid, in the process, the very sort of consequentialism which he characteristically rejects. If the advocate of DE can come up with a convincing method for weighing the good effects against the ill, then this may undercut his own anticonsequentialism.

The only potentially fruitful suggestion for how the advocate of DE might proceed is for proportionality to be explicated not in terms of the weights of the various goods and evils at stake but, rather, in terms of "proportionate reason."[11] The concept of "proportionate reason" instructs us to focus not on the size of the goods and ills involved but, so to speak, on the quality of the reasons for and against action. Along these lines, it can, perhaps, be said that exercising one's right to defend one's basic rights is a higher quality reason for action than (merely) preserving one's life in the face of some indeterminate danger to it. Hence, even though Alyosha's death in Case 5 is not intended, the release of the gas is not done with "proportionate reason" because it is not a defense against a violation of rights. Although this shift to "proportionate reason" is suggestive, I do not see how it can be brought to clear fruition. Part of the problem is that this sort of shift to "proportionate reason" seems inapt for the standard cases in which proportionality has been invoked. For instance, traditional advocates of DE have wanted to say that if

---

[11] This move to "proportionate reason" is attempted in Germain Grisez, "Against Consequentialism," *American Journal of Jurisprudence*, vol. 23 (1978), especially pp.49–56. My first encounter with the idea was in conversation with Joseph Boyle.

Alice's self-defense against Alfred has the deaths of n bystanders as a byproduct, and n is large enough, then the proportionality condition is violated and Alice's act is impermissible. Yet, in such a case the bystanders' deaths would not be intended and Alice would have one of those high quality "proportionate reasons."

Nevertheless, the idea of focusing on the differential merits of different sorts of reasons for acts involving foreseen but unintended killing may be a fruitful one. I will explore one aspect of this idea in the next section, *viz.*, reasons of self-defense versus reasons of self-preservation.

III. THE DOCTRINE OF COUNTERFORCE DEFENSE

Is it possible, then, to formulate an alternative view which yields the permissibility of the incidental killings of bystanders in Acts 2 and 3', and the impermissibility of both the direct killing of bystanders in Acts 3, 3*, and 4 *and* the incidental gassing of Alyosha in Act 5?[12] One possibility turns on the moral difference between self-defense and self-preservation – or, more specifically, on the claim that each individual possesses a right to self-defense, but not a comparable right to self-preservation. The right to self-defense is a second-order right to thwart by injurious force attacks upon one's life, limbs, and liberties. The right to self-defense is second-order in the sense that its appropriate exericse is governed by a conceptually prior specification of the rights to be defended. These are first-order rights; the rights on behalf of which the right to self-defense is exercised. For the purposes of this essay, I take the relevant first order rights of individuals to be their rights to life, limb, and liberty. These rights do not include or imply rights that others provide one with life, limb, or liberty or with the necessities for preserving them. Nor do they imply (enforcible) obligations on the part of others to assist one in preventing the loss of one's life, limb, or liberty. It is because of the negative character of the first-order rights, requiring as they do only that others not trespass upon one's moral space, that the right of self-defense is a limited right. It only vindicates forcible responses against the invasive activities of others. In contrast, a right to self-preservation would be a right to do or have done whatever is necessary to preserve one's life (and one's other basic interests, e.g., one's bodily integrity). Such a right to self-preservation would include a right to require that others do what is necessary to preserve one's life, etc.[13]

Were one's first order rights positive rights to be provided with life and

---

[12] I do not test subsequent doctrines against Case 6, the abortion case. For our sense of what is permissible in that case depends upon many further factors, e.g., our views about the personhood of fetuses and about the moral relevance of this purported personhood.

[13] As stated, this right of self-preservation would be both a first and second order right.

limb or to be protected against loss of life or limb, then any failure by others to provide or protect would count as a violation of one's rights and, in the exercise of one's right of defense, it would be permissible to force that positive service. For example, in Case 4, were Alice's right to life a positive right, requiring that others protect her from the loss of life, Alyosha's refusal to give up his kidney would be a violation of Alice's right to life. Thus, Alice's seizure of Alyosha's kidney would count as an act of self-defense against Alyosha's rights violating inactivity.[14] Thus, if first-order rights are construed positively, the distinction between a right of self-defense and a right of self-preservation collapses. Since this is obviously a real distinction (e.g., when Alice seizes Alyosha's kidney she is acting in a self-preserving way, but not in a self-defending way), we have indirectly come across a reason for maintaining the negative construal of these rights.

The application of the distinction between the legitimate right of self-defense and the specious right of self-preservation to the cases at hand is straightforward. In Case 2 (and even more obviously, in Case 1) Alice exercises a right of self-defense. In Cases 4 and 5, however, what she does is not an exercise of her right of self-defense – not, at least, if that right is properly understood as derivative from negatively construed first-order rights. Unfortunately, we must recall that Acts 2, 3, 3′ and 3* are all responses to genuine attacks upon Alice and, hence, can all be viewed as defensive and not merely self-preserving. Thus, if the killing, albeit incidental, of the innocent bystanders in Cases 2 and 3′ can be justified in the name of a right of self-defense, cannot the same justification be provided for the killings of bystanders in 3 and 3*? Can it be argued that Acts 2 and 3′ are so much better justified by a right of self-defense than 3 and 3* are that the former, but not the latter, are vindicated as defensive acts?

Two related arguments can be made for marking off Acts 2 and 3′ from Acts 3 and 3*. The first more explicitly than the second reintroduces, within the Doctrine of Counterforce Defense, the DE's intended/foreseen distinction. Both arguments focus on the counterforce character of Acts 2 and 3′ versus the countervalue character of Acts 3 and 3*.

(i) In Cases 3 and 3*, Alices's chosen course of action is guided and made explicable by reference to the presence of (and movements of) a bystander. This targeting of a bystander gives credibility to the characterisation of her action as "aggression against this bystander." Given this aggression, and the bystander's right to life, Alice's counterattack in Cases 3 and 3* is

---

[14] If one were to adopt the widely held thesis that there is no morally significant difference between knowingly failing to prevent an injury and causing that injury, then it would seem to follow that all such failures constitute attacks against which self-defensive force is legitimate. The adoption of this thesis is another way to collapse the distinction between self-defense and self-preservation. For a survey of arguments for this thesis, and a critique of it, see my "Bad Samaritanism and the Causation of Harm."

impermissible. In contrast to this, Acts 2 and 3', although they involve the deaths of bystanders, are in no way explicable as the destruction of nonaggressors. Their self-defensive character dominates our understanding of them. The especially strong moral weight accorded to exercises of the right of self-defense renders Alice's actions permissible, even though each brings about the death of an innocent. Each of Acts 2 and 3' instantiates the concept of Counterforce Defense and is vindicated by the right of self-defense.

(ii) The more Alice's counterattack fails to be responsive specifically to the rights-threatening activity of Alfred, the weaker its claim to being paradigmatically defensive. Indeed, Acts 3 and 3* can hardly be described as counterattacks. There is a dissociation between what Alice does in order to save her life and the human source of the threat to her life. The fact that, in Acts 3 and 3*, the essential interaction is between Alice and Alyosha, a mere bystander, the fact that these acts are not *counterforce* reactions, renders them instances of (mere) self-preservation – albeit self-preservation occasioned by some third party's aggression. Thus, according to Counterforce Defense (CD), neither Act 3 nor act 3* enjoys moral protection under a right of self-defense.

The primary reason for investigating the CD strategy and its chief advantage over DE is that CD does not permit actions like 5, whereas DE may (unless it can be constrained by a theory of "proportionate reason"). The problem for the advocate of CD is that there are other instances of killing bystanders which are both (a) not killings in the exercise of a right of self-defense, and (b) permissible. CD will not account for these kinds of permissible killings. It is possible, of course, that CD can account for some permissible killings of bystanders while we would need an utterly different theory (or set of theories) to account for the other permissible killings. But it would be nice to have a single, unified, theory – especially in light of how similar various defensive and non-defensive permissible killings are.[15] Consider, for instance:

> Case 1' Alfred has accidently stumbled and his falling body is about to dislodge a boulder which will crush Alice, who is immobilized. (Or he has accidently stumbled and his falling body itself will crush Alice.) Alice can only save herself by firing her bazooka into Alfred's body.

---

[15] In an earlier essay, "The Moral Basis of National Defense," I was more satisfied with something like the CD approach, just because I focused primarily on killings which are responsive to attacks by other agents. Nevertheless, the *policy* implications drawn in that essay are the same as those which should be drawn from the present essay. See R. Poole, Jr., ed., *Defending the Free Society* (Lexington, MA: Lexington Books, 1984).

In Case 1', Alice is less threatened by Alfred's activity, his action or agency, than she is in Case 1. As we decrease the role of Alfred's agency, it becomes more difficult to vindicate Alice's use of her bazooka *as an exercise of a right to self-defense*. Although Alice's life is in danger, she is no more in danger of having her right to life violated than she would be were she threatened by a boulder dislodged by the forces of nature. In Case 1', it seems that Alfred is not even about to be an innocent violator of Alice's rights.[16] And yet, it also seems permissible that Alice fire her bazooka in Case 1'. If this is correct, we already have some reason to believe that no doctrine of legitimate self-defense, even one which allows the indirect killing of the innocent in the course of counterforce reactions, can fully account for the permissible killing of the innocent. Similarly, consider:

> Case 2'   Some force of nature has dislodged a boulder which is accelerating toward Alice, who is immobilized. Alice can only protect herself by knocking the boulder aside with her (unloaded) bazooka. But if she so deflects it, it will strike and kill Auberon, who is further down the hill and who, otherwise, would not be in the boulder's path; and
> Case 2''   The same as 2', except that Alice can only save herself by firing her bazooka at the approaching boulder at the very moment that the boulder is passing Auberon. The explosion that will destroy the boulder will also kill Auberon.

Both of these actions seem morally permissible. But no issue of self-defense arises. And just as one could specify other-defense counterparts for the various self-defense cases, one could specify other-preservation counterparts for Cases 2' and 2''. It would be permissible for Alice to deflect a boulder in order to save two people even if the deflected boulder would then strike and kill another.[17] It would be permissible for Alice to explode a boulder on the path to the two even if that explosion would kill another. (It is assumed that Alice has no antecedent special obligation to protect the one or to injure or allow the injury of the two.) But consider the other-preservation counterpart to case 2'':

[16] On the claim that even a moderately permissible right of self-defense (i.e., one encompassing the killing of individuals posing innocent threats) would not vindicate killings of the sort needed by Alice in 1', see Nancy Davis, "Abortion and Self-Defense," *Philosophy and Public Affairs*, vol. 13 (Spring 1984). "It is considerably less obvious how we are to justify killing to preserve our own life when the attacker has done nothing at all to threaten us but is, instead, a *passive threat*: someone whose mere movements *qua* physical object or mere presence constitutes a threat to our life" (p.190).

[17] Deflection cases, including the various runaway trolley cases, are discussed in Thomson's "Killing, Letting Die and the Trolley Problem."

Case 5' Alice and Allen will be killed by the approaching boulder unless someone fires a bazooka shell into that boulder. Unfortunately, Alyosha will be right next to the boulder at the crucial moment and will be killed by the explosion which saves Alice's and Allen's lives.

If Acts 2' and 2'' are permissible, then so is Act 5'. And Act 5' does, indeed, seem to be permissible. *But how can Act 5' be distinguished from Act 5* (in which one person is exposed to a poisonous gas so that two may be saved)? If one believes that Act 5 ought to be rejected, then it seems that one must not give a DE account of the acceptability of Acts 2', 2'' and 5'. For, as previously noted, DE yields the permissibility of Act 5.[18] On the other hand, if one rejects Act 5 because it would not be an instance of self-defense, one must reject Act 5' and Acts 2' and 2'' as well.

IV. THE DOCTRINE OF ANTECENDENT CAUSATION

A consideration of Case 2' may set us on the path to an alternative to both DE and CD. In this simple deflection case, a key element in our judgment that Act 2' is permissible is surely the idea that the dangerously careening boulder remains the dominant or substantial cause of Auberon's death, even though Auberon would not have died had Alice not deflected the boulder with her unloaded bazooka. We perceive the careening boulder as a generalized peril, and when this peril eventuates in someone's death, we track the "responsibility" for that death back through various intermediate events to that dangerous condition. We do this even though, had those intermediate events not occurred, the death would not have occurred. The predominant causal responsibility lies with the antecedent cause and not with the intermediate action. The Doctrine of Antecedent Causation (AC) maintains that when generally perilous and inevitably injurious forces confront a person such that, no matter how that person acts, some nonaggressor(s) will be injured, the antecedent perilous forces bear the predominant causal responsibility for the subsequent injuries – unless those injuries are intended by a person whose action is an intermediate cause. If those injuries are intended, the intermediate actions (usually) "negative" the causal connection between those forces and the subsequent injury.

Contrast Case 2', in which Alice deflects the boulder *away from* herself, with:

[18] I assume that the "proportionate reason" argument which was discussed at the close of section II does not work so as to allow the advocate of DE to escape acceptance of Act 5. But, if it does work out, then the advocate of DE must disallow Acts 2', 2'' and 5'.

> Case 2*   The same as 2', except that Alice deflects the onrushing boulder *in order* for it to strike and kill Auberon. She does so through the very same physical movements involved in saving herself in 2'. (Perhaps, to insure that *the* intended goal is Auberon's death, we should suppose that it does not occur to Alice that she will be killed if the boulder is not deflected.)

In contrast to Act 2', Act 2* seems to be clearly impermissible. One way of speaking about this act is to say that Alice makes use of the dangerous condition for her own purposes. She incorporates it into her plan of action and, so, she inherits the status of the substantial cause of Auberon's death which otherwise would have been ascribed to the boulder.

A slightly different way of speaking will help us to distinguish the present account of the impermissibility of Act 2* from one based upon DE. In their renowned work, *Causation in the Law*,[19] Hart and Honoré discuss what types of intermediate events between the occurrence of an earlier event A and a later event B "negative" the causal connection between A and B. It is clear that, even when such negativing obtains, A may remain a necessary causal condition of B. It is the status of antecedent cause A as the *substantial* cause of B that is negatived. If this negativing of causal connection, i.e., the demotion of A from the status of the substantial cause of B, does not occur, then "responsibility" for B continues to be properly ascribed to A and not to some event that mediates the causal connection between A and B.

Hart and Honoré hold that, except in special cases such as those involving inducement, intervening voluntary actions negative causal connections. One of their examples is as follows: if I put poison in Jones's coffee and, unaware of this poison, Jones drinks the coffee and dies, then I have killed Jones. However, if Jones is aware of the poison and, nevertheless, "deliberately" drinks the coffee, he is a suicide. I have not killed Jones (absent some elaborate explanation about my having preyed upon his psychological weaknesses and peculiarities).[20] One thing this example illustrates is that there can be intervening acts which are voluntary in some sense, e.g., Jones's uninformed drinking of the coffee, which do not negative causal connections.

The hard question is whether Jones's awareness of the poison, and, hence, his foresight that he will die if he drinks the coffee suffice to render his

---

[19] H.L.A. Hart and A.M. Honoré, *Causation in the Law* (London: Oxford University Press, 1959) especially Chapter III, "Causation and Responsibility," pp.58–78, and Chapter VI, "The Law of Tort: Causing Harm," pp.126–170.

[20] *Ibid.*, p. 72.

action sufficiently voluntary for it to break the chain of responsibility that leads back to my poisoning of the coffee. That is, does the fact that Jones drinks the coffee with the foresight that his death will result, negative the causal connection between my putting the poison in his coffee and his death? If an affirmative answer is given to this question, and if we assume in Case 2' that Alice knows that deflecting the boulder will result in Auberon's death, then we will have to say that Alice's act negatives the connection to the careening boulder. Responsibility will not be traced back to that perilous antecedent condition. Rather, it will lie with Alice. And Hart and Honoré do seem to endorse an affirmative answer. They hold that for Jones to take the poison "deliberately," and thereby break the causal chain, it is enough that he know that there is poison in his coffee.[21] But I dispute their interpretation of negativing intervening events.

I maintain that Jones deliberately consumes the poison in a way that breaks the link between my poisoning the coffee and his death only if Jones *intends* to consume the poison. It is difficult, in the example as Hart and Honoré describe it, to imagine Jones bringing about his foreseen death by poison without the intention of doing so. Let us change the case slightly. Suppose that the poison causes a painful one week illness from which the victim will fully recover. Suppose also that Jones has a contract with some third party to receive a $10,000 payment for drinking the coffee before him. Now it is easy to imagine that Jones might knowingly consume the poison, foreseeing the painful illness, without his guiding intention being to consume the poison or suffer the illness. He drinks the coffee in order to collect the $10,000. He acts, albeit with more unease, just as he would have, had the poison never been placed in the coffee. Although he foresees the consumption of the poison and the illness, neither prospect plays any (positive) role in guiding or explaining his action.[22]

Suppose Jones does consume the poisoned coffee in order to receive the $10,000 payment. He does not thereby deliberately bring about the illness through a voluntary act which negatives my responsibility for his subsequent

---

[21] However, Hart and Honoré also write that "the free, deliberate and informed act or omission of a human being, *intended to produce the consequence which is in fact produced*, negatives causal connection" (p.129, my italics). Here, intention seems to be required for negativing causal connection. But, perhaps, they would say that the fact that an act has *some* intended consequence is sufficient to negative the causal connection between the background setting for the act and *all* of the act's foreseen consequences. So, if I intend the good consequence of escape from the concentration camp, my deliberate act of escape negatives the causal connection between the setting of the traps along my escape route and the foreseen injuries I suffer in travelling that route!

[22] Contrast this with the case in which Jones has been promised $10,000.00 if he consumes poison and, to his great good fortune, I come along and dump some otherwise unavailable poison into his coffee. He then drinks the potion before him (partially at least) in order to collect on this promise. Here I will not have imposed the poisoning upon Jones.

suffering. I remain responsible for his painful illness. Similarly, if I construct a chamber of horrors along the route through which someone must pass if he is to escape from a concentration camp, the responsibility for his injuries in that chamber is mine, even when he knows full well what awaits him on that route. Only if Jones or the prisoner act for the sake of the painful episodes do their actions negative the chain of responsibility leading back to me. Only if the victim intends the untoward effect, and not merely foresees it, will his voluntary action negative the causal link back to the antecedent perilous condition and its author.[23]

How, then, does the Antecedent Causation account of the difference between 2′ and 2* differ from the DE account? The basic difference is the focus in AC on vindicating the agent by tracing "the" cause of the death that occurs back to the situation and events with which the agent was confronted. We are concerned about the relationship between the setting within which the agent had to make some choice and the death that is subsequent to that choice. Both CD and AC are historical principles in a way in which DE is not. Both assert that without knowing something about the historical setting of an act, we cannot evaluate that act. For without knowledge of the historical setting, we cannot determine whether the act or the setting is "the" cause of some morally significant upshot. According to CD, an action which has as one of its foreseeable results the death of an innocent bystander is not the substantial cause of that death if the setting is itself a rights-threatening situation. According to AC, there are other sorts of perilous and threatening situations whose causal connection with the death of a bystander may not be negatived by a voluntary response which has as one of its foreseeable results the death of that bystander.

The relevance of the intended vs. foreseen distinction for AC is just this: an act which has someone's death as one of its intended results will negative the causal status of the perilous and inevitably injurious circumstances which make it possible to bring about this death; but an action which has someone's death as one of its merely foreseen results will not negative the causal status of these perilous circumstances. Alice's action in Case 2′, in which she deflects the boulder even though she knows that this will result in Auberon's death, does not negative the causal link between the perilously descending boulder and that death. But Alice's action in Case 2*, in which she deflects the boulder with the intention of killing Auberon, does break this link. The theoretical intuition is that when people are confronted with inescapably death-dealing circumstances, responsibility for the ensuing deaths can be

---

[23] Even such intention *may* not shift responsibility to the intermediate agent. See Case 7 below in which Jim's intentional killing is thoroughly and purposively orchestrated by the commandant.

attributed to the circumstances (or, better yet if possible, to an author of those circumstances) rather than to the intermediate agents, as long as the intermediate agents did not intend to bring about any of these deaths.

AC provides an explanation of why deflection cases are so easy, i.e., why it is so easy for us to accept the permissibility of Alice's deflection of the boulder away from herself and of the passenger's deflection of the runaway trolley onto a track with fewer innocent bystanders on it. For, in these cases, there is a clear sense in which the very dangerous condition which threatened Alice or threatened the five people is what, in fact, causes Auberon's death or the death of the one person. AC is an improvement over DE because it accommodates our intuition that a major part of what vindicates Alice and the trolley passenger is the fact that they are confronted with an inevitably deadly situation.[24]

That our ascription of causal responsibility for Auberon's death and the death of the one person should pass back through Alice and the passenger to, respectively, the careening boulder and the runaway trolley, remains true even though, had Alice not deflected the boulder and had the passenger not redirected the trolley, neither Auberon nor the one would have died. This is why no theoretical leap is involved in claiming that, along with Act 2′, Acts 2, 2″ and 3′ (all of which thwart/turn aside deadly forces, but at the cost of incidental deaths) are permissible. In each of these cases, the ascription of responsibility goes back to the inescapably deadly situation.

In her "Killing, Letting Die and the Trolley Problem," and especially in connection with the various deflection cases, Thomson makes use of the idea that there is an evil to be distributed.[25] Although someone distributes this evil, the distributor is not the source of the evil. The description of the deflection cases in terms of an evil to be distributed provides a way of assimilating the deflection cases and those more like Case 2. For in the latter, just as in the former, an agent finds herself in a situation in which evil will be distributed to some individuals (among those in a reasonably well-defined set) whatever she does or fails to do. The question is whether or not, through her chosen action, she becomes the causal agent of the evil. To use both the language of Hart and Honoré and of Thomson, the causal connection between the eventual harm and the situation which necessitated some distribution of an evil is negatived by an agent's intermediate action only if the agent *does* that evil to whom it befalls, rather than simply acting in such a way that it gets distributed to him. And I take it that the agent does

---

[24] The AC "vindication" of an agent looks more and more like a theory of excuse rather than a theory of any sort of justification. But the same point can be made about the DE and the CD "vindications."

[25] Thomson, pp.215–216.

that evil to the party to whom it befalls if, and only if, that evil result is intended as an end or as a means in the agent's plan of action.

Before returning at last to the issue of national defense, I want to provide some further reasons for distinguishing between DE and AC. One reason is that the latter, unlike the former, *may* provide a basis for distinguishing between Cases 5 and 5′ (between the unintended lethal gassing of Alyosha when he has the bad luck to share a hospital room with Alice and Allen, and the unintended killing of Alyosha when he has the bad luck to be near the careening boulder which must be exploded if Alice and Allen are to be saved). My suggestion is that what motivates us to want to distinguish between these two cases is the differing extent to which we presume that the hard choices are *imposed* upon the relevant agents.

We presume that the agent in Case 5′ is simply confronted with the careening boulder and with the choice of whether Alice and Allen or Alyosha will die. Not only is the agent in no way responsible for the horrendous situation, but this is also not the sort of situation that care and effort can be expected to prevent. In contrast, someone *decided* to put Alice, Allen, and Alyosha in the same hospital room. If our previously unspecified agent is that person, he has a strong moral reason to prevent the release of the gas. If this unnamed agent has institutional ties to whoever placed these patients together, he has some moral reason to prevent the release of the gas. The more the agent has played any sort of a role in the placement of Alyosha in the situation in which he must die if Alice and Allen are to live, the less it can be said that the line of responsibility for that death will pass back through and away from this agent. Insofar as we naturally presume some such institutional role for this agent, the AC approch will not allow us to conclude that it is permissible for the agent to release the gas.[26]

In contrast, there are other sorts of cases in which AC may be more liberal than DE in its grants of permissibility. This may be true of:

> Case 7 Jim wanders into a South American village where the local commandant has been amusing himself by making various threats against the innocent villagers. The commandant finds Jim's revulsion at this practice even more amusing. To heighten this delicious amusement, the commandant

[26] Suppose that an employee of a mountain-climbing resort has told a guest to wait for her at point x and now, if she deflects the boulder from its path toward Alice and Allen, it will strike the guest at x. This employee, it seems, is less justified in deflecting the boulder than she would be if she had not given this instruction to the guest. In her "Killing, Letting Die, and the Trolley Problem," Thomson also discusses the importance of the history behind the presence of the individual toward whom the trolley may be deflected. She contrasts a case in which this individual has been promised safety on the alternative track with a case in which this person is a trespasser on the alternative track. See pp.210–211.

has five innocent villagers lined up against the wall and a
sixth innocent dragged before Jim. He hands Jim a spare
pistol (which Jim cannot turn on the commandant), and he
tells Jim that, unless he kills the sixth villager, the other five
will be shot.[27]

Jim's killing of that sixth villager would be intentional. Jim would be aiming
at that villager, making sure that the bullet he fired entered some vital part of
the villager's body. But I am not so sure that this intentional killing would be
wrong.

Doubts about the impermissibility of such killings stem from our
perception of the extent of the commandant's intentional structuring of and
control over the situation. The horrendous situation and the necessity for
choice may be so thoroughly imposed upon Jim that even his intentional
intermediate act of shooting the villager will not negative the connection
between the commandant's action and the villager's death. The very
consideration which some philosophers think argues for the impermissibility
of killing the villager (*viz.*, that under these circumstances, killing the villager
makes Jim an instrument of the commandant's evil design) in fact argues *for*
the permissibility of the killing. When Jim's intention to kill that villager is
itself specifically intended by and orchestrated by the commandant, Jim's
intentional killing of the villager may lack the independence an action must
have if it is to negative causal connections. Clearly, neither the impermissibility of 5 nor the permissibility of 7 have been established by these
brief and imprecise remarks. My point is simply that AC is distinguishable
from DE because it suggests conclusions quite different from those entailed
by DE.

To provide a last clarification of this third approach, and to bring this
discussion back to the issue of national defense, let us consider how AC
vindicates large-scale defensive counterforce strikes which foreseeably kill
innocent bystanders. This vindication can be displayed in a series of cases,
the first of which is lifted from Thomson's trolley paper.

---

[27] Compare this with the case and discussion offered by Bernard Williams in J.J.C. Smart and
B. Williams, eds., *Utilitarianism: For and Against* (London: Cambridge University Press,
1973) pp.98–118. In Williams's case, the person Jim must kill in order to save many is *among
the many*. That person will die no matter what. This special factor suggests a number of *special*
ways to vindicate this killing. To avoid these routes, I have excluded this special factor from
all the cases in this essay. Any doctrine which depended on this special factor would, of
course, be of no use in vindicating the killing of innocent Soviet citizens by the
U.S. government for the sake of saving inhabitants of the U.S. from death, injury, or loss of
liberty.

> Case 8 Harry is President, and has just been told that the Russians
> have launched an atom bomb toward New York. The only
> way in which the bomb can be prevented from reaching
> New York is by deflecting it; but the only deflection-path
> available will take the bomb onto Worchester. Harry can do
> nothing, letting all of New York die; or he can press a
> button, deflecting the bomb and killing all of Worchester.[28]

Harry may press the button for the same type of reason that Alice may
perform Act 2′ (the deflection of the boulder on to Auberon) and the
passenger may turn the trolley onto the track with the one bystander. In this
case, the reason is a combination of (a) the fact that, unless Harry's
intermediate act negatives the causal connection, it will be the launching of
the bomb by the Russians which will be the cause of the ensuing deaths and,
(b) the fact that Harry's pressing the button does not negative this
connection. But, surely, if Act 8 is permissible, then so, by similar reasoning,
is the action suggested by:

> Case 9 The same as 8, except that the only deflection-path takes
> the bomb to a Worchester-sized Moscow suburb.

And if Act 9 is permissible, then so, by similar reasoning, is the action
suggested by:

> Case 10 The same as 8, except that the Russian bomb can be
> destroyed only shortly after it is launched – right above
> that Worchester-sized Moscow suburb and with the
> resulting death of everyone in that suburb.

Note that I suggest no specific limit on how many Soviet bystanders may
be killed in thwarting/turning aside a Soviet attack. Perhaps there are some
limits of the type proposed in the proportionality elements of traditional DE.
But no implication of such limits is evident in the current argument. If that
Soviet bomb was heading for Worchester and President Harry could only
deflect it onto Moscow, that deflection too would seem permissible. Of
course, any real-world counterforce strike would also result in the deaths –
indeed, the *intended* deaths – of both guilty and innocent aggressors. But
those killings would be permissible under our original and only moderately
permissive right of self-defense.

It must be emphasized that the argument of this essay, with respect to the
morality of war, is for the permissibility of defensive force (even when that

---

[28] Thomson, p.208.

force indirectly kills bystanders) which actually thwarts rights-violating attacks. It is not at all an argument for *retaliatory* force – especially not for retaliation, if it can even be called that, against bystanders. Nor does this essay speak to the morality or rationality of *threatening* retaliatory force. Of course, carrying out such a retaliatory threat, should one's bluff be called, would be impermissible and irrational.

V. CONCLUSION

This essay has provided a sympathetic presentation and examination of three different, but dialectically related, approaches to vindicating the sort of killing of innocent bystanders which is inevitable in the use of any forseeable system of national defense – no matter how strong that system's counterforce orientation. The development and evaluation of these vindications has been placed within the broader philosophical context of the permissible killing of innocent bystanders. The coherence and moral significance of the central distinction of the Doctrine of Double Effect, *viz.*, between foreseen but unintended untoward consequences and intended untoward consequences, has been defended. But I have argued that the absence of intention in connection with bringing about a bystander's death does not suffice for that killing to be permissible – even if the act which unintentionally kills is done in order to save lives. The Doctrine of Counterforce Defense represents a first attempt to state what else must be true, in the way of historical-causal context, for life (or limb or liberty) saving incidental killings of bystanders to be permissible. It maintains that the life (or limb or liberty) saving killing must constitute a response to an impending violation of the right to life (or limb or liberty). But there are more instances of permissible incidental killing of bystanders than are accounted for by CD. There are, for instance, those troublesome runaway trolley cases.

The Doctrine of Antecedent Causation seeks to account for these instances, as well as those accounted for by CD, by providing a more inclusive specification of the historical-causal context which must obtain for an act which indirectly results in a bystander's death to be permissible. The context is that of an agent's being presented with an inescapably perilous condition which imposes on him an inevitably fatal (or injurious) choice. Under such antecedent conditions, an agent's intermediate choice need not negative the causal connection back to that perilous setting. The agent's intermediate choice will not negative that connection as long as the death or injury subsequent to his choice, although foreseen, is not a formative goal (an end in itself or a means to some further goal) of his choice and action. To speak in grand terms, under such circumstances, the metaphysical responsibility for the bystander's death or injury remains in the hands of the aggressor, or nature, or God. Only by engaging in an intermediate action *for the sake of* some bystander's death or injury does an agent confronted with such a perilous condition acquire responsibility and blame for such death or injury.[29] Unfortunately, all of these Doctrines, including that of Antecedent Causation, rest on questionable, albeit plausible, presumptions about the character and description of human action, the causal connections between actions and events, and the ways in which human action and its causal connectedness to events give rise to moral responsibility. These presumptions are probably part of our everyday thought about human action and responsibility. So, unless we are prepared seriously to doubt the essential veracity of this thought, we need not feel too guilty about proceeding on the basis of these (largely unidentified) presuppositions. Nevertheless, an examination of these action-theoretic and metaphysical presumptions is needed for a fully satisfactory theory of the permissible killing of innocent bystanders. It is both unfortunate and a matter of great relief that such an examination is beyond the scope of the present essay.

Philosophy, Tulane University

---

[29] And, again, as illustrated in the case of Jim, in some circumstances, an intermediate agent may aim at the death of a bystander and still not acquire responsibility and blame for that death.

Social Philosophy & Policy 3:1 Autumn 1985 ISSN 0265–0525 $2.00

THE INTERNATIONAL DEFENSE OF LIBERTY

BARUCH A. BRODY

It seems to me that those who place great value on the right to human freedom can be badly divided on the question of the use of force by states to defend the liberties of those who are not citizens of that particular state. Concerned about the liberties to be defended, they might be enthusiastic supporters of the use of such force by liberty-loving countries throughout the world. Concerned about the liberties that might be violated when the state marshals its forces for use internationally, they might adopt a more isolationist approach to this issue. This paper is an attempt to help clarify this conflict by looking at some of the philosophical issues it raises. Because I wish to avoid factual debates about current conflicts, I will give no real-life examples. However, they are on my mind, and I hope the reader will keep them in mind as well.

I. HOW TO THINK ABOUT THE JUSTIFIED USE OF FORCE BY THE STATE

The first point that we need to keep in mind is that the use of force, by an individual or a state, always requires justification, since the use of force always seems to violate a right of the person against whom force is used: the right to life (if deadly force is used), or to bodily integrity (if injurious force is used), or to freedom (if incapacitating force is used). What sorts of justification are possible? I claim[1] (but cannot here argue for this claim) that the following are possible justifications:

(1) *The person has waived the right in question.* It seems to be a general truth about all rights (although some[2] have denied this and argued instead that at least some rights are non-waivable, inalienable rights) that the holders of these rights can permit others to do actions that would otherwise violate the rights in question, and that the people so permitted do not act wrongly (or, at least, do not violate any rights) by acting on that

---

[1] This claim will be defended more fully in chapters 4–6 of a book on which I am currently working, tentatively entitled *Beyond Paternalism and Autonomy.*
[2] The debate on this topic is usefully surveyed in R. Martin and J. Nickel, "Recent Work on the Concept of Rights" *American Philosophical Quarterly*, vol. 17 (1980), and in A.J. Simmons, "Inalienable Rights and Locke's Treatises," *Philosophy and Public Affairs*, vol. 12 (1983).

permission. It is, of course, this fact about rights which helps
distinguish the recipients of gifts from thieves, and cohabitants
from rapists.

(2) *The person has lost the right in question.* It seems to be a general
truth about all rights that the holders of these rights can lose
them entirely (or, at least, lose them in part by|losing them against
certain others in certain cases) by performing or threatening to
perform certain wrongful acts, even though the holders of these
rights can in no sense be said to have *permitted* others to violate
their rights. It is, of course, this fact about rights that explains
the moral permissibility of punishment[3] (where those who have
performed certain wrongful acts may justifiably be treated in
ways that would otherwise violate their rights), and of defense of
self and others[4] (where those who threaten to perform certain
wrongful acts may justifiably be prevented from performing
them, even though the prevention involves treating them in ways
that would otherwise violate their rights).

(3) *Other rights and/or the rights of others take precedence.* It seems to be
a general truth about all rights (although some[5] have denied this
and argued instead that at least some rights are absolute, non-
overridable trumps on actions) that we may act in ways that
actually do violate the rights of some so that their other rights or
the rights of others may be realized. This type of justification is,
however, essentially different from types (1) and (2) because,
when this type of justification is employed, there are rights that
are actually violated and this violation requires compensation. It
is this fact about rights that helps explain such legal (and moral)
defenses as necessity.[6] For example, a bank teller is justified
(and not merely excused, so this is not a case of coercion) in
embezzling the funds of the bank and giving them to the hold-
up man who threatens his life, because the teller's need to

---

[3] Provided, of course, that one holds a non-deterrent theory of punishment. A believer in the
deterrent theory might say that punishment involves no loss of rights but, rather, an overriding
of rights to avoid the greater evil of continued crime.

[4] On this point, see B. Brody, *Abortion and the Sanctity of Human Life* (Cambridge: M.I.T. Press,
1975), pp.6–12.

[5] It is not entirely clear that this view has actually been held by anyone. Close analogues to it are
found in R. Nozick's *Anarchy, State and Utopia* (New York: Basic Books, 1974); C. Fried's
Rights and Wrong (Cambridge: Harvard University Press, 1978); and R. Dworkin's *Taking
Rights Seriously* (Cambridge: Harvard University Press, 1978). But remarks by Nozick in his
footnote on p.30, by Fried on pp.9–13, and by Dworkin on pp.90–94 suggest that they don't
really hold the view in question.

[6] On the difference between necessity and coercion, see G. Fletcher's *Rethinking Criminal Law*
(Boston: Little Brown and Co., 1978), pp.774–834.

realize his right not to be killed takes precedence over the bank's right not to have its funds embezzled. Compensation is required, but that burden falls on the thief and not on the teller.

(4) *The violation of the right is a lesser evil.* It seems to be a general truth about all rights that we may act in ways that actually do violate the rights of some so that *much* greater evils (not just greater evils, as utilitarians would say) may be avoided. Justifications of type (4) are different from justifications of type (3) because in cases of type (4) what we are trying to avoid is greater evils, rather than the violation of greater rights. Like justifications of type (3), justifications of type (4) require compensation to the party whose rights are violated because there actually are rights which are violated. It is this fact about rights that helps explain why, for example, a boat may dock at a private dock without permission in order to avoid damage when a storm is threatening to destroy the boat, although the owner of the boat must certainly compensate the owner of the dock for any damage that results from his action.[7]

There is an important point that needs to be noted about each of these justifications. That point is that none of them make any reference to whether the individual using force in ways that seem to violate rights has acted on his own or under a grant of authority from the state. If the person against whom the force is used has waived or lost his right, then it is that waiver or forfeiture which justifies the use of force; authorization by the state is irrelevant. Similarly, if protecting other rights or avoiding greater evils take precedence over some rights, then it is that precedence which justifies the use of force, and a state authorization or lack thereof is irrelevant. We need to think of the state's justified use of force – which for now will mean nothing more than the cases in which a person justifiably uses force with state authorization – as derivative from the individual's justified use of force.

Note two points about this last remark: (1) There are those[8] who argue that the state's justification for the use of force is derivative from the individual's because the individual gives the state the right to use force whenever he would be justified in doing so himself as part of a social contract. I make no such claim. My point about the derivative character of the state's justification for the use of force is based simply upon the fact that the justifications I listed above are justifications with or without state authorization. (2) There may nevertheless be good reasons for individuals

---

[7] The classic cases making this point are *Ploof v. Putnam* 71 A. 188 (1908) and *Vincent v. Lake Erie Transportation Co.* 124 N.W. 221 (1910).
[8] E.g., J. Locke, *Second Treatise*, Chapters 2 and 8.

not to use force until they obtain the state's authorization, even when they are justified in doing so. This may help avoid excessive or mistaken use of force; and it may make sense at least as long as the state does authorize the use of the force by someone, and as long as that person uses it effectively.

This, then, is how I propose to begin to think about the justified use of force by the state. I will be concerned for now with the question of when individuals are justified in using force with state authorization and, at the outset, this is all I will mean when I speak of "justified use of force by the state." More extensive concepts of the use of force by the state will be discussed later. I will assume that such cases must involve justifications of the types listed above, and that those justifications would be justifications even without the state's authorization. I will allow, however, that the state's authorization may play a valuable role; that is why we should be looking at the role of the state, rather than individuals or private associations, in the defense of liberty in the international arena.

II. THE PERMISSIBILITY OF THE USE OF FORCE IN THE DEFENSE OF LIBERTY

Let us begin by considering a standard case of self-defense: an individual A is acting in a way that will cause my death and I cannot stop him from doing so except by taking his life. This looks like a case in which it would be permissible for me to use even deadly force to save my life. There are some who would go further, and say that my use of deadly force is morally obligatory.[9] They would claim that I am obliged to save my life, even if that means taking A's life. Others would say that, while it is permissible to take A's life in order to save my own, I am not obliged to do so. I will return to this issue below. For now, I want to focus on the question of the permissibility of the use of force.

Nearly all agree that it is morally permissible for me to use deadly force to stop A. Let us see what happens as we vary the case one step at a time:

Variation (1) Suppose that individual A is acting in a way that will cause someone else's death and not my death. If the moral permissibility of my use of deadly force against A in the standard case is due to the fact that each person may put his life before the life of others, it cannot be extended to variation (1), which does not involve a threat to my life. If it is due to the fact that A, by his action, has forfeited his right to life, it can be extended to variation

[9] For example, M. Maimonides, *Mishneh Torah IX* 5, 1, 9–14.

(1). I think that the latter must clearly be the correct account. We do not believe, after all, that an individual may in general put his life before the life of others. This is why, for example, if we are both starving, and you have just enough food to keep you alive and won't share it with me, I may not kill you to get the food, even if that is the only way for me to survive.[10] More is required before I can justifiably take your life, and the more seems to be that you must be acting in a way that will cause my death. So the justification for my use of deadly force in the standard case is a forfeiture justification of type (2) and extends to variation (1).

Variation (2) Let us now suppose that A is acting in a way that will cause the death of B, someone other than myself, only if B resists; if B does not resist, A's actions will only result in a serious diminution in B's liberty of movement. A may, for example, be using a threat of deadly force against B to get B to agree to be confined in a very limited location. In this variation, may B or I use deadly force to stop A if that is the only way to do so? Let us divide this question into two parts. First, let us ask ourselves whether B has a right to refuse to be confined. It seems that he does, since A is basing his demands on force and not on any supposed justification, and B has a right to be free. Second, let us suppose that B refuses to be confined and that A responds by acting in a way that will result in B's death unless A is stopped by the use of deadly force. It seems that B or I should still be justified in using deadly force to stop A. After all, A's action will result in B's death unless A is stopped, so A forfeits his right to life. To be sure, A could say that the threat to B's life is at least in part due to the fact that B resisted A's threat to his liberty by refusing to be confined. But B has a right to refuse unjust interferences with his liberty, while A has no right to behave in the way in which he is behaving. In short, it seems that I may use deadly force to stop someone (in this case A) from acting so as to cause the death of someone else (in this case B) because the latter has resisted the former's unjust attempt to deprive him of his liberty.

---

[10] I take this to be clearly true. Recent research, summarized in A.W.B. Simpson's *Cannibalism and the Common Law* (Chicago: University of Chicago Press, 1984), has shown, however, that many eighteenth and nineteenth century jurists held the opposite view.

Variation (3) Let us now suppose that B is afraid of A's behavior and has agreed to be confined because he believes that A will kill him otherwise. May I now use deadly force against A, if that is the only way to free B? Of course, the fact that B agreed to be confined does not mean that his continued confinement does not violate his right to liberty, for the agreement was based upon coercive force. So B's confinement is a violation of his rights. But may I use deadly force? Two things are clear. If, encouraged by my support, B attempts to escape confinement, and A uses deadly force to prevent this, I certainly may use deadly force against A. A's action, just as it did in variation (2), amounts to a forfeiture of his right to life. Moreover, B certainly retains the right to attempt escape, since his confinement is a violation of his rights. But may I use the deadly force against A *before* B begins his attempt and *before* A begins to carry out his threat to use deadly force? I may want to do so either (i) because B is afraid to attempt to escape and will not make that attempt unless I act first, or (ii) because I am also afraid of A and think that I have a better chance to succeed if I use the deadly force before A is alerted by B's attempted escape. I think that this "preemptive" use of force is permissible, at least as long as there is no other way to free B. But if this is correct, then it means that A's confinement of B amounts to a limited forfeiture by A of his right to life: either B or I may kill A, if that is the only way to secure B's freedom, even though B's life and my life are in no way threatened by the situation.

Variation (4) Finally, let us suppose that B, still afraid of A's behavior, has agreed to some other equally serious limitation on his freedom. May I now use deadly force against A to free B, if that is the only way to do so? It seems that the answer should still be yes, since the nature of the liberty of which A is depriving B should make no difference. But one word of caution is required at this point. In variation (3), we dealt with a serious violation of a person's freedom, confining him to a limited location and thereby limiting a fundamental right of freedom of movement. We should only extend the legitimacy of the use of deadly force to cases which involve similarly serious limitations of freedom. Substantially less serious limitations upon freedom may only justify the use of lesser amounts of force.

What we have seen so far is that individuals may (if that is the only way possible) use deadly force to help other people who are resisting threats to their freedom which are backed up by threats to their life, and that individuals may also (if that is the only way possible) use deadly force to free other people from serious limitations upon their freedom. If individuals may do so on their own, they may do so when authorized by the state. That authorization can hardly destroy the permissibility. Therefore, states may use deadly force in such situations, since all that means so far is that they may authorize people to do so. The people who are authorized are permitted to do so even without the authorization, and it can never be wrong (although it may or may not be superfluous) to authorize someone to do what he may do anyway.

III. THE OBLIGATION TO USE FORCE IN THE DEFENSE OF LIBERTY

Thus far we have been discussing the question of the moral permissibility of using force in defense of others. We have not really said anything about the question of a possible obligation to use that force. Since that question will be extremely important in our later discussion, we must now turn to it.

This question cannot arise for someone who believes that we are never under an obligation to come to the aid of others, no matter what their need may be. If we are never under an obligation to come to the aid of others, then we are certainly not under an obligation to use force in providing that aid. Consequently, this question will not have any relevance for someone who holds this "libertarian" view of our obligations to others.

I am certainly not, in this paper, going to argue that the "libertarian" position is mistaken on this point. Instead, I will assume for the sake of discussion that there are at least some cases in which an individual is threatened and in which others have an obligation to aid that individual. The main purpose of this section is to try to sharpen the contours of that obligation and to determine when, if ever, that obligation includes the use of force.

I think that there are two general claims that we can set out at the beginning which will help us considerably. They are: (1) all other things being equal, the more serious the threat to the party in question, the more we are under an obligation to aid him; (2) conversely, all other things being equal, the more burdensome the aid, the less we are under an obligation to aid the threatened individual. I think that these general claims help explain many of our intuitions about the obligation to aid. The clearest case of the obligation to give aid is always one in which a person's life is threatened (e.g., he is drowning in a river) and you can come to his aid with only a modest cost to yourself (e.g. you have little else to do, you are a very good swimmer, and there are no special circumstances that make jumping in to save the person dangerous). In such cases, unless one subscribes to the "libertarian" position,[11] it seems most evident that one is under an obligation to aid even a stranger. Other cases are less clear, in large measure because they involve either lesser threats to the person in danger or greater sacrifices by the person providing the aid.

If we accept these general claims about the obligation to give aid, then it looks as though there are few cases in which the use of force to aid others is obligatory. In general, the sorts of cases in which one is called upon to use force in defense of others are the cases in which they are threatened by force. Most typically, intervention in such situations creates a considerable risk that the force will be turned against the one who intervenes. If that is typically the case, then it is also typically going to be the case that while one may be justified in using force in the defense of others, one is not obliged to use that force.

Perhaps one of my earlier examples will help to clarify this point. Consider variation (3) of the previous section, in which B agrees to be confined because he is afraid of A. What typically happens in such a case when one attempts to use deadly force against A in order to free B? It will, of course, depend on circumstances. One may be able to surprise A and defeat him before he realizes that anyone has come to B's rescue. In that case, the risk to oneself may be very low indeed. But more generally, the world is not so kind to those who would free their fellows. A will usually be aware that an attempt is being made to free B by the use of force. A will respond, typically, by turning the threat of force directly against the person who would free B. That person, therefore, is putting his own life or safety at considerable risk, and that will count significantly against the claim that he is under an obligation to aid B.

I think that all of this is true, but it leaves out one major possibility which will be extremely important for our purposes. Consider, once more, the case in which A is confining B by the threat of deadly force, and we are considering freeing B by using deadly force against A. We might attempt to do so directly by intervening, but this imposes considerable risks upon us, and it is unclear that we are obliged to do so in light of the general contours of the obligation to give aid that I outlined above. There is, however, another way in which we might come to the aid of B. We might be able to hire others who are willing to take those risks in order to free B. These need not be people who are interested in B, but only people who are willing to accept the risks in question. Are we obliged to do this? Here, matters are more complicated. What is at stake is not a serious risk to our own life or limb, but only a risk to our pocketbook. Moreover, the sacrifice to our pocketbook

[11] As did the judges in the infamous drowning cases *Osterlind v. Hill* 160 N.E. 301 (1928); *Yania v. Bigin* 155 A. 2nd 343 (1959); and *Handiboe v. McCarthy* 151 S.E. 2nd 905 (1966).

might be limited because the cost of hiring these mercenaries might be spread over a large number of people. In that case, and in light of the factors outlined above, we may well be under an obligation to come to the defense of the freedom of others through financing attempts to free them.

Three points should be noted about what I have just said: (1) The first and most crucial point that I am trying to make is that cases will vary. I am by no means arguing that we have a general obligation to come to the aid of others, much less a general obligation to come to the aid of others by the use of deadly force in their defense. All that I am saying is that there are cases in which people face threats to life, liberty, or bodily integrity that are extremely serious, and in which we can help to meet these threats by accepting only modest costs to ourselves (these are primarily cases in which we subsidize the use of force by others to aid them). I am suggesting that, in these cases, there may well be an obligation to aid others. (2) All of this discussion is directed towards the issue of our obligation when others are threatened. I have said nothing in this discussion of our obligation to use deadly force when it is we who are threatened. This seems to be a very different and more complex issue. On the one hand, we can hardly be said to have an obligation to ourselves to come to our own aid whether we want to or not, for we can always waive obligations to ourselves, if we don't want to come to our own aid (if, for some reason or other, we would prefer to take our chances and not use deadly force). On the other hand, there may be other moral factors having nothing to do with obligations to ourselves that require us to aid ourselves when we are threatened. A consideration of those other moral factors, however, goes far beyond the scope of this paper. (3) In setting out the basic contours of the obligation to give aid, I talked about all other factors being equal. Of course, all other factors are not always equal. We may be under further obligations to aid someone whose life, bodily integrity, or liberty is threatened because we have promised to do so, because they have aided us in a similar situation in the past, because there is some tremendous social good to be promoted by giving them aid, or for some other reason. I simply wanted to point out that there might be some cases in which we are obligated to use (directly or indirectly) deadly force to aid others, even when none of these special factors are present.

IV. MORE WAYS OF THINKING ABOUT THE JUSTIFIED USE OF FORCE BY THE STATE

Thus far, I have been concerned to explain three main theses and to indicate why I think they are plausible. They are: (a) that there are cases in which it is morally permissible for individuals to use force to defend the liberty of others; (b) some of these are also cases in which individuals are obliged either to use force or to subsidize the use of force to defend the liberty of others; (c) there are good reasons why the state should coordinate this effort by authorizing some individuals, but not others, to use force. In this way, the state's use of force, in the sense of its coordination of the use of force by individuals, in the defense of the liberty of others is justified.

Obviously, however, when we talk about the use of force by the state, we usually mean that the state does much more than just authorize individuals to use force. We must now turn to the questions of what these additional activities of the state are, and what justifications are available for them.

When a modern state goes to war, it does at least the following: (1) it identifies the enemy against whom force is to be used and the forces to be used against that enemy; (2) it raises an army which uses the authorized force against that enemy; (3) it raises the funds to supply that army with the equipment required to fight a modern war. Of these three, (1) has been the primary focus of my discussion until now, for the process of the state's authorization of the use of force by individuals is precisely the process of identifying what force is to be used against whom. But (2) and (3) are clearly central to modern warfare, so we need to look at the moral problems that arise when a modern state takes these steps as part of its use of force to defend the liberty of others.

Raising an army would involve no special moral problems if all that it involved were asking for volunteers. But, of course, it rarely (if ever) means just that, especially when the force is to be used in the defense of others. What, then, is involved in raising an army? Two possibilities seem to be most likely. It either requires us to coerce citizens of the state to participate in the army, or else it requires us to offer citizens sufficient inducements to elicit voluntary participation. The former is what we mean by conscription, while the latter is what we realistically mean when we talk of an all-volunteer army.

There are those[12] who would challenge the legitimacy of this distinction. They generally argue as follows: who would agree to join the armed services, knowing the risks it involves, except those who are very poor and who see the inducements offered as their best (or perhaps their only real) option in a cruel world of very limited options. Such people do not really voluntarily agree to join the services, much less to participate in the use of force. They are coerced into doing so by their circumstances and by their lack of choices, and we who offer them these inducements are really coercing them as well. The use of an "all-volunteer" army is just a way of fooling ourselves into believing that we do not use coercion to take advantage of the disadvantaged.

It is important to note that those who offer this argument are not

---

[12] All those, particularly Marxists and other socialists, who have talked about economic coercion.

necessarily (although they may be) denying the existence of a distinction between threats and offers, or a distinction between coercive choices based upon threats and voluntary choices made as a result of offers. All that they need to be claiming is that those who join are usually doing so in a context in which the inducements are comparatively so attractive, and in which the state of the volunteers before they join up is comparatively so bad, that their choice is not voluntary but coerced.

I do not see, however, that the challenge can successfully be maintained. The question before us is whether we coerce the potential participants by offering them inducements, thereby depriving them of their right to be free from coerced choices. How can it be possible that we are coercing them? Let us consider those disadvantaged people who are the most likely to join. Before we offer them the inducements, they have, *ex hypothese*, few (if any) attractive options open to them. Now that we have given them the choice, they have an additional option, one that they find attractive. How can offering an additional option to people, an option they find attractive, be a form of coercion? By expanding their options, we have increased the significance of their freedom, not limited its exercise.

So there really are two distinct ways in which the state can raise an army. It can do so coercively, by conscripting soldiers, or it can use offers to attract volunteers. Now, those who emphasize the importance of liberty are obviously going to prefer the latter way of raising an army, and I would certainly not want to challenge that preference. I would, however, simply like to point out that there might be cases in which even the use of conscription to raise an army to fight in the defense of others is arguably justifiable. These cases, probably very rare, will fall under one of the following two rubrics. (A) Cases in which, because there are comparatively low costs to those who fight, and comparatively great gains to those who are being freed, we are obliged (and not merely permitted) to use force in defense of the liberty of others. In such cases, one might mount the following argument: the state is, no doubt, coercing people by conscripting them. But what it is forcing them to do is that which they are obliged to do anyway. In such cases, the use of coercion, even if not obligatory, is permissible and is no violation of their rights. (B) Cases in which so much liberty will be regained by so many that securing them their rights to liberty takes precedence over the rights of those who are conscripted, even if the cost to those who are conscripted is great and they have no obligation to fight. Such cases are, of course, possible only if one accepts the view, suggested in section I, that rights may in some cases be legitimately violated so that far greater rights of others may be realized. In such cases, unlike cases falling under rubric (A), those who are conscripted would have a legitimate claim to compensation, either from those who conscript them (or from those whom they free) or from the initial aggressors.

That right to compensation is reflective of the fact, noted in section I, that those whose rights are justifiably violated must be compensated.

Having said what I can by way of a defense of conscription in a few cases, I return to the preferred way of accomplishing (2): raising an all-volunteer army by offering sufficient inducements to elicit a sufficient number of volunteers. In order to do that, the state will require considerable funds. That being so, the defenders of liberty will have to consider morally legitimate ways in which the state might obtain those funds. This is, of course, the very same problem that must be considered by the friends of liberty as they consider (3), raising the funds needed to supply the army. So let us look at those problems together.

Raising the funds to supply the army or raising the funds to attract volunteers, our favored way of accomplishing (2), would involve no special moral problems if all it meant was asking for donations. But, of course, it rarely (if ever) means just that, especially when the funds are to be used to defend others. What, then, does it mean? Two possibilities seem to be most likely. It either requires us to coerce citizens of the state to provide the funds, or else it requires us to offer citizens other services for which they are willing to pay and to use the profits to pay for the army. Since the latter has never (unfortunately, to my mind) been explored as a possibility, I will focus my attention on the former, the use of taxes to fund military efforts to defend the liberty of others.

It seems to me that we will, once more, have two types of cases in which the state may legitimately collect these funds. They will be cases which fall under one of the following two rubrics. (A') Cases in which, because there are comparatively low costs to those who pay the taxes, and comparatively great gains to those who are being freed, we are obliged (and not merely permitted) to pay for the use of force to defend the liberty of others. In such cases, one can mount the following argument: the state is, no doubt, coercing people by forcing them to pay these taxes. But what it is forcing them to do is that which they are obliged to do anyway. In such cases, the use of coercion, even if not obligatory, is permissible and is no violation of the taxpayers' rights. (B') Cases in which so much liberty will be regained by so many that securing them their rights takes precedence over the rights of these who are required to pay the taxes, even if the cost to the taxpayers is great and they have no obligation to pay the taxes. Such cases are, once more, possible only if one accepts the view, suggested in section I, that rights may in some cases be legitimately violated so that a far greater good may be realized. In such cases, unlike cases falling under rubric (A'), those who pay the taxes have a legitimate claim to compensation, presumably from those who are freed or from the initial aggressors. That right to compensation is reflective of the fact, noted in section I, that those whose rights are justifiably violated must be compensated.

Cases of type (A') are obviously analogous to cases of type (A), and cases of type (B') are obviously analogous to cases of type (B). As we saw in section III, there is, however, a crucial difference that needs to be noted. There are going to be far more cases of type (A') than of type (A), and there are going to be far more cases of type (B') than of type (B). Typically, forcing people to help pay for a war, because it involves no threat to their lives or bodily integrity and because the cost can be spread across the entire citizenry, will involve far less serious a violation of their rights than forcing them to actively participate in a war. Therefore, there will be more cases in which they will be obliged to pay than to fight (more cases of type (A') than of type (A)), and more cases in which the gains to liberty will outweigh the loss of the right not to pay than cases in which the gains to liberty will outweigh the loss of the right not to fight (more cases of type (B') than of type (B)).

In short, there will certainly be cases in which it is legitimate for the state to use force to defend the liberty of others, even though this requires the state to raise an army and finance its operations, and even though these latter activities (may) involve coercion.

V. THINKING ABOUT THE REAL WORLD

I began with the observation that those who value liberty might be sorely divided on the issue of the international defense of liberty. Some might attend to the liberties to be defended, while others might attend to the liberties violated in mounting the defense. I have tried to attend to both of these factors.

Using the results of the previous sections, I would now like to describe in a schematic fashion a clear-cut and realistic type of case in which it would be justifiable for one country to use its forces to defend the liberties of citizens of another country. I will then look at other realistic cases (leaving aside less realistic but possible cases to which I alluded in earlier sections) which may be more or less clear-cut.

Consider the following set of circumstances:

(1) The citizens of country B are resisting a major threat to their liberty by the citizens of country A. Unfortunately, some are likely to lose their lives and the rest their freedom.

(2) The citizens of country C have no special obligations, based upon past promises or past help, to the citizens of either

country, and the loss of freedom by the citizens of B in no way threatens the freedom of the citizens of C.

(3) The citizens of C can, at a relatively modest cost to each, raise and equip a volunteer army that can defeat the efforts of the citizens of A and preserve most of the lives and/or freedoms of the citizens of B that would otherwise be lost. No group of volunteers from C comes forward to fund this army, but an exercise of the political processes in place in C leads to a decision to fund such an army with tax revenues.

I have argued that in this obviously realistic set of circumstances, C may justifiably raise the requisite funds by a coercive system of taxation, and may then use those funds to raise and equip a force of volunteers who will use force to defend the liberties of the citizens of B. The use of force against the aggressors from A is justified by the fact that those aggressors have forfeited their rights to life and bodily integrity, and the use of coercion by C to raise funds from its citizens is justified by the fact that its citizens are obliged to provide those funds to aid the citizens of B. Since the use of this force and coercive taxation are the only two morally questionable aspects of the enterprise, and since they are justified, C is justified in its international use of force to protect the lives and liberties of the citizens of B. Note, however, that the fact that C is justified does not entail that C is obligated to aid B. That is a separate question, and I have nothing to say about that complex issue of state obligation in this paper.

What factors might make the case even more clear-cut? There are certainly cases in which the success of the aggressors from A might encourage them to challenge the freedom of the citizens of C, and might give them the added strength required to succeed in that challenge. In such cases, C's use of force to protect the liberties of the citizens of B is even more certainly justified, since there are even more rights being protected and the obligation which justifies the coercive taxation is greater. Similarly, there are cases in which the citizens of C have special obligations to the citizens of B (based upon past promises or upon gratitude), and these additional obligations increase the legitimacy of the coercive taxation. In these two ways, both of which involve the falsity of condition (2), the case becomes more clear-cut because the coercion involved in raising funds is even less troublesome.

What factors might make the case less clear-cut? The major one is certainly the following. Suppose that the cost of raising and equipping the volunteer army becomes greater and greater. As it does, the obligation of the citizens to pay those funds becomes weaker and weaker, as does the legitimacy of the state's coercive efforts to collect them. At some point, the burden is too great, the obligation to help is no longer present, and the situation becomes very complex. If the loss to the citizens of B vastly outweighs the loss to the citizens of C, C may still justifiably force its citizens to fund this army, but the citizens may demand compensation afterwards from the citizens of A or of B. If the loss to the citizens of B is less than that to the citizens of C, then C may no longer compel its citizens to pay for this war of liberation. The following very hard question may arise: if the loss to the citizens of B vastly outweighs the loss to the citizens of C, but no compensation of the citizens of C is possible, may C coercively fund this use of force?

Can we take this analysis of types of cases and bring it to bear upon real life instances of the use of force in the international defense of liberty? I believe that we can, but only if we are sensitive to a number of complications that the real world often presents:

(I) The Status of Liberty if we Succeed. Throughout this analysis, I have supposed that the result of the use of force to eliminate the threat from A is a restoration of the threatened liberties. In the real world, this is often not the case. The citizens of B may wind up living under a regime which restricts their liberties in other ways. Alas, this often seems to be so whether the threat from A is a threat from the right or the left. None of this affects the moral legitimacy of the use of force against the aggressors from A. But, since the liberty of the citizens of B may not be promoted very much by saving them from the aggressors from A, that may seriously undercut the legitimacy of coercing the citizens of C to fund the war against A. If that legitimacy derives from the obligation of the citizens of C, it may be undercut by this complication, since they have no obligation unless the liberties of the citizens of B can be promoted. If that legitimacy derives from the maximization of rights, it may be undercut by this complication because defending the citizens of B against A may not maximize their rights.

(II) The Marginal Cost of this Effort. Throughout this analysis, I have treated a particular instance of the use of force by the state as a discrete entity whose cost to the citizenry can be clearly ascertained. Often, that is not the case. The state in question may use forces and equipment already mustered for other purposes. What we need to know, but may find it very hard to ascertain, is the marginal cost of this additional effort; for that expresses what is relevant, the burden this defense of liberty imposes upon the citizens of C.

(III) The True Aggressor. Throughout this analysis, I have

assumed that it is clear that some parties to a conflict have forfeited their rights to life by threatening the lives and liberties of others. But that is often not the case. Various parties to a conflict may have threatened to use and may have used force in various ways, and it may be very unclear who has forfeited his rights. Complications (I) and (II) affect our ability to ascertain whether or not C's coercive taxation to fund its use of force is justified. This complication affects our ability to ascertain whether the use of deadly force by C's army is justified by some aggressor's forfeiture of rights.

We need, then, to be realistic about our ability to apply the results of this philosophical analysis to real life questions about the use of force in the international defense of liberty. Being realistic is not, however, being pessimistic. It is just being careful. With care, and with sound moral theory, those who treasure liberty can decide in a principled fashion when to support the international defense of liberty.

Philosophy, Rice University and
Center for Ethics, Baylor College of Medicine

Social Philosophy & Policy 3:1 Autumn 1985 ISSN 0265-0525 $2.00

CONFLICTING CONCEPTIONS OF DETERRENCE*

HENRY SHUE

The Baptism of the Bomb

Here is a two-step plan to rescue nuclear war from immorality. First, the United States should build the most moral offensive nuclear weapons that money can buy and bring nuclear warfare into compliance with the principle of noncombatant immunity. Then it should build a defensive "shield" that will make offensive nuclear weapons "impotent and obsolete" and take the world "beyond deterrence." In this second stage, called the "Strategic Defense Initiative" (SDI) by believers and "Star Wars" by doubters, anti-missile technology will confront missile technology like a Hegelian antithesis confronting its thesis, and we will all be lifted up out of the age of nuclear war into a realm made safe for conventional war.[1] Even according to believers in the SDI, however, intermediate deployment, not to mention full deployment, of a strategic defense is some time away, pending breakthroughs on technological problems at which public money is now

---

* Early ancestors of this paper were read at Davidson College, at a Third Thursday Briefing and a Workshop for Teachers conducted by the Center for Philosophy and Public Policy at the University of Maryland, at the Poynter Center at Indiana University, and at the First Fulbright Anglo-American Colloquium on Ethics and International Affairs of the Centre for Philosophy and Public Affairs at St. Andrews University. I benefitted so much from the discussions at these occasions that I doubt whether those present will now recognize the paper, least of all its conclusion. For the financial support of this work I am grateful to the Ford Foundation, which bears no responsibility for my views. Besides the abiding influence of the Maryland Center and my colleagues there, during final revisions I enjoyed the informal hospitality of the Institute for Advanced Study in Princeton.

[1] For some of the doubts, see Sidney D. Drell, Philip J. Farley, and David Holloway, "Preserving the ABM Treaty: A Critique of the Reagan Strategic Defense Initiative," *International Security*, vol. 9 (Fall 1984), pp.51–91; John Tirman, ed., *The Fallacy of Star Wars* (New York: Vintage Books, 1984), especially the chapter by Hans A. Bethe and Richard L. Garwin; Ashton B. Carter, *Directed Energy Missile Defense in Space* (Washington: Government Printing Office, 1984); and Henry Shue, "Are Nuclear Defenses Morally Superior?" *QQ: Report from the Center for Philosophy and Public Policy*, vol. 5 (Spring 1985). For advocacy of SDI, see Colin S. Gray, *Nuclear Strategy and Strategic Planning*, Philadelphia Policy Papers (Philadelphia: Foreign Policy Research Institute, 1984), "Option Five: Damage Limitation with Defense Dominance," pp.86–93; Richard D. DeLauer, "Antiballistic Missile Defense – The Opportunity and the Challenge," *NATO's Sixteen Nations: Independent Review of Economic, Political and Military Power*, vol. 29 (November 1984), pp.7–11; Keith B. Payne and Colin S. Gray, "Nuclear Policy and the Defensive Transition," *Foreign Affairs*, vol. 62 (Spring 1984), pp.820–842; and Zbigniew Brzezinski, Robert Jastrow, and Max M. Kampelman, "Defense in Space Is Not 'Star Wars'," *New York Times Magazine*, January 27, 1985, pp.28–29, 46, 48, and 51.

44 HENRY SHUE

being thrown. Meanwhile, during the intervening decades, we must look to
the morality of our offensive missiles, and on the offensive front too there is
good news: nuclear weapons are becoming more discriminate. The bomb
has been born again. Now it is more just, and it need not indiscriminately
slaughter the innocent. Thus spake, for example, Wohlstetter.

In a wide-ranging article in *Commentary*, eminent theorist of deterrence
Albert Wohlstetter decries how some moralists have blithely embraced the
threat of the nuclear incineration of women and children in the adversary
society on the mistaken assumption that the most – perhaps the only –
credible form of deterrence was mutual assured destruction: destruction, not
of enemy forces, but of enemy families.[2] "Not even Genghis Khan,"
Wohlstetter notes, "avoided combatants in order to focus solely on
destroying noncombatants."[3] Seriously intended assured destruction is
neither moral nor credible. Further, Wohlstetter's critique of mutual assured
destruction as "self-confessed suicidal bluff" and of "the insanity of
deception labeling itself deception," strengthens his essay as a powerful and
worthy successor to Fred Iklé's classic critique of mutual assured destruction.[4]

Moralists who have opposed assured destruction have, according to
Wohlstetter, been part of the problem in a different way. (Few, if any,
"moralists" seem to have been part of the solution.)

> Moralists who have chosen to emphasize the shallow paradoxes
> associated with deterrence by immoral threats against population
> have been at their worst when they have opposed any attempts to
> improve the capability to attack targets precisely and discriminately
> . . . They have often stopped research and engineering on ways to
> destroy military targets without mass destruction; and they have
> done collateral damage to the development of precise, long-range
> conventional weapons . . . They have tried to stop, and have slowed,
> the development of technologies which can free us from the loose
> and wishful paradoxes involved in efforts to save the peace with
> unstable threats to terrorize our own as well as adversary civilians.[5]

---

[2] Albert Wohlstetter, "Bishops, Statesmen, and Other Strategists On the Bombing of
Innocents," *Commentary* (June 1983), pp.15–35.
[3] ibid., p.16.
[4] ibid., p.31. See Fred Iklé, "Can Nuclear Deterrence Last Out the Century," *Foreign Affairs*,
vol. 51 (January 1973), pp.267–285. A reply to Iklé then was: Wolfgang Panofsky, "The
Mutual Hostage Relationship Between America and Russia," *Foreign Affairs*, vol. 52 (October
1973), pp.109–118. A recent reply to (Iklé and) Wohlstetter is: McGeorge Bundy, "Existential
Deterrence and Its Consequences," in Douglas MacLean, ed., *The Security Gamble*, Maryland
Studies in Public Philosophy (Totowa, N.J.: Rowman & Allanheld, 1984), pp.3–13.
[5] ibid., p.29.

While I certainly do not think that all the paradoxes of deterrence are shallow, loose, and wishful,[6] I shall have nothing to say in response to Wohlstetter's internal criticisms of mutual assured destruction. I want to concentrate instead on Wohlstetter's positive thesis, his good news about "the revolution in precision" of offensive nuclear missiles. This good news is that we now have an alternative that is morally superior to mutually assured destruction, an alternative that is neither murderous intent nor suicidal bluff. The new generation of precision guided munitions (nuclear and non-nuclear) restores a morally significant choice "between killing innocent bystanders with nuclear weapons or attacking means of aggression and domination" – "a choice between destroying military targets and destroying innocents."[7]

I am not persuaded that we have any such choice between a form of nuclear war that could more or less satisfy the just-war requirement of avoiding harm to the innocent and another form of nuclear war that involves mass slaughter. Worse, I fear that in pursuit of a way to fight a nuclear war with clean hands we may undermine what little hope we still have of avoiding nuclear war. In order to see the depths of the difficulties, we first need to take a few steps back.

Four Polar Postures

Whenever people discuss the reason for possessing nuclear weapons, they say "deterrence," but increasingly they do not mean deterrence or, at the very least, they do not mean deterrence in its classic, i.e. early post-World-War-II, sense. Your reasons for wanting to possess nuclear weapons depend upon how you would use them, if you chose to use them. Almost everyone, although not quite literally everyone, says that he or she would never wish actually to use nuclear weapons. But possession is pointless unless some use is not only conceivable but, in some sense, feasible. I do not mean that the possession of nuclear weapons is pointless unless you will, or even would, use them. I mean it is pointless unless you might use them – unless there are circumstances in which you could use them and might do it, whether or not you actually would. If there are no circumstances in which you might use nuclear weapons, then you cannot even effectively bluff that you would use them – you can, as Wohlstetter emphasizes, only bluff suicidally. So, any given rationale for the possession of nuclear weapons turns upon their conceivable use.

---

[6] The most sophisticated discussions of the paradoxes I know are: David Gauthier, "Deterrence, Maximization, and Rationality"; Gregory S. Kavka, "Nuclear Deterrence: Some Moral Perplexities"; David Lewis, "Devil's Bargains and the Real World"; and Gregory S. Kavka and David Gauthier, "Responses to the Paradox of Deterrence"; all in MacLean, ed., *The Security Gamble*.

[7] Wohlstetter, pp.19 and 31.

Use has at least two essential components: what and when. What are the targets and when might they be attacked? I shall call these two elements of any planned use of nuclear weapons "target" and "time." Over-simplifying enormously, we can divide conceptions of deterrence into four types by reference to choice of target and choice of time:

Targets \ Time	earlier	later
civilian	(Terroristic)	Retaliatory
military/ command	Anticipatory	(Damage-limiting)

Figure 1 Polar Offenses

The targets of a nuclear attack can be either predominantly "countervalue" (cities and other civilian areas) or "counterforce" (weapons, troops, and command centers). The attack can be launched either earlier (before the other side has launched nuclear weapons) or later (after the other side has launched nuclear weapons).[8]

Any plan to attack civilian targets, but only after a nuclear attack, I call retaliatory deterrence. Any plan to attack military targets in an initial use of nuclear weapons, I call anticipatory deterrence. I am introducing these new

[8] Sometimes it is difficult to decide when one is clarifying by sticking to the fundamentals, and when distorting by oversimplifying. Obviously, far more than four options can be, and repeatedly have been, worked out. Counterforce targets, for example, could be divided into nuclear and non-nuclear, e.g. troop concentrations; or they could be divided into military strictly speaking (which could be subdivided into nuclear and non-nuclear) and politico-military, including the whole Soviet or American chain of command, right up to the top. Initial uses could be subdivided into limited and massive, etc. Besides targets and timing, one could also consider a third dimension: type of weapons used, nuclear or non-nuclear. Soviet nuclear missiles could, perhaps, someday be struck with American precision-guided conventional weapons, thereby observing the taboo on nuclear *use*.

I do not mean to deny that at least some of these other distinctions are important or even that something is lost when they are left aside. I maintain only that I am focusing on *some* of the fundamental issues, and I am trying to discuss them in an uncluttered way. Much else could usefully be said, but I do not think it would require essential changes in what I say. In the final section of the paper, I introduce one simple additional factor that I take to be crucial.

labels, which I shall explain more fully in due course, as part of an effort to take a fresh look at some issues. Nevertheless, reciprocal policies of retaliatory deterrence would obviously constitute what is ordinarily called mutual assured destruction, and NATO's declared policy of first use of nuclear weapons in response to a successful conventional attack in Europe is one form (among several possible forms) of anticipatory deterrence.[9] I want, however, to stick largely to the fundamentals here, rather than to enter the thickets of actual policies just yet. First, we must see why we seem to be driven into choosing between retaliatory deterrence and anticipatory deterrence. Then we can concentrate upon that disagreeable dilemma, and, in the end, we can try to escape the dilemma.

Nuclear deterrence is one method for stopping an adversary nation from doing things you do not want it to do without, if the deterrence succeeds, actually having to go to war. Nuclear deterrence is a form of international coercion for nation-states that are politically sovereign but understand, to some extent, their nuclear vulnerability. Deterrence succeeds if it stops your adversary from doing what you did not want done without getting you into a war. In its specific form, between the Soviet Union and the United States, its goal is containment without conflict. Each superpower is attempting to protect its own sphere of influence without being forced to fight World War III in order to do so. If avoiding war were the policy's only purpose, deterrence would not be as delicate a balancing act: the trick is avoiding war *and* getting what you most want (what the speeches call "vital interests"). One may well decide, in the closing words of the film "War Games," that "the only winning move is not to play the game." If one chooses to play, however, it is essential to see that the game is ineradicably in part *military*. Doctrines of deterrence are politico-military: (1) here is how we will stop them without a war and (2) here is how we will fight the war if (1) does not work. Accounts of deterrence that ignore the question, "And what if deterrence fails?" are deceptions, self-deceptions, or both – and "it had better not fail" is not an answer to the question.

The military and the moral debates are alike in being fundamentally about what would have to be done if deterrence fails.[10] The military question is this: if your adversary can in fact be coerced only by means of a successful war

---

[9] For a clear account of the major differences between first use and first strike, and an explanation of why the current combination of first strike on one side and first use on the other is one of the worst possible combinations, see Freeman Dyson, *Weapons and Hope* (New York: Harper and Row, 1984), pp.250–253.

[10] At least in the United States they are. For a fascinating discussion of national differences in emphasis, see Pierre Hassner,"Ethical Issues in Nuclear Deterrence; Four National Debates in Perspective – France, Great Britain, United States, and West Germany," paper prepared for European-American conference on "Ethical Aspects of Nuclear Deterrence," April 1985, Stiftung für Wissenschaft und Politik, Ebenhausen, West Germany.

effort, in how good a position will you be to conduct a successful effort after your deterrence policy has failed? The military assessments obviously admit of degrees, but for our purposes very rough and obvious standards will serve. Moral criteria apply to both the threat and the military implementation, if the threat should fail to deter, but judgments about the threat are in some (difficult to specify) fashion dependent upon judgments about what will happen if the threat fails. Thus, it would seem prudent to give a lot of attention to the case of failure.[11]

Looking at Figure 1 with military and moral considerations in mind, then, we can see fairly quickly why terroristic deterrence is the most objectionable militarily and morally. We can next turn to its diametrical opposite, damage-limiting retaliation, which is more appealing militarily in that it plans for attacks upon the opposing forces rather than upon civilians, and more appealing morally in that it respects the nuclear taboo by using nuclear weapons only in retaliation. This appealing combination will turn out, however, to suffer centrifugal tendencies. The combination of counterforce targeting and second-strike timing seems driven apart: if we demand counterforce targeting, we are pushed toward first-strike timing, that is, anticipatory deterrence; if we demand second-strike timing, we are pushed toward civilian targets, that is, retaliatory deterrence. And we seem to be left with these two unappealing choices. First, then, we acknowledge terroristic deterrence; next we struggle with damage-limiting retaliation; and then comes our confrontation with the only two choices that seem to be left.

Military Pressures for Early Launch

Terroristic deterrence. What is militarily sensible can be of human interest only if it is morally sensible as well. Nevertheless, be it ever so moral, a position about nuclear deterrence is unacceptable unless it makes military sense. Satisfaction of both military criteria and moral criteria is necessary for an acceptable deterrence policy. To attack first and to attack the civilians on the other side (upper left box of Figure 1) is militarily nonsensical – more precisely, instrumentally irrational – not to mention morally abominable. Terroristic deterrence toward another nuclear power is a disastrous failure on both military and moral criteria. From a military point of view, one does not initiate a nuclear exchange by consuming substantial numbers of one's most sophisticated and powerful weapons in a manner certain to enrage and embitter the political and military leaders of a nuclear-armed adversary, while leaving the adversary's best weapons and leadership untouched – this would be true military madness. From any recognizable moral point of view,

[11] For a comprehensive examination of the varieties of deterrence theories, and their intellectual failure to face the question of what happens if deterrence fails, see Lawrence Freedman, *The Evolution of Nuclear Strategy* (New York: St. Martin's Press, 1981).

this would be true terrorism as well. What terrorists do – as well as most torturers, which is why most torture is a species of terrorism[12] – is assault defenseless civilians who are in no way responsible for causing what the terrorists oppose.

Terroristic deterrence will, I hope, strike ordinary readers as bizarre. Nevertheless, it is well to remember that the only two actual military uses of nuclear weapons so far, the American attacks upon Hiroshima and Nagasaki, were and were intended to be terroristic. They were war crimes which went unpunished simply because the victor committed them. Nevertheless, they were unsurpassed in calculated cruelty by the most dastardly war crimes of the Japanese. The purpose of the nuclear strikes on Hiroshima and Nagasaki was "to induce a sense of hopelessness in a people, still resisting despite immense suffering, by impressing upon them their vulnerability to an unprecedented form of horror."[13] As George Marshall maintained before the attacks on the two cities: "It's no good warning them. If you warn them there's no surprise. And the only way to produce shock is surprise."[14] The United States consciously implemented a policy of terrorizing civilians. In one sense it "worked," but presumably only because the adversary could not defend itself in kind.

Damage-limiting retaliation. A retaliatory strike against military targets (lower right box of Figure 1) is a deterrent threat that would be welcomed, or at least tolerated, by many moralists, viz., those whose overriding criterion is the principle of noncombatant immunity which is interpreted to mean not targeting civilians. Indeed, from this point of view one would judge that the only form of retaliation the implementation of which could possibly be morally justified (after deterrence had already failed) would be an attack upon the military forces, not the civilians, of the other society. I readily acknowledge that damage-limiting retaliation is in an entirely different moral realm from terroristic deterrence and that the appropriate moral assessment of it is not obviously negative. Let us say for now that we will not exclude it on moral grounds.

How to assess damage-limiting retaliation by military criteria is a difficult question. In destroying any remaining forces on the other side, especially any nuclear forces that had been held in reserve, one would be limiting the future damage that one could suffer (in a subsequent round). Thus, a military rationale might well generally support the choice of military targets for any strike, retaliatory or not. Professional military leaders in general tend greatly to prefer to fight the opposing military forces rather than to attack

[12] See Manuel Velasquez and Cynthia Rostankowski, eds., *Ethics: Theory and Practice* (Englewood Cliffs, NJ Prentice-Hall, 1985), pp.150–168.
[13] Freedman, *The Evolution of Nuclear Strategy*, pp.18–19.
[14] ibid., p.19.

unarmed civilians. Since it is the other side's military forces, not its noncombatants, who can destroy your own forces, it is eminently sensible to prefer to deal first with the opposing military. It is the threat to you – and to the civilians you are defending.

The trouble is, first, that the feasibility of counterforce retaliation lies largely in the hands of the adversary, who can eliminate many potential nuclear targets and many other non-nuclear military targets from your retaliatory attack by the simple expedient of using them in its own initial attack.[15] An adversary who has decided to launch a nuclear attack is unlikely to be very cooperative about saving targets for you. Second, if you were seen by the adversary to be building the capability for damage-limiting retaliation, it would have an added incentive to make any first-strike a massive one. Both these difficulties result from the fact that military targets tend to be movable targets. The first aspect of movability is that you can do less damage to the enemy in your second-strike – and the enemy decides how much less and where – while the second is that the enemy has an added reason to do more damage to you in its first-strike, in order to put its capabilities to good use instead of merely letting you destroy them where they sit.

Worst of all, whatever you were actually planning, an objective capability to conduct any very significant damage-limiting retaliation might appear to even a moderately suspicious adversary as evidence of plans for a disarming first-strike, since any counterforce capability that could be used later could also be used earlier. It will always be difficult to convince an adversary that any major counterforce capability is only for retaliating, not for preempting.[16]

It turns out, then, that any plan for damaging-limiting retaliation suffers at least three significant military defects:

1. Enemy-selected targets:
   Your adversary decides what you can attack (quantity and quality) in your second-strike in deciding what to use in its first-strike.

2. Magnitude incentive:
   An adversary who observes that you have major counterforce

---

[15] See Desmond Ball, "Can Nuclear War Be Controlled?" Adelphi Paper No. 169 (London: International Institute for Strategic Studies, 1981), Section V, "Soviet Strategic Doctrine: Implications for the Control of Nuclear War," pp.30–35. "The doctrine that, once the nuclear threshold is passed, it is the task of the nuclear forces to terminate the war by achieving military victory through massive, crippling strikes is deeply rooted in Soviet strategic culture, and the preferences and habits of the military bureaucracy would tend to rule out any possibility of improvisation in favour of 'American-formulated rules of intra-war restraint'" (34–35). Also see note 9 above, on the difference between NATO first use and U.S.S.R. first strike – and the tragedy of their being combined.

[16] It will be impossible to convince anyone, when the counterforce capability is itself vulnerable to an initial counterforce strike, as will be the MX when it is based in Minuteman silos.

capabilities has a strong reason to make any first-strike it would otherwise have made more massive than it would otherwise have been in order not to "waste" its weapons by leaving them for you to destroy with your second strike.

3. Preemption incentive:

An adversary who observes that you have major counterforce capabilities has a reason to make a first-strike it would not otherwise have made in order not to be vulnerable to a disarming first-strike, even though you may not currently be planning a first-strike.

The second and third defects together mean that any significant capability for damage-limiting retaliation provides an adversary with some reason (of indeterminate strength – and indeterminate net strength, when contrary incentives are considered) to launch a massive, preemptive counterforce strike. These are two respects in which damage-limiting retaliation *cannot be* militarily *superior* to anticipatory deterrence. The third point, indeed, consists of a cautious adversary treating damage-limiting retaliation as if it were anticipatory deterrence, as a result of the inexorable (and understandable) tendency to engage in worst-case planning when faced with an enemy's capability of launching a preemptive, disarming strike. The militarily rational response to a genuine capability for preemptive disarming can be, other things being equal, preemptive disarming of that very capability. More about this vicious circle later.

The first defect, enemy control of the quantity and quality of targets available for a second-strike, is a respect in which damage-limiting retaliation is irretrievably inferior to anticipatory deterrence, in military terms, because at best it can destroy only "left-over" targets. *How* inferior depends, of course, on how massive the initial attack is. Against an adversary who actually has the plans that NATO claims to have – beginning a nuclear war with a limited first use – damage-limiting retaliation might be, in military terms, quite a good plan, only marginally inferior to anticipatory deterrence; against an adversary whose first attack would in any case be massive, which is the announced Soviet policy, damage-limiting retaliation would be radically inferior.[17] The essence of the first point, however, is that how inferior the

---

[17] For a discussion of the Soviet doctrine of preemption, see note 15. Also see Colin S. Gray, "Targeting Problems for Central War," *Naval War College Review*, vol. 33 (January/February 1980), pp.9–10; John Erickson, "The Soviet View of Deterrence: A General Survey," *Survival*, vol. 24 (November/December 1982), pp.242–251; and Nikolay Vasilyevich Ogarkov, *Always in Readiness to Defend the Homeland*, trans. JPRS L/10412, 25 March 1982 (Moscow: Voyenizdat, 1982).

implementation of damage-limiting retaliation would be to the implementation of anticipatory deterrence is under the control of your enemy, who gets
the first "move."

Therefore, while I am not claiming that the military assessment is
conclusive, the case in the abstract for considering damage-limiting
retaliation unacceptable by military criteria is very strong: on points two and
three it cannot be superior to anticipatory deterrence, and on the first point it
must be *inferior to a degree to be determined by an attacking adversary*. Damage-
limiting retaliation is *ineradicably* inferior (to an indeterminate degree) in that
it permits the adversary to control targets because, after all, it is a second-
strike, which brings us back to the two underlying features of time and
target.

Of the three military defects of damage-limiting retaliation that we have
considered, only the first is determined by time; the second and third are
determined by target. *Any* plan for a retaliatory strike allows the adversary to
move what is movable, if it chooses. Any plan for a very large counterforce
strike provides the adversary with some reason to strike first and with
considerable reason to do so massively. It should now be abundantly clear
why the only serious options appear to be anticipatory deterrence and
retaliatory deterrence (if you do not simply assume that deterrence will be
effective indefinitely and ignore the consequences of its failure).

Looking at Figure 1, we can say that if you are going to be in the bottom
row, it appears that you should be in the left column. That is if your targets
are to be military, it appears that you should plan to strike first. This is the
only way to prevent the adversary from seriously limiting the military
effectiveness of your retaliatory attack. This is clear from our comparison of
damage-limiting retaliation with anticipatory deterrence. It is especially clear
for the concrete case in which your adversary's first-strike will, either
because of your counterforce targeting or for other reasons of its own, not be
limited.

From our earlier discussion of terroristic deterrence, on the other hand,
military and moral reasons combine into a conclusive case for saying that the
upper left box is absolutely to be avoided, although the moral reasons lean
towards choosing the right column and the military reasons lean towards
choosing the bottom row. That is, from a moral point of view, if you are ever
going to slaughter civilians, you should surely do it only in retaliation; and
from a military point of view, if you are ever going to slaughter civilians, you
should surely eliminate the forces defending them (and capable of attacking
you) first. Putting the military point less perversely, we can say simply that
military considerations argue for attacking the opposing military forces,
whenever it is that you attack. There are no sound military reasons for
attacking non-combatants.[18]

Faced, then, with an apparent residual dilemma between anticipatory deterrence and retaliatory deterrence, I shall try in the remainder of this essay to move through the following four steps: a brief indication of the sharp difference to doctrine from that originally accepted by the West (whatever the historical continuity in military policy) represented by the doctrine of anticipatory deterrence; a catalogue of four implausible premises on which the thesis of the moral superiority of anticipatory deterrence over retaliatory deterrence rests; some speculative arguments for the thesis that anticipatory deterrence is morally inferior to retaliatory deterrence; and the introduction of finite deterrence as possibly the least evil form of nuclear deterrence.

The Doctrine of Anticipatory Deterrence

Retaliatory deterrence is a doctrine that threatens only retaliation. Retaliatory deterrence never requires your side to be the first to go nuclear.[19] Anticipatory deterrence is a doctrine that threatens to initiate nuclear war. The implementation of anticipatory deterrence depends upon your side's using your nuclear forces first, before your adversary has used its nuclear forces – and using your forces against its nuclear forces (among other military targets).

"Deterrence" was once sharply defined as what I am calling "retaliatory deterrence," for example, by Albert Wohlstetter in 1959:

> To deter an attack means being able to strike back in spite of it. It means, in other words, a capability to strike second.[20]

---

[18] It may be worth mentioning what I would call the "air-force fantasy," which contradicts this Clausewitzian point. Fans of air-force city-bombing often advance the false hypothesis that if civilians are subjected to terror-bombing, the morale on the other side will be broken. After all the megatonnage dropped from the skies, there never yet has been a clear positive example. The disconfirming cases include: German bombing of the British, British bombing of the Germans, and American bombing of Japan during World War II; and American bombing of Vietnam. The unfalsifiable counterargument always is: it wasn't terrible enough – next time, unleash us (e.g., Vietnam). On Vietnam, see John Mueller, "The Search for the Single 'Breaking Point' in Vietnam: The Statistics of a Deadly Quarrel," *International Studies Quarterly*, vol. 24 (December 1980), pp.497–519.

And don't Hiroshima and Nagasaki show that if it is *nuclear* terror, morale will break? What if they show, instead, that morale will break if nuclear attacks are made on a *non*-nuclear power, which cannot retaliate in kind?

[19] You might fire back before you are hit, if you have a policy of launch under attack, but not before you are fired upon with nuclear weapons. And if your own force is survivable – that is, will remain available for use even after you have been attacked – as it ought to if your strategy actually is retaliatory deterrence, you will have no need for the dangerous hair-trigger policy of launch under attack, or launch on warning. You can wait to assess what actually resulted from the attack before you make the decision to retaliate.

[20] Albert Wohlstetter, "The Delicate Balance of Terror," *Foreign Affairs*, vol. 37 (January 1959), p.213. I am not implying a criticism of inconsistency – everyone is allowed to change his mind once every quarter century – I simply want to emphasize the magnitude of the change between the 1959 article and the 1983 article.

About Wohlstetter's views specifically, my thesis is that his 1983 position about *targets* is in tension with his 1959 position about *time* and is pushing him away from the doctrine of retaliatory deterrence toward the doctrine of anticipatory deterrence. This may be a shift that he himself would not welcome. "Anticipatory deterrence" is my term, not his, but it is only my attempt to draw out explicitly the implications of what he now says. If, once the implications are explicit, he would like to reject them – and their premises – I for one would welcome that.

I am giving the benefit of the doubt to Wohlstetter and to advocates of counterforce targeting generally by treating their doctrine as a form of deterrence, and I have manufactured the clumsy name "anticipatory deterrence" in order to do so. Some critics of counterforce targeting would simply say that all the associated doctrines lead to doctrines of war-fighting, and should not be considered as deterrence doctrines at all. These are doctrines of war-fighting, it is said, because they are doctrines about how actually to employ nuclear weapons in a militarily fruitful way, by engaging the military forces on the other side.

Now, the critics are quite right to notice a radical doctrinal difference between the retaliatory deterrence of Wohlstetter's 1959 position and the anticipatory deterrence that is, or is implied by, his 1983 position. It is this difference that my labels are intended to mark. It is inaccurate, however, simply to label all doctrines of counterforce targeting, or even all doctrines of first-strike counterforce targeting – that is, of anticipatory deterrence – as "nuclear war-fighting," if the implication is that the advocates of these doctrines are all planning for the fighting of a nuclear war, so that as soon as they are ready, they can go ahead and get one started.

A doctrine of anticipatory deterrence is a doctrine about the circumstances in which nuclear weapons would be used, and a full-blown account of anticipatory deterrence, which Wohlstetter does not pretend to offer, would specify how the nuclear weapons would be used – against which targets, etc. In this sense, namely that it discusses when and how to use nuclear weapons, anticipatory deterrence is a doctrine about fighting a war. Doctrines of retaliatory deterrence, however, also specify when and how nuclear weapons would be used. The time is a second-strike: the targets are civilians.

What is different about anticipatory deterrence, then, is not that it specifies when and how to use nuclear weapons, but the specific answers it gives: early and against military forces, perhaps including nuclear forces. These answers do not keep anticipatory deterrence from being a doctrine of deterrence – they simply make it, as I shall soon try to show, a misguided form. It is perfectly possible for people, perhaps including Wohlstetter, to believe that the best way to preserve peace is to be prepared for war –

thereby *deterring* aggression! This "lesson of Munich," I believe, is misguided as a universal rule, but it is a perfectly coherent and widely held belief: it is, for example, the basic justification given every year to Americans and Russians alike to justify gargantuan military budgets.

Anticipatory deterrence is the nuclear variant of the generic belief that the best way to prevent wars is to be prepared to fight them. The argument goes like this:

> The best way to prevent a nuclear war is to be prepared to fight one. The doctrine of retaliatory deterrence is not a plan for fighting a war – it is a plan for murdering the civilians on the other side after the enemy forces have already defeated you. Why should the enemy leaders believe that after your threat to slaughter their civilians has failed to achieve its purpose (of deterring their forces) you will execute the threat anyway? Why would you? Indeed, morally, how could you?

This is a very fundamental challenge to the received wisdom, for it is, at bottom, the thesis that threats to retaliate will not actually deter: you do not deter the first move by threatening to make the (by that time pointless) second move. You deter the other side from making the first move by being ready to make the first move yourself and by being ready to make it in a militarily rational way. As Paul Nitze has put it, "My view is that a capability to fight a nuclear war and to survive is in fact the best way to prevent a war."[21]

Now, the preceding argument is based on pure conjecture; it is constructed of conclusions, without any supporting data, political, historical, psychological, or of any other kind. This is a first, very important point to be made against anticipatory deterrence: like all doctrines of deterrence, it is 99 percent speculation. What the preceding paragraph claims is that anticipatory deterrence will more effectively deter. Such speculative assertions are difficult to assess, but there is no particular reason to believe them. It adds nothing, however, to label anticipatory deterrence "war-fighting," merely because it answers the questions of time and target. What we must do is to examine critically the specific answers given by this form of deterrence policy, and the rationale for choosing just these answers.

---

[21] Testimony of Paul H. Nitze, in U.S. Congress, Joint Committee on Defense Production, *Civil Preparedness and Limited Nuclear War*, Hearings on April 28, 1976 (Washington, DC: U.S. Government Printing Office, 1976), p.70, quoted in Donald W. Hanson, "Is Soviet Strategic Doctrine Superior?" *International Security*, vol. 7 (Winter 1982/1983), p.63.

56 HENRY SHUE

Is Counterforce Targeting Less Murderous?

Albert Wohlstetter says that we should choose counterforce targeting because it is, among other things, morally superior to the targeting of civilians. I have already explained why I think targeting military forces tends to lead to planning to go nuclear early, that is, to lead to the choice of anticipatory deterrence rather than damage-limiting retaliation. However, the criticisms of this claim of moral superiority which I will raise in this section of the essay apply to much counterforce targeting; they would also apply to damage-limiting retaliation if it could be sustained against my earlier criticisms of its military defects.

Anthony Kenny has lucidly summed up the objections to all doctrines of deterrence by saying that deterrence is "murderous, dangerous, and wasteful": murderous, because we risk killing innocent people; dangerous, because we run a high risk of getting ourselves killed; and wasteful, because in the process we are misguidedly spending billions.[22] Wohlstetter assures us that counterforce targeting is less murderous than countervalue targeting. (He clearly also believes that it is less dangerous, because more credible, and that the research and development on precision-guided munitions are an excellent investment.) Why is that?

At first, the moral superiority of counterforce targeting seems too obvious to deserve discussion. Superficially it may appear to be perfectly apparent that the best way to prevent a certain category of people from being killed is to prevent anyone's aiming nuclear weapons at them. Not only is this not obviously true, however, but whether or not it is true at all is one of the central issues about the effectiveness of deterrence. What the relationship is between targeting certain people and killing those same people is at the heart of the arguments about whether, and how, deterrence actually works.

The central thesis of the doctrine of retaliatory deterrence is that, given that both sides possess nuclear weapons, the civilians on both sides are safer if they are the targets of the weapons, because – roughly – no leader in his right mind wants to get the civilians on both sides killed and so the situation is stable in the sense that neither side has any persuasive reason to use its weapons. I am far from trying to defend retaliatory deterrence with reference to effectiveness. All that I claim is that retaliatory deterrence is not obviously mistaken as an empirical hypothesis and that, therefore, to ignore the distinction between who is targeted and who, if anyone, is actually killed is question-begging.

I maintain, then, only that *if* the doctrine of retaliatory deterrence should

---

[22] Anthony Kenny, "Nuclear Deterrence," paper presented at First Fulbright Anglo-American Colloquium on Ethics and International Affairs, University of St. Andrews, October 1984. Also see Anthony Kenny, *The Logic of Deterrence*, forthcoming.

somehow turn out to be meaningful and correct, it would follow that those who were targeted were not killed and were not killed because they were targeted – this is one of the many "paradoxical" aspects of retaliatory deterrence. This is also a *very* big "if." The doctrine of retaliatory deterrence bears a remarkable structural similarity to the air force fantasy. The original fantasy concerns conventional city-bombing and says: the way to break the morale of the enemy forces is to bomb their families. Retaliatory deterrence says: the way to deter enemy forces is to threaten to bomb their families. The original fantasy turned out in World War II and Vietnam to be false, but retaliatory deterrence could be different, since it depends upon a threat, not upon punishment already inflicted. Perhaps, as Bernard Brodie reasoned, there is "more strategic leverage to be gained in holding cities hostages than in making corpses."[23] My only point now is: who knows?

And that is to say, I am unwilling at this point either to try to defeat Wohlstetter's thesis of the moral superiority of counterforce targeting by invoking the alleged greater effectiveness of countervalue targeting or to accept Wohlstetter's thesis because he invokes the alleged greater effectiveness (credibility, etc.) of counterforce targeting. Either way, the moral issue would be settled by appeal to supposed knowledge about what will work – actually deter – the specific decisionmakers on the other side. If anyone had such concrete knowledge, that would be fine. Given the difficulties that the CIA has in making accurate predictions about simple questions like who will be the next Soviet defense minister, however, any pretensions to knowing even which Soviet leaders have which degree of influence on which issues, much less how each thinks and what the dynamics of the interactions of the various leaders are, would be a joke. So, we must turn elsewhere.

Before we do, however, we can formulate the first premise needed to support the thesis of the moral superiority of counterforce targeting, a premise which, I submit, is now and in the foreseeable future unverifiable and unfalsifiable:

First Premise for Moral Superiority: Greater Effectiveness.
Counterforce targeting by the United States, which it has the capability and will to execute, will deter present and future leaders of the Soviet Union from aggressive actions outside the sphere of influence already conceded to the U.S.S.R. by the U.S. in the absence of aggressive actions by the United States outside the sphere of influence already conceded to the U.S. by the U.S.S.R., and countervalue targeting will not deter them.

[23] Bernard Brodie, "Schlesinger's Old-New Ideas," unpublished paper, *Bernard Brodie Papers*, Box 33, folder 8, quoted in Fred Kaplan, *The Wizards of Armageddon* (New York: Simon & Schuster, 1983), p.47.

Obviously the details of this formulation could be debated endlessly, but in our current state of knowledge about the specific workings of nuclear deterrence, it does not seem worth the trouble.

The second premise concerns a considerably better-defined issue, although its formulation too is subject to debate:

> *Second Premise for Moral Superiority: Separable Targets.*
> Collocation of counterforce and countervalue targets in the Soviet Union is negligible; that is, the number of Soviet noncombatants who would be killed in the smallest counterforce strike that it would be militarily rational for the United States to make is significantly smaller than the number who would be killed in the smallest countervalue strike required by retaliatory deterrence.

My understanding is that this second premise is as completely and straighforwardly false as any statement about nuclear matters can be.[24] Many of the most essential Soviet military targets are located in or near major concentrations of population.

> Assuming the urban population was 90 percent sheltered ... estimated Soviet fatalities from a U.S. counter-ICBM attack would range from 3.7 million to 13.5 million, depending on the attack parameters; if the urban population were only 10 percent sheltered, fatality estimates for the same set of attacks ranged from 6.0 million to 27.7 million.
>
> A comprehensive U.S. counterforce attack would kill many more people than this. Two of the three Soviet FBM submarine bases are located within urban areas (Severomorsk near Murmansk, and Vladivostok). More than 70 percent of the Soviet air bases are in the western U.S.S.R. south of Leningrad. And about 500 IRBMs and MRBMs are deployed west of the Urals ... Attacks on these could well double the fatality estimates cited in the previous paragraph ...

[24] For how little difference "careful" targeting makes, see in addition to the reference in the next note, the following studies: Sidney D. Drell and Frank von Hippel, "Limited Nuclear War," *Scientific American*, vol. 235 (November 1976), pp.27–37, which includes the effects of a Soviet counter-ICBM attack on the U.S.; William M. Arkin, Frank von Hippel, and Barbara G. Levi, "The Consequences of a 'Limited' Nuclear War in East and West Germany," *Ambio*, vol. 11 (June 1982), pp.163–173, reprinted in book form under different titles by different publishers, *The Aftermath: The Human and Ecological Consequences of Nuclear War* (Pantheon) and *Nuclear War: The Aftermath* (Pergamon); and Frank von Hippel, "The Effects of Nuclear War," in David W. Hafemeister and Dietrich Schroeer, eds., *Physics, Technology and the Nuclear Arms Race* (New York: American Institute of Physics, 1983), pp.1–46. Also see Kevin N. Lewis, "The Prompt and Delayed Effects of Nuclear War," *Scientific American*, vol. 241 (July 1979), pp.35–47.

> In the case of a U.S. counterforce attack against the Soviet Union, the fatalities could well approximate those of the Second World War, when the Soviet Union suffered about 20 million fatalities (some 10 million of them were civilians), but they were lost over a period of four years – rather than a few hours, days or perhaps weeks – and they were considered as being nothing less than a holocaust.[25]

Countervalue destruction is guaranteed. The only question is whether to *add counterforce* targets too.

Further, on many versions of counterforce targeting, including Wohlstetter's, the targeting would also be counter-command; that is, the political and military leadership who could order a retaliatory strike against the United States and Western Europe would be included as prime targets. Given the poor quality of intelligence about such crucial details as the physical movements of specific Soviet leaders, those choosing the targets would presumably have to include secondary and tertiary targeting options if there was to be any serious hope of preventing retaliation by killing everyone who could order it.

In addition, Wohlstetter relies on the theoretical possibility that the yield of warheads can be reduced in the future as the precision of missile guidance systems continues to improve. If you can deliver a warhead right on top of its target, you need less explosive force to destroy the target than if you can only come close. The question remains: will yields actually be reduced to such a degree that "collocated," that is, nearby, noncombatants will not be killed? Presumably, yields will not be reduced below a force that will reliably destroy command bunkers and missile silos that have been "super-hardened" to the maximum extent feasible. "ICBMs are and will remain – at best – area devastators, not hard point destroyers."[26] Moreover, even an extremely low-yield warhead which strays over a "soft," that is, civilian, target will wreak awful destruction. Whatever the *average* degree of precision, no one can be expected to believe that there will be no stray missiles – it is well to remember that the old Army acronym SNAFU stands for Situation *Normal* . . . (. . . All Fucked Up)! The moral superiority claimed for counterforce targeting must turn on the features of the actual attack, not on an ideal attack on paper.

In sum, the question is not: how precisely guided are individual missiles? The questions are: how much destruction altogether would you need to try

---

[25] Desmond Ball, "Can Nuclear War be Controlled?" p.28; in this extremely careful analysis, see generally Section IV, "The Control of Damage in Nuclear War," pp.26–30.
[26] A.G.B. Metcalf, "The Minuteman Vulnerability Myth and the MX," *Strategic Review*, vol. 11 (Spring 1983), p.9.

to inflict in order for an attack not to be suicidal (by inviting and leaving the possibility of a retaliatory attack); and how much destruction would you probably actually cause? There may be precise individual missiles – there are no militarily-rational, precise missile attacks. Actual United States battle plans, for example, the Single Integrated Operational Plan (SIOP), have in fact always included the launch of thousands of missiles at a thorough mixture of kinds of targets.[27]

Speaking of suicide, we come to the third premise, which is even more important than the second:

> *Third Premise for Moral Superiority: No Escalation.*
> The initial counterforce strike would be militarily decisive (while remaining small enough to satisfy the second premise of separable targets); that is, neither the massive response promised by official Soviet policy statements nor further rounds of escalation by the United States would occur. At best, the entire nuclear war would consist of a single attack by the United States, which the Soviet Union would then lack either the capability or the will to answer; and, at worst, the United States would endure any Soviet military responses without resorting to retaliation against Soviet civilians.

If the second premise (separable targets) is as clearly and totally false as it seems to be, the third premise does not even make sense: it is impossible to avoid "escalating" to civilian targets if civilian targets will already be destroyed by missiles nominally aimed at military (and command) targets. Let us, nevertheless, assume that an initial nuclear attack large enough to make sense militarily could also somehow be "clean" enough to satisfy the second premise – perhaps targets would be restricted to troop concentrations on the great plains between Moscow and Warsaw. (If it included missile silos around Moscow, it would be indistinguishable from a counter-value attack on Moscow.) So, an initial counterforce strike by the United States is sufficiently restrained to be clearly distinguishable from a countervalue strike (as required by the second premise), with the result that missiles near cities have been voluntarily spared (not to mention submarine-launched missiles involuntarily spared).

---

[27] See David Alan Rosenberg, "The Origins of Overkill: Nuclear Weapons and American Strategy, 1945–1960," *International Security*, vol. 7 (Spring 1983), pp.3–71; reprinted in a highly useful collection, Steven E. Miller, ed., *Strategy and Nuclear Deterrence, An International Security*, Reader (Princeton: Princeton University Press, 1984), pp.113–181. Also in the Miller anthology, see Desmond Ball, "U.S. Strategic Forces: How Would They Be Used?" pp.215–244; and see Desmond Ball, "Targeting for Strategic Deterrence," Adelphi Paper No. 185 (London: International Institute for Strategic Studies, 1983).

Now what? Are we really supposed to believe that the surviving Soviet leaders would calmly say, "OK – you win"? They might. NATO clings to the hope that they would. Much of the world would be praying that they would. Soviet leaders would be assured a place of special honor in human history – for having kept human history in business – if they did. But, would they really leave all those expensive, gleaming missiles sheathed in their silos? The unlocatable submarines harmlessly submerged? I am not claiming to know – this is yet another example of the pointless tennis-without-a-net that masquerades as deterrence "theory." My only point here is my previous one: who knows? It is for those who are so confident about counterforce targeting to shore up their premises.[28]

It should be added explicitly that the civilians at risk from escalation include the civilians in the society whose government breaks the nuclear taboo. The Soviet Union has *never*, to my knowledge, claimed that it knows how to conduct a nuclear strike that will not slaughter civilians – it only claims that it will not use nuclear weapons first.

The fourth premise carries us into a different realm of uncertainty and speculation:

> *Fourth Premise for Moral Superiority: No Nuclear Winter.*
> The initial counterforce strike, plus any Soviet retaliation and any further exchanges between the two sides, will remain below the (currently unknown and probably unpredictable) threshold for nuclear winter.

Although I think that the findings about nuclear winter are important, primarily because they demonstrate the significance of factors that were totally ignored previously in government studies on the effects of nuclear war, I have not relied upon them, and I shall only mention them, for two reasons. First, clear, nontechnical accounts of the significance of these findings are readily available.[29] Second, although I am treating nuclear winter

---

[28] That mutual assured destruction is the *reality*, irrespective of whether it is any nation's *policy*, has recently been persuasively argued in Robert Jervis, *The Illogic of American Nuclear Strategy*, Cornell Studies in Security Affairs (Ithaca: Cornell University Press, 1984).

[29] The most accessible account of the findings about nuclear winter and their implications for policy is Carl Sagan, "Nuclear War and Climatic Catastrophe: Some Policy Implications," *Foreign Affairs*, vol. 62 (Winter 1983/84), pp.257–292. The most recent account, which uses three-dimensional models of the atmosphere, is S.L. Thompson, V.V. Aleksandrov, G.L. Stenchikov, S.H. Schneider, C. Covey, and R.M. Chervin, "Global Climatic Consequences of Nuclear War: Simulations with Three Dimensional Models," *Ambio*, vol. 13 (1984), pp.236–243. Pioneering articles appeared in a special double issue, "Nuclear War: The Aftermath," *Ambio*, vol. 11 (1982), reprinted in book form under different titles by two publishers: *The Aftermath: The Human and Ecological Consequences of Nuclear War* (Pantheon) and *Nuclear War: The Aftermath* (Pergamon). The one-dimensional study that first attracted

as the subject of a fourth premise in order to acknowledge its importance, the satisfaction of the fourth premise is directly dependent upon the satisfaction of the second and third premises. As the reports of the findings about nuclear winter have stressed, the suspended soot in the smoke from burning cities is much more critical to the blockage of sunlight than is the suspended dust from blasted military targets. If a militarily meaningful counterforce strike cannot avoid causing conflagrations in metropolitan centers (i.e., satisfy the second premise), the jig is up for everyone in the Northern Hemisphere after the first strike. If these findings are correct, a nuclear attack would amount to "self-retaliation" – the soot clouds could be at least as thick over the attacker as over the attacked in a few days. The judgment of Carl Sagan is that "A major first strike would be clearly in the vicinity of, and perhaps well over, the climatic threshold."[30]

If we, nevertheless, assume the absence of the "self-retaliation" phenomenon, we then face, in effect, questions about the satisfaction of premise three. When you add the smoke from the burning of United States cities set afire (even if not nominally targeted) by a Soviet retaliatory strike, how great and how persistent would the temperature drop from blocked sunlight be? Or, would the Soviet leaders just decide that if the initial American attack on them had so far left the hemisphere below the threshold of climatic catastrophe, they should refrain from retaliating and keep us all below the threshold, leaving themselves defeated and the United States not only victorious but unscathed? Perhaps. Or perhaps they would choose what is called "victory-denial." In any case, the questions about premise four are simply a rerun of the questions about premises two and three.

---

widespread public attention was reported in R.P. Turco, O.B. Toon, T.P. Ackerman, J.B. Pollack, and Carl Sagan, "Nuclear Winter: Global Consequences of Multiple Nuclear Explosions," *Science*, vol. 222 (December 23, 1983), pp.1283–1292. A more readable account appeared as Richard P. Turco, Owen B. Toon, Thomas P. Ackerman, James B. Pollack and Carl Sagan, "The Climatic Effects of Nuclear War," *Scientific American*, vol. 251 (August 1984), pp.33–43. The original report from *Science* and relevant discussion is available as Paul R. Ehrlich, Carl Sagan, Donald Kennedy and Walter Orr Roberts, *The Cold and the Dark: The World after Nuclear War* (New York: W.W. Norton, 1984). A study requested by the Department of Defense was unable to fault the basic methodology of the original studies: see Committee on the Atmospheric Effects of Nuclear Explosions, National Research Council, National Academy of Sciences, *The Effects on the Atmosphere of a Major Nuclear Exchange* (Washington: National Academy Press, 1985). A plan for further research was submitted to the White House, but has not been funded: see National Climate Program Office, NOAA, *Interagency Research Report for Assessing Climatic Effects of Nuclear War* (Washington: Executive Office of the President, Office of Science and Technology Policy, February, 1985). For the Pentagon's argument that the solution is to do all the things it was planning to do anyway, see Caspar W. Weinberger, *The Potential Effects of Nuclear War on the Climate*, A Report to the Congress (Washington: Office of the Secretary of Defense, March 1985), mimeo.

[30] Carl Sagan, "Nuclear War and Climatic Catastrophe," p.276. Then there would be the climatic effects of the retaliatory strike.

One may object that the findings about the phenomenon of nuclear winter are too speculative and based on too many debatable assumptions to be reliable. Admittedly the nuclear winter findings are hypothetical projections. But they are not one whit more speculative than the assumptions which pass for "deterrence theory," which is part elegant game-theory and part inelegant conjecture about actual Soviet political interests: the Rational Russian meets the Real Russian. Actual discussions of deterrence tend to be like a caviar and peanut-butter sandwich: the elegant bits of game theory sink into the mire of conjecture about Soviet decision making.[31] We have no reason to believe that the mathematical models of particle suspension and reflectivity used by the scientists working on nuclear winter are any farther from the actual phenomenon than the rational agents in war games are from Soviet Air Force generals. Cautious agnosticism seems to me to be in order all around.

Is Anticipatory Deterrence Less Dangerous?

In the preceding section I have not actually kept separate what Anthony Kenny calls "murderous" and "dangerous." I have emphasized, as Wohlstetter did, the murderous, that is, the killing of civilians on the side attacked; but, especially when we considered retaliation in the discussion of premises three (no escalation) and four (no nuclear winter), we were discussing the dangerous, that is, the killing of civilians on the attacking side. For the most part, I think a civilian is a civilian, and it is immaterial whether he is a powerless member of the aggressive state or a powerless member of the state

---

[31] Perhaps I ought to provide an example. Here is an almost randomly selected one, in no way worse than average but interesting in that the "argument" is said in an accompanying footnote to go back to 1967, thus demonstrating how groundless speculations become orthodox dogmas of deterrence: "Presumably people believe the Soviet Union is interested in annihilating the United States because this would make it the dominant world power. The analogy, if U.S. defenses had eliminated the Soviet ability to annihilate the United States, would be a countervalue attack designed to weaken the United States. To deter this type of attack, the United States would need a retaliatory capability that could weaken the Soviet Union as much as the Soviet countervalue attack could weaken the United States. A countervalue capability roughly equivalent to the Soviet countervalue capability should be sufficiently large to satisfy this requirement"; Charles L. Glaser, "Why Even Good Defenses May Be Bad," *International Security*, vol. 9 (Fall 1984), pp.103–104. This deterrence requirement of "equal countervalue capability" is, thus, derived from the assumptions that the Soviet Union is simultaneously (1) devoted to dominating the world by doing as much damage to the United States as the U.S. lets it and (2) devoted to making military decisions using Benefit-Cost Analysis and the principle of maximizing expected utility. That a demonically power-mad regime would use BCA to set its strategy is logically possible, but what reasons do we have to believe it is true? How do we know that an equal amount of damage "should be sufficiently large"? If they are such wild annihilators, perhaps the U.S. would need to be capable of doing them twice as much damage in order to deter them. If they are such careful reasoners, perhaps they would not risk half as much damage in an uncertain adventure. Why exactly equal amounts? Are they just like us? If so, why are we contemplating destroying each other?

aggressed against. After all, one of the main purposes of the laws of war has always been to prevent the slaughter of noncombatants committed in the name of punishing the guilty.[32] To the extent that all noncombatants are to be treated the same, the distinction between murderous and dangerous does not cut much ice. It would certainly not recommend a United States policy the ultimate effect of which would not be to kill a lot of civilians on the other side but to get a lot of American civilians killed.

In the preceding section, the main doubts I raised focused generally on counterforce targeting. In this section I concentrate specifically upon the early-use version of counterforce targeting, which is anticipatory deterrence. I want, in other words, to focus upon the choice about timing that makes the most military sense out of counterforce targeting. I shall lay out what might be called the objective incentive structure of anticipatory deterrence. So far I have concentrated upon the military and moral considerations which apply when deterrence fails. Now we must consider the much more obscure issue of whether deterrence will in fact fail and, more specifically, whether either anticipatory or retaliatory deterrence is in any way more likely to be effective in preventing a nuclear war. At the beginning of the preceding section, I simply noted that the first premise for the moral superiority of anticipatory deterrence is greater effectiveness. I confessed there that the similarity between retaliatory deterrence and conventional city-bombing gives me great doubt about whether retaliatory deterrence "works."

Now I want to lay out the strongest reason I know for believing that anticipatory deterrence may not only not "work," but may even be strongly counterproductive, that is, may produce nuclear war. Since all arguments about the effectivenss of nuclear deterrence directed by the two superpowers at each other are highly speculative, I have no great faith in arguments about effectiveness in either direction – hence, my earlier emphasis on the moral and military results of deterrence failure. The following abstract argument is recounted here with two particular limitations. First, I claim only to be describing the objective incentives created by anticipatory deterrence. What will happen subjectively – or, if you like, whether Soviet and American actors will decide rationally – I do not claim to predict. I maintain only that anticipatory deterrence unnecessarily creates a situation in which a response that *would* be rational for the other side is very bad for the side with this

---

[32] Thus, although I generally admire the pioneering philosophical work on deterrence by Gregory Kavka, I utterly reject his thesis that Soviet civilians "are partially responsible and hence partly liable"(to threatened attack); see Gregory S. Kavka, "Nuclear Deterrence: Some Moral Perplexities," in MacLean, ed., *The Security Gamble*, p.132. It is the rare Soviet civilian, I would suggest, who has even the slightest responsibility for any of the policies of the dictatorial state to which he is subjected, and few indeed who have enough responsibility to be placed justly at risk of death. The vast majority of the civilians in the Soviet Union are women and children with no power and no voice at all.

policy. Second, I once again do not so much attempt to establish anything positive as to urge deep hesitations about the accelerating American and Russian plunges into anticipatory deterrence by showing that one can tell just as good a story on the contrary side of the argument about its effectiveness.

Whatever else can be said about retaliatory deterrence, that policy gives the other side no additional reason to attack. Retaliatory deterrence may or may not "work" – that is, deter attack – and it obviously creates possibilities for accidental nuclear war and provides each side with a capacity for enormous harm to the other. Thus, it gives the other side much serious cause to *worry*. But it would give them no cause to *attack*, if they believed that their adversary's strategy were genuinely retaliatory. The Soviets could be assured that our strategy were strictly retaliatory if we built no weapons with counterforce capability, or a number so small as to make it obvious that we were not preparing for early use. Since our force is survivable, an attack by them would be even more pointless. Regardless of whether a force capable only of retaliatory deterrence has any positive deterrent effect, it would not be provocative.

And what have the Americans been building lately? Large numbers of counterforce weapons of the kind needed for a first-strike. And what have the Soviets been building lately? Large numbers of counterforce weapons of the kind needed for a first-strike.

Now, it is essential to see that the main issue is not whether leaders on either side are gratuitously scheming to launch a first-strike out of the clear blue sky. The issue is the incentive structure that is being created in the form of objective military capabilities. The problem is what the insiders call "crisis stability." I do not think that the United States now intends a first-strike against the Soviet Union, nor that the Soviets now intend one against the U.S. Yet the fact remains that Americans are building weapons that are objectively capable of destroying some Soviet weapons before they are fired, and the Soviets are doing the same. Objective capabilities remain, while intentions can change. Intentions are most likely to change when people have powerful incentives to change them. Let us look at the incentives the Soviets and the Americans are creating by relentlessly adding these weapons with counterforce capability. This will show why enhancing a counterforce capability in the direction of a first-strike capability, and the strategy of anticipatory deterrence that can rationalize this enhancement, could add greatly to whatever the probability of nuclear war would be if both sides clearly had only the capability for retaliatory deterrence.

Our counterforce weapons threaten their strategic nuclear weapons, which are the only nuclear weapons that protect them from our nuclear weapons. They would not want to lose their weapons. Unfortunately, there is an obvious way not to lose weapons that is not a way not to lose cities. Use them. Soviet development of an effective capability to destroy a very high percentage of American weapons in the ground becomes an incentive to use them, and *vice versa*.

I am not suggesting for a minute that the leadership of either country is crazy enough simply to go ahead one day and calmly use its missiles on the other side for no other reason than that they *might* otherwise lose their own missiles. The great danger is that, in a period of heightening tension between the U.S. and the U.S.S.R., the situation might reach a point at which war seemed inevitable – or at least, very likely – and the leadership on one side or the other might decide that they should act before it is too late. A number of scholars have argued, very roughly, that World War I began because of mutual belief in its inevitability (and brevity) and mutual desire to get a military jump on the other side once attempts at prevention seemed doomed.[33]

I do not know, or claim to know, *how* likely this phenomenon of use-them-before-you-lose-them is. The point is simply that development of an objective capacity to destroy a major portion of the other side's forces is in itself an incentive for use – it is both a stimulant and a provocation. A capacity to destroy virtually all the other side's forces – that is, a capacity to disarm – would be a severe provocation.[34]

It is important also to notice that the incentive pulls on both sides and that it creates a vicious circle. It is not merely that the Soviets who shot down Korean Airlines Flight 007 might, if you will pardon the expression, jump the gun. The Americans too might jump the gun: who would want to go down in history as the American president who "let the Communists repeat Pearl Harbor on his watch"? And it is not just that one or the other might

---

[33] "Russia, Germany and France each misjudged the extent of the other's military preparations and mobilized, fearful that failure to do so would enable their opponents to gain a decisive military advantage"; Richard Ned Lebow, "Practical Ways to Avoid Superpower Crises," *Bulletin of the Atomic Scientists*, vol. 41 (January 1985), p.25. For a full study of how crises issue in wars, see Richard Ned Lebow, *Between Peace and War: The Nature of International Crisis* (Baltimore: Johns Hopkins University Press, 1981); on World War I, see especially "The July Crisis: A Case Study," pp.119–147. However, also see Richard Ned Lebow, "Windows of Opportunity: Do States Jump Through Them?" *International Security*, vol. 9 (Summer 1984), pp.147–186, as well as other articles in the same number, all reprinted in Steven E. Miller, ed., *Military Strategy and the Origins of the First World War*, An *International Security* Reader (Princeton: Princeton University Press, 1985).

[34] Fortunately, neither side is anywhere near the capacity to disarm the other; see Harold A. Feiveson and Frank von Hippel, "The Freeze and the Counterforce Race," *Physics Today*, vol. 36 (January 1983), pp.36, 38, 40, 42, 44, and 46–49. Compare the recent statement of President Reagan's science adviser, as part of the Administration's advocacy of the Strategic Defense Initiative: "Inevitable advances in technology have now put *both* superpowers' retaliatory forces at risk to preemptive attack"; G.A. Keyworth, "Ganging Up on Star Wars," *Washington Post*, 24 December 1984, p.A15 (emphasis in original).

jump the gun; it is also that each side must worry that the other side will. One of the most terrible features of counterforce warfare is, as we saw earlier, that there can be enormous advantages for the side that is ruthless enough to strike early – if going late means going with only what is left after you have suffered a counterforce strike. This contrasts with the incentive structure of a retaliatory deterrence posture. After all, you cannot fire off your *cities* and thereby avoid losing them. The essential point was recognized as early as November 1945 by Jacob Viner, who asked: "What difference will it then make whether it was Country A which had its cities destroyed at 9 a.m. and Country B which had its cities destroyed at 12 a.m., or the other way around?"[35] Thus, there is a radical difference in incentive structure between countervalue targeting and counterforce targeting (with large numbers of warheads).

Therefore, developing a large counterforce capability appears actively to undermine any actual deterrence there might be. The vigorous development of a counterforce capability inherently tends toward the attainment of superiority, because it moves in the direction of a capacity to attack your adversary in such a way that it will be made unable to attack you back. A fully successful counterforce attack – a disarming attack – would deprive the other side of even the capacity to retaliate. Insofar as the stability of deterrence depends upon its mutuality – that is, depends upon each side's capacity to retaliate after having absorbed a first strike (an axiom of deterrence theory) – a full counterforce capability undermines this stability. The other side is rendered unable to strike second. They could not rely on the strategy of retaliatory deterrence even if they wanted to.

Once again, this does not mean that they will just gratuitously go ahead and strike first. One intermediate possibility is to adopt the policy of launch-on-warning, or launch-under-attack. Launch-on-warning is not a first strike policy. Missiles are not launched until there is an indication that the other side has already attacked, but they are launched very promptly. Adopting launch-on-warning amounts to putting nuclear forces on a hair-trigger. There is not a lot of time for checking around to confirm whether the signals indicating incoming missiles are false, if these missiles are aimed at military targets. If they have civilian targets or your retaliatory force will survive for some other reason (such as hardened silos) you have all the time in the world.

This pressure to act fast is an additional specific manner in which the development of counterforce capability might increase the probability of nuclear attack. It provides a strong incentive for the adoption of a policy of

---

[35] Jacob Viner, "The Implications of the Atomic Bomb for International Relations," *Proceedings of the American Philosophical Society*, January 29, 1946, p.54, quoted in Fred Kaplan, *The Wizards of Armaggedon*, p.27.

launch-on-warning, and the policy of launch-on-warning might raise
enormously the probability of accidental nuclear war. Only panic, not
malevolence, is required. Here too, the incentive pulls on both sides and
creates a vicious circle. If both sides were on hair-trigger settings, we might
never know who made the mistake and fired first, thinking they were firing
second. But, then, we would not need to know.

Now, since I can see no reason why concrete policies for the real world
should be based on disembodied scenarios like those in the preceding few
paragraphs, I cannot honestly recommend taking this abstract argument
about crisis instability as definitive. Many firm advocates of retaliatory
deterrence seem to find it a devastating demonstration that anticipatory
deterrence is more dangerous. In the abstract one could speculate, however,
that the complete attainment of a counterforce capacity great enough for a
nonsuicidal first strike would immobilize the other side with fear.

Who knows? I feel compelled to emphasize the methodological point that
the arguments about effectiveness are awash in ignorance and uncertainty.
Even the most authoritative treatment of all the attempts to construct a
coherent theory of deterrence ends with foreboding:

> This legion of uncertainties ought to have created a common
> humility – to be so much in the dark with so much at stake.
> Unfortunately the frustration with this predicament led many
> strategists to show astonishing confidence in their own nostrums,
> combined with vindictiveness against those who differed. The
> question of what happens if deterrence fails is vital for the
> intellectual cohesion and credibility of nuclear strategy. A proper
> answer requires more than the design of means to wage nuclear war
> in a wide variety of ways, but something sufficiently plausible to
> appear as a tolerably rational course of action which has a realistic
> chance of leading to a satisfactory outcome. It now seems unlikely
> that such an answer can be found. No operational nuclear strategy
> has yet to be devised that does not carry an enormous risk of
> degenerating into a bloody contest of resolve or a furious exchange
> of devastating and crippling blows against the political and econ-
> omic centres of the industrialized world. . . . Those who have
> responsibility for unleashing nuclear arsenals live by the motto that
> if they ever had to do so they would have failed. Remarkably, up to
> now they have succeeded. C'est magnifique, mais ce n'est pas la
> stratégie.[36]

---

[36] Freedman, *The Evolution of Nuclear Strategy*, pp.395 and 400.

Nevertheless, bearing in mind that we are in great danger of drifting away from solid ground, we can pursue the debate about crisis instability a few steps farther. One rejoinder to the above thesis that anticipatory deterrence is crisis-unstable is as follows. What is being criticized is counterforce targeting, but what is being shown to be unstable is the situation constituted by a first-strike capacity on at least one side. Having even a large number of counterforce weapons may, however, be far from having a first-strike capability. One has a genuine first-strike capability only when one has so many counterforce weapons of such high reliability that one can launch a first-strike that is nonsuicidal, that is, a first strike that will not simply invite and allow a devastating retaliation. One must be capable of a virtually *disarming* first-strike, or it would be suicidal to launch one. There is no "window of vulnerability" – neither the Americans nor the Soviets are anywhere near the capability to disarm the other. So what is the harm in building more counterforce weapons as long as neither side has a true first-strike capability?

A competition in building counterforce weapons has two possible outcomes. Either one side will "get ahead" and attain the capacity for a nonsuicidal first strike or the competition will continue indefinitely without either side's attaining enough superiority to embolden it to launch. If it is more likely that one side will actually attain the capability of destroying enough weapons on the other side to hold any retaliation within "acceptable" limits, then the objection about crisis instability will at that time apply. And prevention is surely better than a cure attempted within the unstable situation. The argument against the current counterforce competition is, then, that it will probably lead to an unstable situation that is easier to head off than to fix later.

If, on the other hand, it is more likely that the competition in counterforce weapons will continue indefinitely, the policy of anticipatory deterrence amounts to a formula for an endless arms race. The situation may never become a great deal more unstable than it is now, if neither side achieves a "breakout." The new counterforce weapons on one side simply become new targets for the other side, which then needs more warheads, which then become new targets for the first side, etc. This, obviously, is another vicious circle – and a limitlessly expensive one.

Thus, the fundamental problem concerning the effectiveness of anticipatory deterrence is that pursuit of it leads to one or the other of two vicious circles.[37] If one side can attain a genuine first-strike capacity, the result is the vicious circle of crisis instability created by the military incentive for

---

[37] This point has become clear to me from repeated – not to say endless – conversations with my colleague, Robert K. Fullinwider.

attacking first. (The incentive applies as well to the weaker side, which lacks
first-strike capacity, because it will be weaker still if it lets the superior side
go first – indeed, partially disarming the stronger adversary before it more or
less totally disarms you may seem the only hope.) How strong this incentive
will be, relative to other considerations, I do not, as I have emphasized, claim
to know. If neither side can attain a genuine first-strike capability, on the
other hand, the result is the vicious circle of an unending, highly competitive
arms race. How strong the incentive to keep trying to attain first-strike
capability will be, I once again do not claim to know. But how effective is a
policy that leads only to vicious circles?

Finite Deterrence: Escape from the Dilemma?

Maybe there is something a little more positive here. The answer to the
question, "what is an acceptable conception of deterrence?" must surely be:
none of the above. Retaliatory deterrence is supremely murderous. Anticipatory deterrence is supremely dangerous and supremely wasteful – and,
unless escalation could be controlled, equally murderous in the end as well.
The U.S. committed in Hiroshima and Nagasaki the kind of civilian
slaughter that terroristic deterrence would threaten to commit, and
Americans have been haunted by their massive, unpunished war-crime ever
since. Damage-limiting deterrence involves severe military compromises.
Decency and honor would suggest, however, that rather than making moral
compromises of the magnitude we have canvassed, we should consider
military compromises.

The worst feature of damage-limiting deterrence is that it may be
perceived as, or by worst-case reasoning treated as, anticipatory deterrence,
which in turn feeds crisis instability. Yet, of the four polar positions among
conceptions of deterrence, late use against military targets – second-strike
counterforce – seems the least awful morally. Is there a form of later military
use that could be threatened without being mistaken for anticipatory
deterrence, as damage-limiting deterrence is liable to be?

Once again, I do not really know. If there can be an acceptable form of
nuclear deterrence – and it is nowhere written that there necessarily can be –
it would seem likely to lie farther than damage-limiting deterrence in the
direction of second-strike counterforce. We would have to go, so to speak,
out through the lower right-hand corner of Figure 1. Is there in reality such
a position?

We saw at the end of the last section that there is a critical distinction
between counterforce capability and first-strike capability. A first-strike
capability is a counterforce capability so extensive that it would disarm the
adversary, leaving it with no nuclear forces with which to retaliate. The

trouble is that counterforce tends to move in the direction of first strike, as more and more counterforce is built. The distinction tends to be eroded. All ordinary counterforce tends to be destabilizing because it tends to grow toward first-strike capability, which would be very destabilizing indeed.

No form of counterforce capability can be acceptable unless it is clearly distinguishable from anticipatory deterrence, especially by a suspicious adversary. Perhaps, however, maintaining this distinction may be easier than one suspected. What is needed is a counterforce capability with a low ceiling on quantity. Both anticipatory deterrence and damage-limiting deterrence involve relentless competition in arms-building, because each of the weapons on side A becomes a target for the weapons on side B. As side A builds new weapons/targets, side B needs new weapons. But these weapons are, for A, also targets, and against these new weapons/targets side A needs new weapons/targets against which side B needs new weapons/targets, *ad infinitum*. This is what I mean in saying that a counterforce competition is *relentless*. It becomes impossible even to explain what adequacy could mean – enough is never enough, except temporarily, until the other side responds, or seems to respond. In an all-out competition to acquire capacity for counterforce, it becomes literally impossible even to specify an end, much less to reach it (except by seizing any temporary opportunity to conduct a disarming strike).

President Eisenhower, however, is often quoted as having said: "We need only what *we* need." The wisdom of this comment lies in the insight that adequacy for deterrence can be specified in a manner that does not twist adequacy into the endless pursuit of superiority. Relentlessly competitive counterforce, in which every new weapon for side B becomes a new target for side A, begins by assuming: side A can deter side B only if A's forces could defeat B's forces. This means, however, that side A could have an *adequate* force only if it had a *superior* force. Presumably, however, any such "laws of deterrence" are symmetrical; and side B could have an adequate force to deter side A only if it too had a superior force. Therefore, mutual deterrence would depend upon *each* side's being superior to the other side, which is simply nonsense. Relentless counterforce competition is not merely empirically unstable. Worse, it makes *mutual* deterrence logically incoherent. It can in fact only be the pursuit of superiority by both sides.

The goal of counterforce would not have to be incoherent, however, if adequacy were given a sensible interpretation that sharply distinguished the pursuit of genuine adequacy from the pursuit of superiority. If "enough" is not defined in practice as "more than the other side has," it can be possible to have enough (and more than enough). It can be possible to impose a ceiling. Any arms competition will always remain competitive – as Lenin might have said (but did not): "An arms race is not a dinner party." The competition need not, however, be relentless in the sense of each side's endlessly pursuing superiority over the other side.

How much is enough? What would an adequate counterforce capacity look like? This is not the place, and I am not the person, to conduct that discussion. Here, I want only to provide an example of how it can begin – and is beginning. In the 40th Anniversary Issue of the *Bulletin of the Atomic Scientists*, Harold A. Feiveson, Richard H. Ullman, and Frank von Hippel propose a 90 percent reduction in current U.S. nuclear forces. This would still leave the U.S. with an awesome arsenal of two thousand warheads configured in a triad consisting of five hundred single-warhead intercontinental ballistic missiles, five hundred single-warhead submarine-launched ballistic missiles, and one thousand air-launched cruise missiles, which they call an illustrative finite deterrence force.[38] Naturally, the details of what Feiveson, Ullman, and von Hippel themselves consider only an illustrative proposal need further debate, and I no more than they intend to endorse precisely this proposal. My only point now is that this suggestion from the Princeton Project on Finite Deterrence, as it is called, is one plausible way of saying: "This is adequate – stop here."

The members of the Princeton Project do not explicitly discuss the question of first-use, although they do propose the elimination of all "tactical" nuclear weapons from Europe. Nor do they claim that these forces could only be used for counterforce attacks. On the contrary, they explicitly concede that their "finite deterence" is still a "balance of terror." This concession, however, puts them light-years ahead of Wohlstetter's illusions about fine-tuning and the "revolution in precision."

As I noted above, in my criticism of the second premise of Wohlstetter's argument for the moral superiority of his kind of counterforce – the premise of separable targets – countervalue destruction is always guaranteed. The kinds of surgical nuclear strikes that Wohlstetter must assume are utterly imaginary.[39] It is that kind of groundless enthusiasm about precision that can seduce one into embracing the deep tendencies in counterforce toward the pursuit of superiority – superiority which can pay off in battle only if used early while it is still retained. Incautious optimism about an illusory kind of "counterforce without tears" can lead one to give in to the pressures toward superiority and early use.

If it is foolish to pursue "counterforce with a human face," but is wrong, as Wohlstetter insists, simply to embrace the slaughter of civilians, is there any form of nuclear deterrence that is left?

---

[38] See Harold A. Feiveson, Richard H. Ullman, and Frank von Hippel, "Ten-Fold Reductions in the Superpower Nuclear Arsenals," *Bulletin of the Atomic Scientists*, vol. 41, Special Issue (August 1985), forthcoming. In essence, this proposal would reverse MIRVing.
[39] See notes 24, 25, 27, and 28.

The only hope for a tolerable conception of deterrence that I can see is in the direction of a kind of counterforce without illusions, specifically, without the twin – and mutually supportive – illusions that morality is thereby attainable and superiority is therefore desirable. When one sees how false is the premise (you can fight a nuclear war in a morally discriminating manner), one can resist the conclusion (you might as well prepare to win it). If, instead, the best that can be said for counterforce morally is that the slaughter of civilians would be a little less than if you made a special point of slaughtering civilians – that is, adopted retaliatory deterrence – then you could retain a relatively small counterforce capacity, but with the utmost reluctance and in the clear-eyed realization that if you ever used it you might unleash a holocaust. In addition, you would retain only the smallest force compatible with nuclear stability. We might have called this "finite counterforce," but such a name would have encouraged the self-deception that civilians could be spared. The targeting ought in fact to be as purely counterforce as possible, I would agree with Wohlstetter. But it is better to stick with "finite deterrence," especially since the limitation on numbers of warheads would probably do more to spare civilians than any efforts at discrimination in targeting possibly could. Indeed, I think we have seen that in the end, choice of targets, which was a fundamental dimension in Figure 1, is far less significant than choice of numbers. If real attacks cannot discriminate, what you attack is less important than how much you attack with.

Militarily, this is almost as unsatisfactory as it is morally. Of the three military defects of damage-limiting retaliation – enemy-selected targets, magnitude incentives, and preemption incentives – finite deterrence would largely eliminate the last two. By adopting such a policy, a country would demonstrate, through its acceptance of minimally adequate number of warheads, that it was genuinely not aiming at the capability for a disarming first strike. These are extremely important gains for stability in crises. Enemy-selection of targets, on the other hand, is the military price one pays for not being the one who begins a nuclear war. Once one is free from the illusion of becoming able to launch a disarming first strike, one can see that the real price for not going first is less than it seemed. Against a nation whose first nuclear attack was massive, it would nevertheless be high.

Indeed, many will argue that a force of around two thousand warheads is not enough militarily. Others will argue that it is too much morally. It could be the worst of both worlds: not enough militarily (so that nuclear war will come) and too much morally (so that we will commit atrocities). On the other hand, to leave the purists on both sides unhappy may not be a bad rule-of-thumb.

Philosophy, Center for Philosophy and Public Policy,
University of Maryland at College Park.

Social Philosophy & Policy 3:1 Autumn 1985 ISSN 0265-0525 $2.00

NUCLEAR DETERRENCE AND ARMS CONTROL: ETHICAL ISSUES FOR THE 1980s

ROBERT L. PFALTZGRAFF, JR.

The threat of atomic destruction has heightened the criminal irresponsibility of aggression, the employment of war as an instrument of national or bloc policy. Correspondingly, the moral obligation to discourage such a crime or, if it occurs, to deny it victory, has been underscored. The consequences of a successful defense are fearful to contemplate, but the consequences of a successful aggression, with tyrannical monopoly of the weapons of mass destruction, are calculated to be worse. While the avoidance of excessive and indiscriminate violence, and of such destruction as would undermine the basis for future peace, remain moral imperatives in a just war, it does not seem possible to draw a line in advance, beyond which it would be better to yield than to resist. Reinhold Neibuhr.[1]

... the person who deeply desires peace rejects any kind of pacifism which is cowardice or the simple preservation of tranquility. In fact, those who are tempted to impose their domination will always encounter the resistance of intelligent and courageous men and women, prepared to defend freedom in order to promote justice. Pope John Paul II[2]

For two generations the United States has maintained with its principal adversary, the Soviet Union, a security relationship based upon the deterrence of war by the possession of means deemed adequate to inflict unacceptable levels of damage in response to a Soviet attack upon the United States or its allies. Against the Soviet Union, the world's largest land power, in possession of superior conventional forces that could be launched against Western Europe and other peripheral regions of the continents of Europe and Asia, the United States has held nuclear capabilities as the ultimate weapon to be invoked in support of those interests deemed to be most vital to

---

[1] "The Case Against Pacifism," Harry R. Davis and Robert C. Good, eds., *Reinhold Niebuhr on Politics* (New York: Charles Scribner's Sons, 1960), pp.145–146.
[2] 1984 World Peace Day Message.

American security. Under conditions of virtual U.S. invulnerability to the use of nuclear weapons by the Soviet Union before the late 1950s, the United States could offer without great risk to itself to employ such weapons as part of a deterrent whose purpose, it should be recalled, was to deter, or prevent, the outbreak of war by Soviet design. Before the Soviet Union acquired its own atomic weapons, the United States viewed its nuclear capability as the ultimate deterrent to a Soviet attack launched with superior conventional forces. Subsequently, the United States faced the challenge of deterring both a Soviet nuclear and conventional attack.

The attainment by the Soviet Union of superiority in most indicators of nuclear force by the late 1970s, together with its long established preponderance in conventional capabilities, confronts the United States both with strategic and ethical dilemmas. Strategically, the need remains to preserve a mix of nuclear and conventional forces to assure deterrence under conditions of greater uncertainty as a result of the huge arms buildup of the Soviet Union at all levels. Ethically, the peoples of democratic societies find it difficult to sustain public support for weapons whose use they cannot contemplate because of their inherently destructive potential. The strategic requirements for nuclear deterrence (the perceived will to use such capabilities) clashes with an ethic that, if it accepts the concept of deterrence, denies the existence of any goal that would justify resort to nuclear weapons. The resulting strategic-ethical dilemma is apparent in the acceptance by the American Catholic Bishops of the principle of nuclear deterrence while nevertheless expressing "profound skepticism about the moral acceptability of any use of nuclear weapons."[3] What cannot be contemplated in use cannot form the basis for deterrence. If the United States is unprepared to threaten credibility to employ nuclear weapons against a Soviet-Warsaw Pact nuclear or conventional attack against Western Europe, it follows that the acceptance in American declaratory policy of the Bishops' presumption holds the risk of actually contributing to the outbreak of war by miscalculation. Such is the strategic-ethical dilemma posed by nuclear weapons and their destructive potential. This creates for democratic societies a security problem especially acute under conditions in which, for societal and economic reasons, they are not prepared to devote the resources that would be needed for a fully conventional defense. Indeed, the question would then arise whether the Soviet Union, without fear of retaliation, possessing its own nuclear weapons, would not be tempted to use them against an adversary that had largely or completely dismantled its own atomic weapons. Here we confront the discomforting paradox of an all-conventional defense on the part of the

---

[3] *The Challenge of Peace: God's Province and Our Response: A Pastoral Letter on War and Peace*, National Conference of Catholic Bishops, May 3, 1983, p.61.

West, even if it were possible, perhaps furnishing an incentive for a nuclear-armed adversary to employ such weapons without fear of retaliation in kind.

Although the strategic conditions in which American nuclear deterrence operated underwent a dramatic transformation, from an initial decade of clear U.S. superiority (the 1950s) to a decade of Soviet buildup to parity (the 1960s) to a decade of a Soviet quest for superiority (the 1970s), the fact remains that by 1985 a period twice as long as that which separated the two world wars had elapsed without the two leading military powers and political antagonists having gone to war with each other. Whether the United States and the Soviet Union would have engaged in military hostilities with each other in the forty years after the end of World War II in the absence of nuclear weapons is, of course, an unknowable proposition. It can only be stated with certainty that the history of the troubled U.S.-Soviet relationship has been punctuated by periodic international crises which themselves, in their escalatory and de-escalatory phases, have served as surrogates for the actual resort to weapons, with military capabilities casting before themselves their political shadow and providing the hypothetical escalatory options within which diplomacy and other forms of bargaining could bring about a resolution. In fact, states possessing nuclear weapons have not used them militarily against other states possessing such means; nor since the end of World War II have nuclear powers employed atomic capabilities against states not possessing such means. Instead, the military conflict map of the world since 1945 has been redrawn from its previous locus within Europe to the Third World. Thus the numerous wars that have erupted have encompassed nonnuclear powers and other actors, with lesser or greater levels of support from outside states, including those possessing nuclear weapons but resorting to nonnuclear means in armed conflicts against nonnuclear states.

Although the United States has increased substantially its levels of defense spending for conventional forces at times of heightened international tension, and specifically in periods such as the Korean Conflict and the Vietnam War, by and large nuclear weapons have been viewed as a *deterrence* substitute for the far more costly conventional capabilities that would be needed to help prevent resort to force by an adversary in support of its political objectives. Without nuclear weapons, a purely conventional force deployed by NATO against the Soviet-Warsaw Pact capabilities already deployed, or readily available, would be considerably more costly than the means deemed to be necessary under prevailing NATO flexible response strategy whose premises include the rapid escalation of warfare in Europe to the nuclear level. For the continental United States, moreover, nuclear weapons represent the principal, if not the only, direct military threat posed by the Soviet Union. Except for the narrow Bering Strait that divides Alaska from Soviet territory, the United States is separated by vast oceans that would furnish a formidable, but not necessarily insurmountable, barrier to invading Soviet air or amphibious forces. These forces, nevertheless, would form part of any military offensive, together with strikes with nuclear and chemical weapons. For Moscow to contemplate such an attack would depend upon the perception that the gains to be derived would far outweigh the risk of destruction to the Soviet Union. In short, it would mean that the nuclear capabilities of the United States had been neutralized or eliminated as effective instruments of deterrence or of retaliation.

In the changed circumstances of nuclear deterrence of the present decade, it is not the numbers of systems that are at issue, for in nearly all categories of forces the Soviet Union now leads the United States in quantitative terms, while the technological edge once possessed by the United States in strategic nuclear force capabilities has been eroded, if not largely eliminated.[4] The escalation dominance at the nuclear level that once compensated for numerical inferiority in American and NATO-European conventional land forces has been superseded by Soviet advantages in numbers of highly accurate strategic forces targeted against the United States and its allies and other friendly states that diminishes the efficacy of our strategic nuclear deterrent forces. The strategic force modernization program of the Reagan Administration represents a necessary effort to halt the erosion of American deterrent capabilities that otherwise would result in the obsolescence of each of the components of our strategic force with potentially destabilizing consequences of dangerous proportions for the United States and its allies.

Those who acknowledge that the Soviet Union has registered major advances in the development and deployment of strategic forces, but nevertheless mount a campaign for a nuclear freeze or for unilateral cuts in American nuclear capabilities, hold implicitly, if not explicitly, that nuclear superiority is meaningless; hence, the United States need not match a Soviet strategic nuclear buildup. If a larger Soviet nuclear force can be deterred by a smaller American one, the United States can afford to freeze its strategic capabilities at existing levels with resulting savings to be spent either on increasing conventional capabilities or to be diverted to domestic and international programs for the poor or otherwise disadvantaged. To assert that deterrence can be maintained by the retention of nuclear forces that are

[4] See *The Military Balance 1984–5* (London: International Institute for Strategic Studies, 1984), esp. pp.3–6 and 13–18; *Can America Catch Up?: The U.S.-Soviet Military Balance* (Washington, DC: Committee on the Present Danger, 1985). According to this analysis, "State indicators of the nuclear balance have shifted decisively in favor of the Soviet Union. This includes the overall number of nuclear warheads, where the Soviets now lead the United States by at least several thousand (strategic and tactical). In addition, the Soviets enjoy clear strategic advantages in land-target capability and megatonnage."

smaller rather than larger, older rather than newer, is to hold that the strategic nuclear balance is inherently stable. Presumably, increments on one side or the other will not alter a nuclear relationship in which neither side could launch with confidence a disabling attack against the other without expecting retaliation in kind. Under conditions of deterrence based upon the presumed possession by the United States of what the critics of larger forces term "overkill," the prospects for nuclear war are deemed to be remote. Even at substantially lower levels of nuclear capability than the United States presently possesses, the Soviet Union would be deterred from launching a nuclear attack because the residual American retaliatory capability would be sufficient to "destroy the Soviet Union ten times over," so the argument goes. The logical conclusion to be derived from such analysis is that arms control is not an urgent priority since the Soviet Union can be deterred by lower, rather than existing or higher, levels of American nuclear forces. Under such circumstances, the United States could move unilaterally to a strategic-nuclear force posture providing for minimal deterrence. Such is the logical contradiction in the thinking of those who hold that deterrence is inherently stable, even with minimal nuclear forces against a superior adversary, while contending simultaneously that the alternative to the active pursuit of arms control lies in nuclear Armageddon.

Pushed to its logical conclusion, this approach to American nuclear strategy rests upon the dubious proposition that the danger to international security lies not so much in the Soviet strategic buildup of the last decade but, instead, in the potential consequences of a countervailing American response in the form of the program set forth by the Reagan Administration. It must be presumed that the United States, by embarking upon its present effort to modernize strategic nuclear forces, and other defense capabilities, is somehow either tempting the Soviet Union to launch a nuclear attack in order to prevent the United States from attaining, or even preserving, military parity, or that the United States, once its strategic deficiencies are alleviated, will itself decide to launch a nuclear attack against the Soviet Union. In either case, according to such flawed reasoning, the American strategic modernization program becomes a principal destabilizing factor in the present international security environment. It is conveniently overlooked that the United States did not resort to the actual use of nuclear weapons against the Soviet Union during the period, successively, of an American atomic monopoly and superiority. Nothing in the history of American foreign policy, or the value structure of the United States as an open political system, would substantiate such a proposition about the circumstances under which decision-makers would make such a fateful choice.

To accept the premise that Soviet superiority in strategic forces is meaningless is to argue, furthermore, that Moscow can be trusted to hold similar views about the lack of utility of nuclear superiority as the proponents of minimal deterrence. Nothing in the military literature of the Soviet Union, produced more for the instruction of political and military elites in the Soviet Union than for Western consumption, substantiates such an assumption. To the contrary, Soviet military writings stress the integral relationship between nuclear weapons and the other instruments of warfare in an overall strategy based upon surprise, preemption, deception, the destruction of an enemy's ability to wage war, and the need to achieve military victory in consonance with the political objectives established by the leadership of the Soviet Union.[5] If the Soviet Union accepted the tenets of a deterrence strategy based upon smaller rather than larger nuclear forces, its leaders would have had ample opportunity, both in word and deed, to demonstrate such a commitment in the abundant Soviet literature on nuclear strategy, in the configuration of their nuclear forces, and in their conceptual approaches to arms control negotiations and agreements. In pursuing instead a quest for strategic superiority, the Soviet Union appears clearly to reject the argument that the possession of such forces is politically meaningless; or that they are somehow destabilizing in the superpower relationship. Indeed, after nearly a generation, the proponents of minimal deterrence have failed to "educate" the Soviet General Staff to alter its approach to nuclear forces to conform to the doctrinal assumptions and force levels deemed adequate in the concept of minimal deterrence. The case against an American strategic nuclear modernization program that is more in the form of a "catch-up" than a buildup contains the flawed logic that it is more destabilizing for the United States to attempt to acquire such forces than it is for the Soviet Union to continue to possess them. Aside from their cost to the United States, why oppose them otherwise?

If such reasoning is wrong, the adoption of defense policies so flawed leads either to mortgaging to Soviet behavior the security of the United States and those other nations whom we have pledged to defend or to the establishment of the conditions for a *Pax Sovietica*. The prospect of this latter condition itself contains the seeds of instability leading to conflict, for free peoples have been known, as in the period just before World War II, to

---

[5] See, for example, V.D. Sokolovskiy, *Soviet Military Strategy*, edited with an analysis and commentary by Harriet Fast Scott (New York: Crane, Russak and Company, Inc., 1975), pp.14–25, 172–213, 257–259; A.A. Sidorenko, *The Offensive (A Soviet View)* (Moscow, 1970) trans. United States Air Force (Washington DC: U.S. Government Printing Office, 1973), esp. pp.109–118; Joseph D. Douglass, Jr., *Soviet Military Strategy in Europe* (New York: Pergamon Press, 1980), pp.1–20; P.H. Vigor *Soviet Blitzkrieg Theory* (London: Macmillan, 1983), pp.102–122, 144–183; Harriet Fast Scott and William F. Scott, eds., *The Soviet Art of War: Doctrine, Strategy, and Tactics* (Boulder, CO: Westview Press, 1982), esp. pp.17–71; Jonathan Samuel Lockwood, *The Soviet View of U.S. Strategic Doctrine: Implications in Decision-Making* (New Brunswick, NJ: Transaction Books, 1983) esp. pp.13–123.

awaken belatedly to the need to defend themselves against an expansionist totalitarian threat. Having been proven wrong in their assumptions both about the meaning for the Soviet Union of strategic superiority and the nature of Soviet strategy and intentions, the proponents of minimal deterrence would have furnished the setting for Moscow's miscalculation of the nature of the Western response to Soviet political intimidation based upon military superiority. The strategic-military weakness of the United States, masked in the garb of minimal deterrence, would have produced the destabilizing situation that the proponents of such a force posture themselves had sought to avoid. The United States would not have acquiesced in Soviet political intimidation or nuclear blackmail, just as Britain and France decided in 1939 to fulfill their security commitment to Poland under highly disadvantageous military circumstances.

The concept of deterrence itself, as well as the levels and types of capabilities to be deployed in its support, represents a choice between greater or lesser evils, based upon an ethic of consequences over an ethic of intentions.[6] If the threat to use nuclear weapons as a means of deterring their use against the west represents a form of evil, does not the launching of an attack by miscalculation by an adversary become an even greater evil? In the first instance, there has been no loss of life; in the second the human casualties, civilian and military, might be beyond calculation. *The possession of the implements of warfare is not equivalent to their actual military use.* Much of the recent debate about nuclear armaments and conflict has obscured the fundamental distinction between weapons and the motives of their possessors and, ultimately, the causes of conflict. In themselves, weapons are neutral instruments, to be used by their possessors for essentially one or more of four purposes: to launch an attack as an aggressor; to defend against such an attack; to threaten another party by political intimidation; or to deter the actual or threatened use of such weapons against oneself. The gun in the hands of the police officer cannot be equated with the weapon used by the criminal. The resort to armed force against the person engaged in an attack upon an innocent party differs from the use of violent means by the attacker against his victim. The means for violence possessed by law enforcement agencies has as its purpose the prevention of unlawful behavior or, if such deterrence should fail, the actual use of such capabilities against the transgressor.

In an international political system lacking the enforcement mechanisms available in the more advanced domestic political systems, the deterrence of conflict by those forces seeking to overthrow by violent means the

---

[6] For an extended treatment of this issue, see Michael Novak, *Moral Clarity in the Nuclear Age* (New York: Thomas Nelson Publishers, 1983).

established order rests almost exclusively in the hands of other nation states. Under such circumstances, the preservation of a modicum of law and order is dependent upon the ability of such political units either in a deterrent capacity or, under conditions of deterrence failure, as the actual user of miliary force to thwart the ambitions of expansionist states. In this sense, the force used against such powers cannot be equated with the armed capabilities employed in response. The defensive use of arms against Hitler's Germany, or against the Soviet invasion of Afghanistan, is not similar to the employment of armaments by Nazi Germany and the Soviet Union. Nuclear weapons themselves cannot unleash a conflict. They must be launched by the human beings controlling them. The problem to be addressed, then, is not the weapons themselves but instead their possessor, the Soviet Union, who might use them in the absence of sufficient countervailing forces.

The threat to use nuclear weapons, no less than the threat to resort to force by the police officer, represents a deterrent against parties who otherwise might employ such means for unlawful or immoral purposes. What then constitutes the appropriate level of force for deterrence, whether in the case of the legally constituted authority within a domestic society or in an international system lacking agreed procedures and enforcement mechanisms for the prevention or resolution of conflict? Against what categories of targets is it appropriate to employ force either as a basis for deterrence or in the actual conduct of conflict?

Such questions have arisen in earlier ages. Beginning with St. Augustine but traceable to ancient Greece and Rome, a doctrine of "just war" was developed to govern the use of force. But the advent of nuclear weapons, together with other means of mass destruction have made the need to find ethically acceptable answers to such questions more compelling than ever before. The doctrine of just war included the right to go to war (*ius ad bellum*), but it also included the requirement that war be waged justly (*ius in bello*).[7] The means to be utilized had to be proportionate to the ends sought, and the means had to be based upon discrimination between civilian and military targets. Thus, the concepts of proportionality and discrimination

---

[7] For an extended discussion of such issues, see James E. Dougherty, *The Bishops and Nuclear Weapons: The Catholic Pastoral Letter on War and Peace* (Hamden, CT: Archon Books, 1984); James E. Dougherty and Robert L. Pfaltzgraff, Jr., *Contending Theories of International Relations*, Second Edition (New York: Harper and Row, 1981); Ernest W. Lefever and E. Stephens Hunt, eds., *The Apocalyptic Premise: Nuclear Arms Debated* (Washington, DC: Ethics and Public Policy Center, 1982); William V. O'Brien, *The Conduct of Just and Limited War* (New York: Praeger, 1981); Robert R. Reilly and others, *Justice and War in the Nuclear Age* (Lanham, MD: University Press of America, 1983); James R. Woolsey, ed., *Nuclear Arms: Ethics, Strategy, Politics* (San Francisco: Institute for Contemporary Studies Press, 1984).

formed central elements of traditional just war doctrine as it evolved across centuries of Western theological and political thought to confront the ethical dilemmas of the nuclear age. At least in part, U.S. nuclear doctrine has been based upon the ability to threaten the destruction of a designated percentage of an adversary's civilian population. To an even greater extent the strategic forces of smaller nuclear powers – Britain and France – rely upon such civilian targets as the basis for deterrence. But is it not appropriate to ask whether deterrence could be maintained instead first by the assurance that the strategic forces of both sides remained invulnerable to attack (in keeping with the present concept of deterrence), and ultimately if nuclear weapons could be made "impotent and obsolete" (in President Reagan's words) by developing and deploying the means to prevent the use of nuclear weapons against civilian populations as well? If such questions can be answered in the affirmative, it follows that strategic defense offers the prospect for resolving the ethical dilemmas inherent in nuclear deterrence concepts.

In the name of Mutual Assured Destruction (MAD) the United States signed the ABM Treaty, thus precluding the deployment of a strategic defense system. Without such a capability for nuclear defense on the part of the United States, it was hoped that the Soviet Union would forego the deployment of larger numbers of strategic capabilities. In fact, the Soviet Union built strategic forces, in missile size and in warhead accuracy and numbers, whose combined effect was to increase the vulnerability of the American nuclear capability that the United States was prohibited by the ABM Treaty from defending. Although the Soviet Union maintains a huge air defense system, it has sought in arms control negotiations to place strict limits on American strategic aircraft numbers while allowing for uncounted Soviet bomber capabilities (the Backfire). If the ABM Treaty is strategically consistent with smaller nuclear forces, rather than larger numbers of such systems, and thus with a doctrine of mutual assured destruction, the Soviet nuclear capability bears no resemblance to what would be expected from a nation adhering to a MAD doctrine. In fact, the Soviets adhere to a counterforce posture designed to launch a surprise first strike intended to destroy the strategic force of its adversary.

Despite the abundant evidence that the Soviet Union, both in its nuclear doctrine and force structure, does not share the tenets of Mutual Assured Destruction, the view persists that the United States, by taking prudent steps to modernize its strategic force, is pushing the world toward the brink of nuclear war; yet, the Soviet buildup is explained away as simply "defensive" in orientation or a product of paranoia that is based upon the historic experience of the Soviet Union and, before it, Tsarist Russia. The price of such a "defensive" mentality, however, has been Soviet expansion that has included the absorption of neighboring states and the creation of defensive zones in order to protect what has already been conquered. Despite this Soviet "siege mentality," the United States is invited by the proponents of deterrence based upon MAD either to freeze or to reduce unilaterally its nuclear capabilities; and this notwithstanding the fact that the Soviet Union has surpassed the United States in most of the indicators of strategic nuclear force capabilities.

At a time when the evidence indicates that Soviet doctrine and force planning reject the tenets of MAD in favor of a concept calling not for the mutuality of destruction but, instead, for the survival of the Soviet Union and the destruction of the United States, the devotees of minimal deterrence heap criticism upon the Reagan Administration for suggesting the need for a deterrence concept in keeping with the realities of Soviet doctrine and force posture. Somehow, the debate has become convoluted to the extent that those who would meet a larger Soviet strategic capability with a substantially smaller, or at least older, American force are self-anointed proponents of peace, while those committed to the modernization of the U.S. nuclear capability are deemed to be the advocates of war. Statements about fighting "limited" nuclear wars or military doctrines designed to enable the United States to "prevail" in a nuclear exchange are taken out of context and used to rhetorical advantage by the proponents of MAD. Whether a "limited" nuclear exchange could retain such a character is unknowable in the absence of the type of warfare that all Western strategists have striven to deter, or prevent. Just as it cannot be predicted with confidence that a nuclear war could be conducted in "limited" fashion, neither can it be asserted with high levels of confidence that such a conflict would automatically escalate to an all-out exchange. All nuclear strategies have had as their objective to deter by the presumed threat to escalate to general war. If such a basis for deterrence should fail, however, it does not follow that the postulate of automatic escalation would govern the behavior of adversaries in actual warfare. If the Soviet Union has posited the need to provide for its leadership elites and as much of its population as possible the means for post-nuclear attack recovery,[8] contrary to the tenets of MAD, why is it destabilizing for the United States to announce that in a hypothesized nuclear environment it also would seek to "prevail?"

To announce instead that U.S. strategy has as its goal the result opposite to "prevailing," that is to say, defeat and the destruction of American society, however comforting this may be to the proponents of minimal deterrence, serves only to undermine the basis for deterrence. If one protagonist designs

---

[8] See, for example, Leon Gouré, *War Survival in Soviet Strategy: USSR Civil Defense* (Miami, FL: Center for Advanced International Studies, University of Miami, 1976); P.T. Yegorov, I.A. Shlyakhov, and N.I. Alabin, *Civil Defense: A Soviet View* (Moscow, 1970), trans. United States Air Force, (Washington, DC: U.S. Government Printing Office, n.d.).

its nuclear doctrine and force posture to enable it to survive, the power against which such nuclear policies are directed invites either atomic blackmail or perhaps even attack if it adopts a doctrine based upon mutuality of destruction without a force posture that can both survive a nuclear attack and strike back against the military assets of the attacker. Neither capability is present in the American force structure favored by the proponents of minimal deterrence. Only if the dubious premises of the minimal deterrence approach are accepted can its proponents be equated with peace and the advocates of capabilities such as contained in the present U.S. strategic modernization program be considered to be the moral equivalent to the proponents of fighting, rather than deterring the outbreak of, war.

It is not necessary to consider stability based upon deterrence as an ideal state of affairs to believe, nevertheless, that it represents a moral choice based upon the lesser evil. The cost of forces needed for deterrence in a world comprised of governments that, for the most part, do not share the values of Western political pluralism constitutes part of the price of security. The debate about the requirements for deterrence of recent years reveals the lack of ease with which publics live with the presumed hazards of the nuclear era. In our society, such discussion reflects the hope that somehow the perceived dangers will vanish. In its extreme form, such hope yields to frustration that is more easily vented against a proximate, elected, and open U.S. government than against the remote, obdurate and closed Soviet system. Whether by design or unconsciously, the United States comes to be equated with the Soviet Union as the cause of world tensions. If Soviet policy cannot be changed, conceivably unilateral American gestures toward arms control or other forms of tension reduction will furnish the basis for Kremlin reciprocity. Closely related is the dubious notion that the failure of arms control negotiations is the result of the lack of adequate commitment on the part of the United States. The ethic of arms control assumes the form of an end in itself, as if to assert that the achievement of arms accords, regardless of their contents, will help pave the way toward a more peaceful world.

Thus the United States has been faulted in recent years, again often by the proponents of minimal deterrence, for having put forward unrealistic arms control proposals that the Soviet Union could not be expected to accept. Although the United States is alleged to have no need for destabilizing, heavy, intercontinental ballistic missiles armed with a large number of highly accurate warheads, it is argued that the Soviet Union must be allowed to keep what it has, even against a nonexistent comparable American nuclear force. If the United States could neither build such nuclear systems because of their allegedly destabilizing implications, nor confront the Soviet Union with arms reduction proposals designed to reduce such a counterforce threat, American strategic policy and arms control proposals would be reduced to sterile exercises in graceful accommodation to Soviet military superiority masked as international seminars designed to have educational value about the virtues of arms control.

The critics of American proposals designed to produce substantial reductions in Soviet counterforce-capable systems hold that the Soviet Union cannot be expected to reconfigure its strategic force posture. Therefore, American arms control proposals that would make necessary such changes in Soviet nuclear capabilities display a lack of serious commitment to arms control. Presumably, what matters is not the contribution of arms control to a strategic balance in which Soviet counterforce weapons are reduced but, instead, the utilization of arms control as an end in itself, in which the process becomes more important than the consequences. To carry this flawed logic one step farther, those who dismiss Soviet counterforce-capable systems as irrelevant or defensive in nature usually oppose the modernization of American counterforce-capable systems as provocative or destabilizing "first-strike" weapons.

The alternative is to view arms control not as a desirable end in itself, but instead as a subordinate element of a national security policy whose purpose is to furnish the defense and deterrence necessary to protect the interests of the United States, its allies, and other friendly states. Here the ethics of deterrence and of arms control converge to form a concept in which the criteria for arms control flow from a conception of what is needed for the defense of free societies in a hostile international environment. At the strategic nuclear level, according to such an approach, the requirements for deterrence are set within a security environment based upon an awareness of historical and cultural differences in the respective Soviet and American approaches to military affairs and the technological dynamism characteristic of our age. The adequacy of American strategic-nuclear forces is determined by their survivability and retaliatory potential against those categories of Soviet targets established by the deterrence criteria. Stability, measured by force survivability, forms an indispensable part of any strategic force modernization program, but also a criterion for designing arms control proposals. Arms control becomes an important, but nevertheless subordinate, element of national security policy.

Aside from the need to use arms control policy to help build public support for an adequate defense, its proper role lies in an effort to negotiate changes in force structures in keeping with criteria such as strategic stability. Here the dilemma is apparent. Structural asymmetries in the strategic-nuclear forces of the United States and the Soviet Union, notably the huge Soviet lead in counterforce-capable systems, cannot be negotiated away by arms control talks in the absence of an American strategic modernization program in comparable systems. If the price for public support for such American programs is progress in arms control negotiations, the United States will continue to lack the necessary domestic consensus for the very programs it needs either to enhance its deterrence force or to furnish the basis for meaningful reductions in the most destabilizing Soviet forces. This is the impasse that presently faces the United States as it attempts both to make needed improvements in its strategic nuclear force and to engage the Soviet Union in arms control negotiations. It arises because of the inherent difficulty of sustaining for protracted periods the public support needed by pluralistic societies for an adequate defense. The Soviet Union does not face comparable domestic pressures in the form of an antidefense lobby, and Moscow actively seeks to exploit the defense debates of the United States and its allies.

Just as the tenets of a strategy based upon Mutual Assured Destruction do not form the basis for an adequate national security policy today – if they ever did – we have reached an apparent dead end in arms control policy. The results of a decade of SALT were meager. At best, the United States achieved a codification of the strategic nuclear balance at levels that approximated what, even in the absence of such accords, the Soviet Union would have achieved anyway. At worst, the United States gave to the Soviet Union an incentive to narrow the qualitative gap that existed at the time of SALT I, since the Interim Agreement on Offensive Systems had already conferred upon Moscow a quantitative edge in launchers that we could not legally narrow, while placing no effective constraints on Soviet strategic force improvements in, for example, accuracy. The SALT decade represented, furthermore, the period of a deteriorating superpower relationship. Contrary to the expectations of the proponents of arms control as a basis for improving U.S.-Soviet relations, a year after the breakdown of the START and INF negotiations in Geneva at the end of 1983, this decline did not continue. Instead, this period marked the beginning of a modest improvement in relations, if the harsh Soviet rhetoric can be separated from the concrete dimensions of the U.S.-Soviet political relationship. The 1980s have yet to produce crises comparable to those of each of the decades since the end of World War II.

Arms control, as it has been practiced in the SALT-START period, has shown the severe and inherent limitations of this approach to the regulation of superpower armaments. The Soviet buildup of the SALT II period proceeded in tandem with the conduct of arms control negotiations which led to an agreement that had only a marginal prospect for Senate ratification even before the Soviet invasion of Afghanistan in 1979. The START proposals of the Reagan Administration were properly based upon the need to achieve substantial reductions in highly accurate Soviet systems. The

United States sought to evolve a unit of account that provided for consideration of the large size, or throw-weight, of Soviet ICBMs, as well as the large number of warheads that could be deployed on such systems. At all levels of advanced weaponry, we face increasing accuracy potential, which itself creates formidable problems for deterrence stability in the form of threats to survivability. In retrospect, the problems of SALT I, however difficult they were, pale by comparison with the issues that confront the designers of arms control proposals for the remaining years of this century.

If the technical requirements for strategic stability have grown more complex as weapons accuracy has increased, so have the problems of verification outpaced the technologies and other means available for that purpose. To be acceptable, arms control agreements between the United States and the Soviet Union must be verifiable. The apparent evidence of potentially massive Soviet violations of existing arms control accords not only casts a long shadow over the efficacy of such agreements, but also points to the need for verifiability as an essential criterion in any new accords negotiated by the United States. The verification need is greater for the United States than it is for the Soviet Union because of the deeply rooted secrecy of their closed society contrasted with the abundance of information about weapons development and deployment decisions in the United States. Apart from such structural asymmetries that enhance the need for verification, we face a situation in which the verification burdens that would be imposed on an agreement providing for counting missiles and warheads far exceeds that of SALT I. The growing Soviet ability to conceal missiles because of the reloadability of launchers, together with the means available to deploy nuclear systems in hidden locations, vastly increases the difficulty of verifying adherence to an agreement. An accord providing for large-scale reductions, commensurate with the deep cuts needed to minimize the Soviet first-strike potential, would require verification techniques not presently available, or likely to be, available, in the near future, short of extensive on-site inspection in the Soviet Union, itself an unlikely prospect. Conceptually, the greater the reduction in strategic forces, the greater the need for verification, for under conditions of lower numbers of such weapons the greater would be the incentive to conceal additional forces either as a hedge against noncompliance by the other party or as a means of achieving a breakout and eventual strategic superiority. The present political divisions that give rise to the need for armaments can be expected to persist in a dynamic technological environment that will render unlikely the achievement of arms control agreements satisfactory to the security needs of the United States.

Together the tenets of mutual assured destruction and arms control have failed to produce the effects intended by their proponents, namely, the codification of levels of strategic nuclear forces adequate to stability without, however, posing a counterforce threat to the United States. Instead, for reasons already adumbrated, the strategic force deployments of the Soviet Union have conformed to a pattern the opposite of that intended originally by the mutual assured destruction approach to deterrence, however much its proponents have attempted to explain away the trends in Soviet strategic programs. It is difficult to envisage how much greater the Soviet deployment of new systems would have been in the absence of the strategic arms control negotiations and accords of the last fifteen years. Clearly, a new approach to strategic stability, and to arms control, is necessary in light of the inadequacies experienced in the recent past and the problems and opportunities of the present decade. The United States must develop a conceptual framework for deterrence based not on the possession of the means for assured destruction but, instead, only strategic stability created by possession of the means for ensured, or at least enhanced, survival – the notion set forth in President Reagan's March 23, 1983 speech that launched the Strategic Defense Initiative (SDI). The present deficiency of arms control lies in the inability of such proposals and agreements, in themselves, to produce force structures that would reduce the counterforce threat posed by the continuing deployment of Soviet systems. If the arms control accords of the past have codified an existing strategic relationship, while minimizing constraints on the development of new technology, it follows that the United States cannot achieve a strategic balance that codifies lower levels of Soviet offensive systems in the absence of a changed environment for such forces. If arms control cannot achieve such an objective, the only plausible recourse lies in the development of a strategic defense designed to prevent at least a major portion of Soviet strategic forces from reaching their intended targets.

The deployment of such a capability raises numerous issues of profound importance for the United States and the West in general, some of which have begun to be addressed in the public debate that has followed the formulation of the Strategic Defense Initiative. Among SDI's opponents are the advocates of minimal deterrence, many of whom echo the Soviet contention that the deployment of a strategic defense would result in the "militarization" of space and thus the extension of the "arms race" to another arena of competition. Having failed to constrain the Soviet offensive strategic buildup by means of arms control, the proponents of arms control as a desirable end in itself now seek agreements that would foreclose for the United States the opportunity to redress by defensive means the Soviet offensive threat. Negotiations for the "demilitarization" of space would be confined to *future* weapons deployed, whether for offensive or defensive purposes, rather than the principal security threat facing the United States, namely, the huge *existing* counterforce-capable systems that could be launched from the Soviet Union on trajectories passing outside the earth's atmosphere en route to their targets in the United States or elsewhere. Such an agreement, favored by the Soviet Union and a substantial part of the American arms control community, would be designed to preclude the deployment by the United States of technologies still under development, rather than having as their focus the dismantling of Soviet offensive strategic forces already deployed.

At the time of SALT I, the United States faced an analogous situation. The Soviet Union resisted the establishment of meaningful linkage between the negotiation of the ABM Treaty, and reductions in offensive forces. Moscow's purpose was to preclude the deployment by the United States of a strategic defense to protect its ICBM force. As it did in the SALT I period, the Soviet Union again seeks an arms control regime in which the United States must agree to the demilitarization of space without achieving Soviet acceptance of deep reductions in intercontinental ballistic missiles. This is an old Soviet approach to arms control negotiations and broader diplomatic behavior as well (what is mine is mine; what is yours is negotiable). It characterized the Soviet conception of the INF negotiations which, from Moscow's perspective, were intended to codify as near a monopoly position as possible for Soviet deployment of the highly accurate system, the SS-20, while denying NATO the opportunity to deploy the Pershing II and the Ground Launched Cruise Missile. In short, in keeping with Soviet interests, Moscow will pursue a strategy designed to exploit the susceptibility of Western publics and political elites to the seductive appeal of arms control. Conceptually, the separation of the control of systems for defense from those for offense makes no strategic sense to the United States under prevailing circumstances, just as it clashed with American interests at the time of SALT I. By the same token, the negotiation of an arms control agreement that dismantles Soviet counterforce-capable strategic forces in return for nondeployment of an American strategic defense would present formidable verification problems and other inherent complexities, such as those of definition, that render unlikely the success of arms control as a means of enhancing strategic stability.

If the inevitable movement toward the enhanced accuracy potential of weapons sytems has generated new needs for survivability as the basis for deterrence, the technologies of defense have also changed since the signing of the ABM Treaty in 1972. Such change includes the ability to process large amounts of data, the microminiaturization of circuitry, advances in radars, and the possibility of nonnuclear means of intercepting and destroying missiles and warheads at various phases in their trajectory. Thus space is but one of the environments for the possible deployment of a strategic defense capability. Such changes, together with the likelihood of further advances, raise the possibility that it may not always be technically or economically feasible simply to deploy more offensive systems designed to saturate any strategic defense that is deployed. In itself, such a transformation would represent a sharp break from the era in which strategic offense forces deterred simply because of their capability to inflict unacceptable levels of devastation on an adversary.

Such a strategic defense would not have as a requirement that it be leakproof. In fact, the ability to reduce even by a modest percentage, perhaps by half, the likelihood that a Soviet strike could disable all or a major portion of the American strategic force would help to counter the advantages inherent in the huge Soviet counterforce capability. In contrast, the protection of urban populations by means of a strategic defense remains a more remote possibility. Such a capability would have technical requirements calling for complete dependability. Even if as many as 90 percent of incoming missiles could be destroyed, those remaining would be sufficient to devastate civilian targets. Nevertheless, the development of technologies for the defense of military targets will enhance greatly the prospects for the eventual defense of civilian targets against the threat of nuclear attack. The enhanced survivability of nuclear forces themselves would increase the security of civilian populations, for the specter of a disarming attack against American nuclear forces would be diminished.

It is remarkable that those who have called for assured destruction have embraced a concept whose principal basis is the holding hostage of defenseless civilian populations. At the same time this approach to deterrence is based on the premise that steps to protect all, or even a portion, of the United States from the possibility of a Soviet nuclear attack represents an unacceptable extension of armaments competition. A defense against a nuclear attack that substitutes the concept of survival for that of assured destruction as the basis for deterrence is said to render nuclear war more possible and therefore more likely. To accept the chain of logic leading to such a conclusion about nuclear weapons and warfare is to hold that laws mandating the use of seatbelts in automobiles should be repealed because reckless driving is encouraged if drivers believe they can survive an accident. According to such reasoning, the more vulnerable we feel to death from reckless driving, the more likely we are to drive safely. But the case for seatbelts actually lies in the protection they afford in situations that may lie beyond the direct control of the driver, such as the behavior of other drivers. Similarly, the case for strategic defense is found in the need to reduce the risk inherent in uncertainty about the intentions of an adversary who is in possession of nuclear weapons. The point of departure for such a capability lies in the defense of the military targets that the Soviet Union would need to destroy in a successful nuclear strike against the United States. Strategic defense may furnish the means to address the problem that successive arms control proposals and agreements have either left unresolved or, in fact, may exacerbated.

If the experience of the last fifteen years is illustrative of the limits of arms control negotiations and agreements in support of national security, it is equally apparent that a basis for sustained public support for defense must be found in a concept of deterrence linked as clearly as possible to ethical standards acceptable to Western pluralistic societies. The criteria for deterrence have not been fulfilled by existing arms control policy which, instead, offers more a placebo for concerned publics than a real supplement to the security needs of the West. In the absence of a broadly acceptable ethical basis for deterrence, and in the face of a sustained Soviet buildup of strategic forces, the West will continue to breed nuclear pacifism frightened by the real or imagined threat of atomic holocaust. The logic of the minimal deterrence approach leads to the acceptance of Soviet strategic advantage, while an exclusive reliance upon new generations of offensive systems by the United States as the means of redressing the imbalance intensifies discord within the Western Alliance about the appropriate means for national security in the nuclear era. The end result of this discord may be a feeling of helplessness in the West and an inclination by some people to surrender to the forces of totalitarianism in the hope of guaranteeing survival. Hence the need for an ethical basis for deterrence that diminishes the likelihood of nuclear war, whether by design or by miscalculation.

Numerous issues must be addressed in the formulation of such a deterrence concept. They include the transitional requirements in a process of change from an offense-dominant to a defense-oriented strategic environment; the relationship between defense against ballistic missiles and the threat posed by other capabilities such as cruise missiles; the problems of defense for military targets and the protection of civilian populations in keeping with the ethical standards of proportionality and discrimination between armed forces and noncombatants; the technologies most appropriate for various types of strategic defense; the conventional-nuclear threshold issues associated in particular with graduated escalation in the Atlantic Alliance; the implications of strategic defense for crisis management; the ramifications of strategic defense for extended deterrence and the protection of the interests of allies; and, last but not least, the precise types of arms control agreements that would become feasible within a strategic defense-oriented security environment. If such issues can be successfully addressed, the prospects for radical changes in the offense-defense force structure that is the basis for deterrence will become apparent within a strategic framework that reconciles the needs of deterrence with ethical standards appropriate to societies whose purpose is the preservation of peace in freedom and justice.

The Fletcher School of Law and Diplomacy,
Tufts University

Social Philosophy & Policy 3:1 Autumn 1985 ISSN 0265-0525 $2.00

THE MORAL STATUS OF
NUCLEAR DETERRENT THREATS*

DAVID A. HOEKEMA

Ethical reflection on the practice of war stands in a long tradition in Western philosophy and theology, a tradition which begins with the writings of Plato and Augustine and encompasses accounts of justified warfare offered by writers from the Medieval period to the present.[1] Ethical reflection on *nuclear* war is of necessity a more recent theme. The past few years have seen an enormous increase in popular as well as scholarly concern with nuclear issues, and philosophers have joined theologians in exploring the moral issues surrounding the harnessing of atomic forces in the service of war.

Neither philosophical nor popular discussions of the problems of the nuclear age have attended sufficiently closely, however, to a troubling paradox which lies at the very heart of the strategy of nuclear deterrence. The paradox lies in the alleged necessity, for the sake of achieving an inestimable good, of threatening incalculable harm. The contending parties in the current debate either dismiss this paradox too easily, counting it an intellectual puzzle but not a moral difficulty, or invoke it in an oversimplified form as a demonstration of the immorality of deterrence.

The purpose of the present study is to examine both the basis of this paradox and its practical import. Nuclear deterrence will be considered as an example of a policy which threatens grave harm for the sake of great good. In exploring the morality of deterrent threats, I will propose some general

* Portions of this discussion were included in a paper entitled "Intentions, Threats, and Nuclear Deterrence," published in Michael Bradie, Thomas W. Attig, and Nicholas Rescher, ed., *The Applied Turn in Contemporary Philosophy: Bowling Green Studies in Applied Philosophy*, *vol. V* (1983); permission to reprint some material here is gratefully acknowledged. A version of the same paper was presented at a colloquium session of the Eastern Division meeting of the American Philosophical Association in December, 1983, and the remarks of my commentator, Steven Lee, and of members of the audience helped refine the argument of the present discussion. I also benefited from discussion of the paper in a Philosophy Department colloquium at Calvin College. Charles R. Beitz, George Mavrodes, Douglas MacLean, Robert Wachbroit, Susan Hoekema, and the editors of *Social Philosophy and Policy* have offered invaluable criticisms and comments on earlier drafts of the present essay.

[1] Compilations of historical and contemporary defenses of the just war doctrine can be found in Arthur Holmes, ed., *War and Christian Ethics* (Grand Rapids, Mich: Baker Book House, 1975), and Albert Marrin, ed., *War and the Christian Conscience: From Augustine to Martin Luther King, Jr.* (Chicago: Henry Regnery Co., 1971).

principles concerning the morality of threats. By avoiding either a too facile
dismissal of immoral threats or an overhasty condemnation of all threats of
grave harm, I hope to lay an important part of the foundation for a
satisfactory account of the morality of nuclear deterrence.

It is necessary at the outset to have a clear notion of what nuclear
deterrence is. Clearly and uncontroversially, deterrence consists in influenc-
ing another's action by means of threats; the threats we are here concerned
with are threats to use nuclear weapons against an adversary in war. But
ought we to include in the category of deterrent threats only attempts to
prevent the outbreak of nuclear war by threatening retaliation? Or can the
threat to initiate a nuclear exchange also be considered an example of
nuclear deterrence? Equally important, should the concept of deterrence be
limited to threats of massive retaliation against an adversary's territory and
population – to threats of "countervalue," and not "counterforce," nuclear
attack, in strategic jargon? Or can the threat of concentrated attack upon an
adversary's nuclear forces themselves – a threat which might be carried out
either preemptively or in retaliation – be considered a deterrent threat as
well?

These questions are of vital importance to the contemporary debate, for
practical as well as moral reasons. I will set them aside here, however, in
order to begin by examining nuclear deterrence in what is probably its
longest-established and most widely recognized form: the threat of large-
scale retaliation for any nuclear attack. Deterrence in this form has been a
central element in United States nuclear policy since the early 1950s, when
Soviet development of fusion as well as fission weapons had broken the
American nuclear monopoly and the Korean War held out the frightening
prospect of triggering a superpower war. Against this background, Secretary
of State John Foster Dulles declared in 1954 that "local defenses" against
aggression "must be reinforced by the further deterrent of massive retaliatory
power."[2]

The strategy of "massive retaliation" or "assured destruction" remains an
essential element of United States nuclear policy. Whatever may be the
currently favored competing or complementary strategic doctrines, the
continued existence of a large arsenal of strategic warheads constitutes an
unmistakable threat of massive retaliation. The role of the retaliatory
doctrine is confirmed in official statements of United States policy. Secretary
of Defense Caspar Weinberger stated in the *Annual Report to Congress, Fiscal
Year 1984*, for example, that the United States must "maintain nuclear

---

[2] John Foster Dulles, speech before the Council on Foreign Relations, Jan. 12, 1954, reprinted
in *The New York Times*, Jan. 13, 1954; cited in Bernard Brodie, *Strategy in the Missile Age*
(Princeton: Princeton University Press, 1959) p.248.

forces to deter nuclear attack on itself." In order to deter, the Secretary insisted,

> We must make sure that the Soviet leadership, in calculating the risks of agression, recognizes that because of our retaliatory capability, there can be no circumstance in which it could benefit by beginning a nuclear war at any level or of any duration. If the Soviets recognize that our forces can and will deny them their objective at whatever level of nuclear conflict they contemplate and, in addition, that such a conflict could lead to the destruction of those political, military, and economic assets that they value most highly, then deterrence is effective and the risk of war diminished.[3]

Weinberger's statement, though intended to support a great deal besides a force capable of massive retaliation, shows that the threat of massive retaliation remains a central and unavoidable element in United States policy, and we may presume that similar thinking guides Soviet planners as well. Moreover, such threats confront us with the paradoxical character of nuclear deterrence in its clearest form. The scale of destruction which might result if the threat were to be carried out is quite literally incalculable and nearly unimaginable – and the magnitude of the threatened harm provides all the more assurance, according to the supporters of deterrence, that it will never need to be carried out. It is appropriate, therefore, to proceed with our exploration of the morality of threats by considering, as a paradigm example of a seemingly immoral but beneficial threat, the threat of massive retaliation for a nuclear attack.

I. *Kavka's Analysis of Wrongful Intentions*

The morality of nuclear deterrence has been debated by ethicists as well as statesmen ever since the first atomic bomb made such a policy possible.[4] I shall not here attempt to trace the various positions which have been

---

[3] United States Department of Defense, *Annual Report to Congress, Fiscal Year 1984*, published in Feb., 1983 (U.S. Government Printing Office), pp.52, 51.

[4] These issues have been addressed infrequently by philosophers but more frequently by theological ethicists. For collections representing a range of ethical positions, see James Finn, ed., *Peace, the Churches, and the Bomb* (New York: The Council on Religious and International Affairs, 1965); and Walter Stein, ed., *Nuclear Weapons and Christian Conscience* (London: Merlin Press, 1961). The writings of Paul Ramsey, included in the above collections, have been perhaps the most extended and careful defenses of nuclear deterrence strategy; see also his *War and the Christian Conscience* (Durham, N.C.: Duke University Press, 1961), and the essays in his later collection, *The Just War* (New York: Charles Scribner's Sons, 1968). Ramsey's defense of deterrence doctrine is briefly challenged by Michael Walzer in *Just and Unjust Wars* (New York: Basic Books, 1977). Recent discussions of the issues raised by Ramsey and others can be found in Alan Geyer, *The Idea of Disarmament!: Rethinking the*

defended in the course of that discussion, although reference will be made to
a few works, particularly those of philosopher Gregory Kavka, as I proceed.

In order to address the question of the moral justifiability of nuclear
deterrence, we must first face a prior question: can the *actual use* of nuclear
weapons as means of retaliation for nuclear attack ever be morally justified?
In the case which I am considering, retaliation would involve the direct
destruction of the attacker's factories and cities, as well as military forces.
Traditional just war teaching requires that the means of war observe the
standard of proportionality to the end sought and spare the lives of
noncombatants.[5] A large-scale counterattack on an enemy nation would
flagrantly violate these standards. Thus, whatever the provocation, such an
attack would surely violate the requirements of justified warfare.

Therefore, I begin with the premise that whatever moral case can be made
for deterrent threats of massive retaliation extends no farther than the threats
themselves. Precisely here, after all, lies the paradoxical character of
international relations in the nuclear world. Granted that it can never be
morally right to retaliate against another nation using nuclear weapons, we
must consider whether it may nevertheless be right and fitting, perhaps even
our duty, to own them and to threaten their use. (Of course, implicit in my
argument on the immorality of counterattacking with nuclear weapons is the
assumption that it is also immoral to initiate massive use of nuclear
weapons.)

This initial premise does not simplify our task so much as complicate it,
for it requires us to give an account of nuclear deterrence which is divorced
from any justification for using the weapons we hold. Yet to reject this
premise by insisting upon something stronger – to argue not merely for the
deterrent threat but for the actual use of large numbers of nuclear weapons
in retaliation – would be to deny the validity of the tradition which
distinguishes just from unjust wars, or at least to disregard its demands for
proportionality and the immunity of noncombatants.

A second initial ethical assumption is also necessary in order to grasp the
difficulty of the choices which confront us. That is the assumption that the
consequences of our actions are an important determinant of their moral
character. Deterrence merits consideration, from a moral point of view, only

Unthinkable (Elgin, Ill.: Brethren Press, 1982); in George F. Kennan, *The Nuclear Delusion*
(New York: Pantheon, 1982); and, in succinct form, in the pastoral letter of the United States
Catholic Bishops, *The Challenge of Peace: God's Promise and Our Response.* An extended
argument for nuclear pacifism which sets out carefully the views of others has been offered by
Edward J. Laarman in *Nuclear Pacifism: A Contemporary Application of the Just War Tradition*
(New York: American University Studies: Theology and Religion, 1984).
[5] On the requirements of the just war tradition, see the works of Ramsey and Walzer, cited
above, and James T. Johnson, *The Just War Tradition and the Restraint of War* (Princeton:
Princeton University Press, 1981).

if we are willing to give significant moral weight to the consequences of acts.[6] Given the potentially disastrous results – in the most literal sense – which the failure or the abandonment of deterrent threats might cause, it seems necessary to grant this much.

Some of the most penetrating and provocative among recent philosophical discussions of the morality of nuclear deterrence have been written by Gregory Kavka.[7] His analysis of the morality of deterrence will be employed here as a starting point for my own. Kavka adopts both of the assumptions just mentioned: that, whatever may be the justification for making a nuclear threat, there are "conclusive moral reasons" not to carry it out; and that, at least in cases where a great deal of suffering and serious injustice are at stake, morality turns on consequences.[8]

Kavka argues that a number of troubling paradoxes arise from a class of situations which he calls Special Deterrent Situations (SDS's), of which "the balance of nuclear terror as viewed from the perspective of one of its superpower participants" is a paradigmatic example. More generally, he offers the following definition of an SDS:

> An agent is in an SDS when he reasonably and correctly believes that the following conditions hold. First, it is likely that he must intend (conditionally) to apply a harmful sanction to innocent people, if an extremely harmful and unjust offense is to be prevented. Second, such an intention would very likely deter the

[6] Deterrence may still pose a difficult moral dilemma on strictly deontological grounds: one may be torn between the duty to protect the lives of one's countrymen and the duty to spare the lives of innocent citizens of a hostile nation. Such a dilemma is not precisely the same as the apparent paradox of threatening grave harm for the sake of great good, even though consideration of conflicting duties may support the same action as does the argument from the consequences of deterrent threats.

[7] Gregory Kavka, "Some Paradoxes of Deterrence," *The Journal of Philosophy*, vol. 75 (June 1978), pp.285–302. A classic discussion of the strategic issues which provides the starting point for Kavka's discussion is Thomas Schelling, *The Strategy of Conflict* (Cambridge, Mass.: Harvard University Press, 1960). Kavka has returned to the theme of this article in several other writings, though the one cited above is the most succinct and, for our purposes, the most clearly relevant. But see also the article cited in the note immediately following, and his contribution to the Sterba volume cited below "Nuclear Deterrence: Some Moral Perplexities," pp.127–138.

[8] More precisely, Kavka assumes that the act with the highest utility ought to be performed whenever a very great deal of utility is at stake, at least if what is at stake is a great deal of negative utility and the cost of failing to perform the most useful act includes serious injustice. See Kavka, (1978), p.288. Kavka evidently regards the reference to injustice as explainable in terms of utility – a controversial assumption, but not essential for the paradoxes he proposes. In a later article, Kavka has further explored the morality of nuclear deterrence from a more thoroughly utilitarian standpoint: see "Deterrence, Utility, and Rational Choice," *Theory and Decision*, vol. 12 (Mar. 1980), pp.41–60, where he articulates a principle of rational choice which, he argues, is better able to take account of the catastrophic consequences which nuclear deterrence must weigh than are most versions of utilitarianism.

offense. Third, the amounts of harm involved in the offense and the threatened sanction are very large and of roughly similar quantity (or the latter amount is smaller than the former). Finally, he would have conclusive moral reasons not to apply the sanction if the offense were to occur.

In such situations, Kavka argues, several paradoxes arise. They result from the fact that, in SDS's, an agent can prevent grave harm only by threatening similar harm, and moral considerations seem to require making the threat at the same time that they forbid carrying it out. Kavka's first paradox states this central point succinctly:

> (P1) There are cases in which, although it would be wrong for an agent to perform a certain act in a certain situation, it would nevertheless be right for him, knowing this, to form the intention to perform that act in that situation.[9]

But this claim, Kavka observes, is a denial of a highly plausible principle which connects the morality of action with the morality of intention, a principle which Kavka labels the Wrongful Intentions Principle:

> (WIP) It is wrong to intend what it is wrong to do.

This principle, suggests Kavka, has seldom been explicitly discussed by moral philosophers – very likely because it seems so self-evident as to need no defense.[10] The force of the paradox Kavka has formulated, therefore, is evident: there appear to be situations in which we may and indeed ought to form immoral intentions, even though we ought in general not to form immoral intentions.

Kavka resolves this paradox by denying the validity of the WIP in situations where a conditional intention is formed solely for the purpose of

---

[9] Kavka, (1978), p.288.

[10] It is worth noting that from a utilitarian standpoint the WIP is by no means obviously true – indeed, it would appear to be clearly false. If morality demands maximization of utility or of preference satisfaction, then the moral assessment of intentions, like that of actions, turns on their probable consequences. If intending harm leads on balance to good consequences, then it is right and proper to have such intentions, whatever the WIP may suggest to the contrary. For the evaluation of intentions, on a utilitarian view, is quite independent of the evaluation of actions, except insofar as intentions tend to produce actions. It would appear that a strict utilitarian ought to feel no compunctions about forming immoral intentions, if the formation of such intentions influences others' actions in desirable ways, but ought not to follow through in action if by doing so utility is sacrificed. David Gauthier has argued recently, however, that when the effect of intentions on the probabilities of alternative outcomes is properly considered, a strict utilitarian may have cogent reasons both to form and to carry out intentions such as those involved in deterrent threats. See "Deterrence, Maximization, and Rationality," *Ethics*, vol. 94 (April 1984), pp.474–495.

deterring another's action which, if actually carried out, would provide the occasion for acting on one's intention.[11] In doing so, however, Kavka fails to recognize that the WIP does not bear as directly as he supposes on deterrent situations. For it is not *intentions* that deter, as Kavka supposes, but *threats*. The differences between these two concepts are more important to the moral assessment of deterrence than Kavka or other writers have recognized. Kavka's paradoxes do not refute the WIP, therefore, nor do the situations he describes require its violation.

II. *The Illocutionary Force of Threats*

In order to draw the distinction between intentions and threats clearly, let us return to the definition of the Special Deterrent Situation in which immoral intentions seem to be morally required. The first condition which must be satisfied, according to Kavka's account, is that "it is likely" that the agent "must intend (conditionally) to apply a harmful sanction to innocent people, if an extremely harmful and unjust offense is to be prevented." This description is imprecise, however, because it confuses *intentions* with *declared intentions*, such as *threats*. When these are clearly distinguished, it appears highly unlikely that this first condition is ever satisfied.

What is a *threat?* We might define the notion briefly as follows:

(D1) A person P threatens a person Q just in case P declares the intention of bringing about a consequence which Q desires to avoid.

Threats are usually *conditional*: P declares the intention of harming Q unless Q acts in the way that P directs. Conditional threats are means of coercion, for if the threatened consequence is severe enough to constitute intolerable harm, given the action demanded, then Q is likely to be coerced to act as P demands. A conditional demand, however, is not essential to the making of a threat. A threat is still a threat even if it is a simple declaration of intention to do harm, as in the case of assassination threats.[12]

---

[11] Kavka, "Some Paradoxes of Deterrence," section II. In the more recent article, "Nuclear Deterrence: Some Moral Perplexities," Kavka reiterates this conclusion and supports it further on the basis of a "Threat Principle" – the principle that it is wrong to threaten the lives of large numbers of innocent people. He rejects a categorical form of this principle on essentially consequentialist grounds and substitutes a weaker form which rests on a weighing of threatened harms against expected benefits (pp.130–131). Though this line of argument leads to a conclusion which I accept – that some, but not all, threats to do the immoral are justified – it fails, like the earlier analysis, to mark out clearly the distinction urged below between threats and intentions.

[12] I have explored the nature of threats and offers as means of coercion in Chapter 2, "The Nature of Coercion," of *Rights and Wrongs: Coercion, Punishment, and Social Institutions* (Selinsgrove, Penn.: Susquehanna University Press, 1985). See also Robert Nozick, "Coercion," in Sidney Morgenbesser, Patrick Suppes, and Morton White, eds., *Philosophy, Science, and Method: Essays in Honor of Ernest Nagel* (New York: St. Martin's Press, 1969), pp.440–445.

Threats constitute one form of interpersonal influence. In the characteristic case of conditional threats, one person threatens another because she wants to make him act in a certain way. What has this effect, if the threat succeeds, is the threat itself – the declared intention to do harm. The intention to do harm may be declared in any of a number of ways, and explicit statement is by no means necessary; but the effectiveness of a threat does depend on its *credibility*. A threat is credible, we might say, if it is such that the person threatened believes that the threatener has both the intention and the means to carry it out.

An unarmed individual who confronts a battalion of soldiers pillaging his village and tells them, "Leave the village at once or I will mow you all down," has not credibly threatened the soldiers. His threats, no matter how vehement and specific, are unlikely to have any effect. On the other hand, the soldiers can make a highly credible threat to the villager, even without an explicit statement. If they demand his watch while holding a rifle to his head, they are effectively threatening him with death if he fails to comply – even if they say only, "Would you be so kind as to lend us your watch so that we may admire its workmanship?"

Nothing has been said thus far about *intention per se*. A threat is the declaration of an intention to do harm, and in order to be effective the declaration must be credible. But whether the threatener actually holds such an intention is irrelevant to the effectiveness of the threat. A convincing bluff is as effective as a genuinely intended threat. If Bob tells Carol, "Give me your money or I'll blow your head off," while holding a loaded pistol, he has threatened Carol even if he is actually a very gentle person who has no intention of harming her but is merely curious about how she will respond. Conversely, the vilest intentions do not constitute a threat unless they are communicated, through word or action, to others. If Ted says to Alice, "Would you mind bringing me that handsaw?" but secretly intends to strangle her if she does not do so, this intention does not make Ted's simple request a threat.

In making threats, therefore, intention functions simply as one among many means to enhance credibility. If a threat is a bluff there is always a danger, however remote, that the bluff may be found out, and the threat may for that reason fail. But if the threat is not a bluff, it cannot be found out.

Kavka acknowledges that his first condition rules out bluffing, and he comments as follows:

> The first condition will be satisfied only if attempts by the defender to bluff would likely be perceived as such by the wrongdoer. This may be the case if the defender is an unconvincing liar, or is a group with a collective decision procedure, or if the wrongdoer is shrewd

and knows the defender quite well. Generally, however, bluffing will be a promising course of action. Hence, although it is surely logically and physically possible for an SDS to occur, there will be few actual SDS's.[13]

The occurrence of an SDS, then, presupposes that intending to carry out a particularly dire threat is necessary for the credibility of the threat. But this intention, surely, is an empirical fact which we can never know with certainty. If I am an unconvincing liar, or if my attempts to deceive are likely to be unsuccessful for some other reason, then I must do whatever I can to increase the credibility of my threats. Perhaps I ought to make my decisions in greater secrecy, or carry out a few threats to show that I am capable of doing so. Perhaps I ought even to cultivate an appearance of recklessness and instability. But deliberately forming the intention to carry out the threat is only one of many ways of making my threat more credible, and a very indirect one at that. If there are moral reasons for *not* forming such an intention, that is all the more reason why I ought to back up my threats with more persuasive and belligerent bluffs without intending to carry them out.

Kavka's analysis, and that of many other writers on deterrence, seems to overlook the fact that threats are examples of what J.L. Austin has called the *illocutionary force* of language.[14] Language, Austin reminds us, is not merely a way of *saying* something but is also a way of *doing* something. Threats are among the actions that we perform by saying certain sorts of words in appropriate contexts and sometimes even by saying nothing but acting in a way which communicates the threat of harm. Threats are thus acts performed in the presence of others. Intentions, by contrast, have to do with mental states or dispositions, and they do not influence others until they are expressed through overt statements or acts. An undeclared intention to harm no more constitutes a threat than an unstated intention to marry constitutes an engagement. And it is the act of threatening, not the intention behind it, that has an effect on others. An insincere threat may be no less far-reaching in its consequences than an insincere assent to marriage vows.

III. *The Wrongful Threat Principle*

Suppose we amend the definition of a Special Deterrent Situation to refer to threats rather than intentions. Let us say that an agent is in an SDS just in case it is likely that he must *threaten* to harm innocent people in order to

---

[13] Kavka, (1978), p.287.

[14] See J.L. Austin, *How To Do Things With Words* (Oxford: The Clarendon Press, 1962), esp. Lecture 8; cf. "Performative Utterances," in *Philosophical Papers*, 2nd ed., ed. J.O. Urmson and G.J. Warnock (Oxford: Clarendon Press, 1970), pp.233–252.

avoid disastrous consequences. We might similarly amend Kavka's first paradox, quoted above, to read as follows:

> (P1a) There are cases in which, although it would be wrong for an agent to perform a certain act in a certain situation, it would nonetheless be right for him, knowing this, to threaten to perform that act in that situation.

Should we still count this as a "paradox of deterrence"? Certainly something troubling remains. The revised statement no longer conflicts with the Wrongful Intentions Principle mentioned above. But it does conflict with a slightly weaker principle which we might label the *Wrongful Threat Principle*:

> (WTP) To threaten to do what one knows to be wrong is itself wrong.

Philosophical ethicists have not often systematically distinguished threats from intentions, and I know of no historical or contemporary philosophical discussions which state or defend this principle. All the same, it seems at least as plausible as the stronger principle to which Kavka appeals in motivating his paradoxes. What follows from this principle, if we take it as true?

The Wrongful Threat Principle offers a simple and appealing way of distinguishing between justified and unjustified instances of coercion. Coercion is legitimate, we might say, when the coercer threatens a penalty which it would not be immoral to carry out if the threat should fail. Illegitimate coercion threatens a consequence which it would be immoral to carry out. Thus, the police officer who threatens arrest and possible injury to deter an assailant – hoping that his threat will succeed in preventing the assault – is acting morally, because he will be justified in carrying out the threat if its deterrent effect fails. But the bandit who threatens, "Your money or your life," would be committing a grave wrong if he carried out his threat, and the coercive threat itself is therefore wrong.

On this account, the threat of massive nuclear retaliation would clearly be an example of unjustified coercion, since the threatened consequence would be immoral to carry out. The mere possession of large numbers of nuclear weapons, and of delivery vehicles capable of reaching an adversary, may constitute a clear and credible threat of such retaliation and hence an immoral act.[15] Deterrence using the threat of conventional weapons, however, might be legitimate, since the actual use of conventional weapons to repel an invasion is, on many accounts, morally permissible.[16]

IV. *Justifying Immoral Threats: An Example*

Simple and appealing as it is, however, the WTP is mistaken. Its error is evident in a situation such as the following. Imagine that a terrorist has seized a number of hostages and has threatened to kill them unless some extravagant demand is met – let us say, the immediate execution of the chief executives of all NATO nations and of the chief executive officers of the Fortune 500. Police officers are in communication with the terrorist, but several days of attempts at negotiation have been fruitless. Police conversations have revealed, however, that the terrorist is extremely fearful that some harm may come to his family as a result of his actions and seems willing to go to any length to prevent such an outcome. The police, therefore, discuss the possibility of threatening to harm the terrorist's wife and children in order to induce him to surrender and release his hostages. In such a situation, is it not morally permissible – even obligatory – to make such threats?[17]

This would seem to be an instance where the avoidance of disastrous consequences justifies what would otherwise be an immoral threat. It is only the *threat* that is permissible – certainly not the *intention* to harm the terrorist's innocent wife and children. We may not actually harm the innocent in order to protect others, and therefore we may not intend to do so either. All the same, we may do many things to make the threat more credible, including practicing deception of various kinds. We may boast to

---

[15] For this reason, I am doubtful that the novel position recently defended by James Sterba, which permits the possession of nuclear weapons while prohibiting the explicit threat to use them, can finally be sustained. Sterba argues that such a posture achieves the ends of deterrence while eliminating the need to intend or threaten the immoral. The effectiveness of such "deterrence without threats," Sterba argues, results from other nations' doubts about the sincerity with which one declares that one will not use the nuclear weapons which are nevertheless maintained in one's military arsenal. I am not persuaded that the renunciation of explicit threats accomplishes anything more than the easing (on questionable grounds) of one's own moral qualms; but Sterba's argument deserves more extended consideration than I can offer in this discussion. See James Sterba, "How to Achieve Nuclear Deterrence Without Threatening Nuclear Destruction," in Sterba, ed., *The Ethics of War and Nuclear Deterrence* (Belmont, CA: Wadsworth, Inc., 1985), pp.155–168.

[16] Although I cannot take up this matter here, the question of the justification of the use even of conventional arms in self-defense is an important one, and the pacifist's argument that such armed force is immoral deserves far more serious consideration than it has received from either political leaders or ethicists. See, for example, Portia Bell Hume and Joan V. Bondurant, "The Significance of Unasked Questions in the Study of Conflict," *Inquiry*, vol. 7 (1964), pp.318–327, which argues for theoretical attention to techniques of active, nonviolent conflict. A thorough review of the character and techniques of nonviolence is offered by Gene Sharp in *Exploring Nonviolent Alternatives* (Boston: Porter Sargent Publishers, 1971). I have briefly explored some of the common objections to pacifism in "Reformed Pacifism," in *Peace Studies Bulletin* (Bulletin of the Manchester College Peace Studies Institute), vol. 14 (1984), excerpted in "In Defense of Pacifism," *The Christian Century* (forthcoming).

[17] This example was suggested to me, in a panel discussion at St. Olaf College, by Edmund Santurri.

the terrorist how much we will enjoy torturing his children, thus attempting to portray ourselves as monsters capable of such an act. Perhaps we may even sharpen a few knives near the telephone and make gleeful and sadistic noises. But what we may not do is intend or carry out deliberate harm to the innocent.

The example of the terrorist suggests that, plausible as the Wrongful Threat Principle may appear, it must sometimes be set aside in order to prevent grave harm. In a situation where one must choose between threatening an act which would be immoral to carry out and permitting the death of innocent persons, the presumptively immoral threat seems to be morally allowed, perhaps even required. The argument of the previous section against the threat of nuclear deterrence, which was based on the WTP, is therefore too simple. Seemingly immoral threats may sometimes be morally permitted, and we must consider the possibility that nuclear deterrence falls into this category.

Yet the threat of nuclear retaliation is different in important respects from the threat to harm the terrorist's family. Let us take note, first, of the ways in which the two situations are similar and, then, of their differences.

First, both nuclear deterrence and the threat to harm a terrorist's family involve the threat of grave harm to the innocent. To speak of "innocence" does not require that we absolve those threatened from all responsibility for the disaster we hope to avert. Perhaps the people of the nation against whom we threaten nuclear retaliation have assisted in some way in building the military institutions or policies which now threaten us. Similarly, it is possible that the members of the terrorist's family have failed to do all they could to prevent the terrorist from seizing hostages. (Ought every mother to warn her children daily, "Now go outside and play, but don't kidnap any hostages"?) Remote complicity is not a ground for the kind of punishment we threaten, however. The residents of the cities of an enemy nation, and the families of terrorists, are innocent as regards the immediate threat of death which we hope to deter, and the threat we direct against their lives is a threat against persons whom we may not deliberately harm.

Second, both situations require deception in order to ensure the credibility of the threat. The terrorist will not take our threat seriously unless we convince him that we are immoral and sadistic enough to carry it out. And the same is true, presumably, for the nations whom we intend to deter from use of nuclear weapons.

But the nature of this deception is radically different in the two cases. The police must mislead the terrorist about their intentions, but they may assure their own friends and families that they have no intention of carrying out their threat. As soon as the threat succeeds and the terrorist gives himself up, the deception dissolves: the terrorist is arrested, his family is unharmed, and the police put away their sharpening stones and stop cackling. Even if the threat should fail, the need for deception is limited and temporary. If the terrorist defies all attempts to coerce him and begins executing his hostages anyway, the police must then turn to other tactics to stop him. Their threat against the family, which cannot morally be carried out, will have no further use.

The threat of nuclear deterrence, by contrast, is not a temporary and limited expedient but a permanent and pervasive feature of a nation's foreign policy. When a nation's foreign policy relies on nuclear deterrence as an essential foundation, this threat becomes the unchanging background of every other mode of international behavior. The morally troubling character of the threat to destroy entire cities and nations with a nuclear attack is not dispelled, therefore, by noting that there are situations in which a normally immoral threat can be temporarily justified. The threat depicted in our hypothetical example is strictly limited in its scope and its duration; the nuclear threat, however, respects limits of neither sort.

Although the example we have considered restrains us from condemning *a priori* every threat to do the immoral, it is not sufficient to allay our qualms about the morality of a threat made, not by a few policemen to an isolated terrorist, but by entire nations to the world at large. A nation which bases its position in the world on such threats is sharpening its knives for all the world to hear.

V. *Justifying Immoral Threats: Necessary Conditions*

The argument of the previous section has shown that threats to do the immoral *may* sometimes be justified. The Wrongful Threat Principle, attractive as it appears on first examination, excludes too much. Since the principle condemns all immoral threats, a single example of a threat which, though immoral to execute, is nonetheless morally justified is sufficient to refute the principle. And we have found such an example in the case of the terrorist: a hypothetical example, to be sure, but one which is all too realistic in the contemporary world. It is unlikely, but by no means impossible, that those attempting to deal with an actual terrorist would find that, having exhausted every other means of saving innocent lives but this, they must resort to threats of the sort that I have described.

To make immoral threats, therefore, though it is normally to be avoided, is not in itself categorically immoral. Is the threat of nuclear deterrence among the threats that can be justified morally? In the case of threats of massive retaliation, it has been argued above, the differences from the terrorist example outweigh the similarities, and the moral case for deterrence is overwhelmed by the scope and duration of the threat. The threat of large-scale retaliation for a nuclear attack, therefore, is not a justified threat.

But it is necessary at this point to extend our inquiry to include not only the threat of massive retaliation but other nuclear threats as well. For it has been claimed by some ethicists and strategists that, in evaluating nuclear threats from the moral standpoint, the precise nature of the threat makes a decisive difference. Might it be justified, in some situations, to threaten to use nuclear weapons in a limited attack on military installations, for example? Would such an attack be a justifiable response to a nuclear attack? Might it even be a legitimate means of countering a nonnuclear attack of certain kinds? Some writers have given affirmative answers to all of these questions. Equally important, the present military policy of the United States is unmistakably committed to development of a greater capacity to make, and to carry out, a credible threat of both retaliatory and initial use of nuclear weapons in limited attacks of this kind.[18]

Whether the threat of limited nuclear attack can ever be justified is a subject of heated and extended debate, and I cannot hope to resolve the question finally in the remainder of this brief discussion. Instead, I shall suggest the way in which any answer that we may give to this question depends crucially both on the moral considerations I have already discussed and on matters of empirical fact.

The Wrongful Threat Principle, I have observed, is initially plausible: certainly we ought normally to avoid making threats which we cannot morally carry out. What is it about the terrorist example which places it in a special class and permits us to threaten the immoral? Two characteristics of the threat – its limited scope and limited duration – have already been mentioned. There are three more characteristics implicit in the case as I have described it which are also essential, I believe, to the moral justification for this particular threat:

The credibility of the threat: the threatened party believes that the threat is not a bluff but really will be carried out. The police possess the means of carrying out their threat; and their behavior, as I have described it, is calculated to make the threat seem genuine. The terrorist's fears for his family, already expressed before the threat is made, make it likely that he will take it seriously. If the threat were not credible, it would be ineffectual; and without a reasonable likelihood that the threat will avert grave wrong, we ought not to make immoral threats. The credibility of the threat in this case is enhanced, not undermined, by a second essential element:

The irrationality of the threatened party. The point is not that only irrational persons comply with threats: on the contrary, to attempt to influence by

---

[18] See the Department of Defense *Annual Report to Congress, Fiscal Year 1985* (U.S. Government Printing Office, Feb. 1984), pp.29–31. "We must plan for flexibility in our forces and in our options for response," the report states, "so that we might terminate the conflict on terms favorable to the forces of freedom." (p.29)

means of threats presupposes that the other is at least sufficiently rational to be moved by our threat. Yet it is highly significant that, in the case we have described, the object of the threat is a person fanatically dedicated to some cause and willing to sacrifice innocent lives in its name. It is the comparative irrationality of the terrorist (and the danger that arises from his irrationality) that permits us to threaten harms which we may never actually impose. Even so, we may cross this moral border only after satisfying a third condition:

The exhaustion of all alternative means of averting imminent catastrophe. In our example, both legitimate threats (e.g., of imprisonment) and every reasonable means of negotiation have been attempted and found fruitless. Then, and only then, may the police resort to the extreme tactics we have described.

Justified threats to do the immoral, then, are threats intended to avert a grave and imminent catastrophe. Furthermore, as the example of the terrorist suggests, such threats can be considered morally permissible only in the presence of five further conditions:

(1) limited scope of the threatened harm
(2) limited duration of the threat
(3) credibility of the threat
(4) dangerous irrationality of the party threatened
(5) exhaustion of all alternative means of influence.

When all five conditions are satisfied, I contend, the Wrongful Threat Principle may be set aside in order to avert great harm. But if one or more of these conditions is not satisfied, however, it is highly doubtful that the threat of immoral harm can be justified.

VI. *Nuclear Deterrence: Three Cases*

Now we must return to the case of nuclear deterrence in order to consider whether the conditions just described are met. And at this point, for the sake of relevance to contemporary policy discussion, it is necessary to consider variations of the nuclear deterrent posture which I have not yet discussed. Specifically, we must consider nuclear deterrent threats of three kinds:

Case 1: The threat of massive retaliation, or, in the language of military strategy, second-strike countervalue targeting. This is the only case I have considered thus far.

Case 2: First-strike threats. My primary concern in this study is with the morality of nuclear deterrence, i.e., the use of nuclear weapons to deter nuclear attack. Threats to employ nuclear weapons in response to nonnuclear attack fall into a different category. Certainly such threats have a potentially deterrent effect, and since this effect is achieved by means of nuclear weapons, we might perhaps label it "conventional deterrence by nuclear means." If we take the adjective in "nuclear deterrence" to be applied not to the end but to the means of achieving deterrence, then first-strike threats are a form of nuclear deterrence, and in any case they are of vital importance to current policy and political debate.

Case 3: Threats of limited retaliation, or of "second-strike counterforce" attack. Of the three cases considered, this would appear the most plausible example of a justified threat. Furthermore, continuing progress in the development of highly accurate delivery systems makes this an option of increasing political and military importance. And we are in this case clearly back in the realm of nuclear deterrence in the strict sense, since such threats are intended to prevent nuclear attack.[19]

Before we consider whether any of these cases can meet the conditions for justifiable immoral threats, we must first establish that the second and third cases are in fact threats to do the immoral. Clearly, they are threats of grave harm whose aim is to avert great wrong. But is the harm which they threaten one which it would always be immoral actually to impose? Some have denied this premise of our discussion, holding that it is possible to justify not only the threat but the use of nuclear weapons in some circumstances.

Consider the first-strike threat. The immorality of initial use of nuclear weapons is admitted by most, though not all, ethicists and strategists. Some have drawn a sharp moral distinction between an initial attack using strategic nuclear weapons ("first strike") and a nuclear attack using limited numbers of low-yield weapons ("first use").[20] The former, it is argued, can never be justified, and even to threaten such an attack is immoral; but to threaten, and even to carry out, the threat of "first use" may be an unavoidable military necessity in the face of others' threats. The risk that any use of nuclear weapons would ignite the exchange of strategic forces, however, as well as

---

[19] Since threats may be limited to retaliation or may encompass initial use of nuclear weapons, and since the threat in either case may include the targeting of a large number of military and civilian targets or may include only a limited number of military targets, there are in effect four distinct variations of the nuclear threat:
- First-strike with countervalue targeting
- First-strike with counterforce targeting only
- Countervalue retaliation (massive retaliation)
- Counterforce retaliation
The first of these is not seriously defended by any contemporary moralist or strategist – even though it is the only one among the four postures which has ever actually been carried through in action, in the case of the United States' nuclear attack on Japan in 1945. In the text, I consider the first two postures as variations on a first-strike strategy.

[20] See, for example, Freeman Dyson, *Weapons and Hope* (Cambridge, Mass.: Harper and Row, 1984), esp. ch.20. Dyson's treatment of nuclear issues is one which I find very valuable even if finally unpersuasive on some issues; see my review in *The Christian Century*, vol. 101 (Nov. 28, 1984), pp.1131–32.

the frequently declared intention of Soviet military leaders to retaliate against the United States for any use of nuclear weapons in Europe, make this distinction far less important in practice than it may appear in theory.[21]

Let it be granted, then, for the purposes of our discussion at least, that it is immoral under any circumstances to initiate the use of nuclear weapons in warfare. Then first-strike threats are clearly threats to do the immoral. And although the harm directly threatened may be limited in scope, to initiate a nuclear attack of any kind is to risk triggering an escalation of conflict whose consequences may be indistinguishable from those of direct strategic attack.

Must a strictly limited retaliation against an attacker's military forces fall under the same condemnation? Some argue that threats of such attack do not fall into the category of immoral threats at all, since a nation subjected to nuclear attack would be committing no wrong by responding with a nuclear strike limited to military installations.[22] Nuclear weapons of low yield and high precision, it is claimed, fall within the range of morally permissible means of war.

If we grant this claim, the status of deterrent threats of this kind would be quite different from that of other nuclear threats, since they would not constitute threats to do what is immoral. It would not follow that such threats are in all cases morally justified, of course. It is not always permissible to make a threat simply because one could morally carry it out. But the perplexities which arise from Kavka's Special Deterrent Situations, at any rate, would not arise.

If limited retaliatory nuclear warfare is morally permissible, however, it must satisfy the moral requirements of discrimination and proportionality which are at the heart of the tradition of justified warfare and which are so evidently violated by large-scale use of nuclear weapons. To make this case plausible, in other words, one would need to demonstrate the truth of the following claims:

(1) Nuclear weapons are no less discriminating in their immediate effect, and no more harmful in their long-term consequences, than conventional weapons which might be used in the same circumstances.

(2) Retaliatory use of nuclear weapons poses no significant risk of triggering a nuclear conflict larger in scale than the initial attack which prompted the retaliation.

[21] The case against limited nuclear attack has been made persuasively by the authors of *The Challenge of Peace*, among many others. Their rejection of limited nuclear war extends to limited retaliatory attack as well; some possible qualifications of their firm position on this issue are expressed in the following section.

[22] Wohlstetter argues for the morality of limited nuclear retaliation but also contends that future advances in precise delivery of high-yield conventional explosives can diminish and ultimately replace military dependence on the nuclear threat: see "Bishops, Statesmen, and Other Strategists on the Bombing of Innocents," *Commentary*, vol. 75 (June 1983), pp.15–35.

(3) Nuclear weapons accomplish as effectively as any alternative the legitimate ends of justified warfare.

Are these premises true? The available evidence seems to me to favor none of them. If even one of the three is false, then limited retaliatory use of nuclear weapons must fall under the same moral prohibition as massive retaliation and first use.

The first premise underlies the others, since the indiscriminate effect of nuclear weapons is the characteristic which makes them both so dangerous in use and so ill-suited to the military aims of legitimate warfare. Perhaps it can be argued that this claim may become true at some point in the future, if weapons development efforts are directed toward maximizing precision in nuclear weapons delivery and minimizing collateral damage. But the same technology which may make nuclear weapons more discriminating also holds the promise of making them unnecessary, since advances in precision may potentially make conventional explosives into counterforce weapons as effective as current nuclear weapons.[23] In any case, neither the first premise nor the others is true in the world as it is at present, and even highly limited retaliatory use of nuclear weapons must be judged immoral. We are justified, therefore, in construing all three of the cases described as threats to do the immoral.

VII. *Limitations and Credibility of the Threat*

We must now consider whether the conditions which permit the making of otherwise immoral threats obtain in any of these cases. First, is the harm threatened properly limited in its scope? In the first case – the threat of massive retaliation – the destruction threatened is more devastating than anything yet experienced in human history, and the ill effects of carrying out such threats reach around the globe and across many generations. Therefore, as we have already observed, our first condition is by no means met, and such threats cannot be morally condoned.

In the second and third cases, the initial destruction caused by a nuclear counterattack may be far more limited than in the case of large-scale strategic retaliation. Yet the use of even a limited number of nuclear weapons crosses a vital boundary both of physics and of politics. The initial damage done by nuclear weapons exceeds that caused by conventional weapons both in scope and in duration, through the lingering effects of radiation. And in conditions of conflict and crisis, a nuclear attack of any kind may trigger an escalation of conflict to a level whose results will be indistinguishable from those of direct strategic attack. Even the threat of limited nuclear counterattack, therefore, poses a significant risk to the lives

[23] On this point, see the Wohlstetter article cited above.

and well-being of soldiers and civilians alike, not only in the country attacked but in vast areas of the globe. Such threats clearly exceed the limited scope which is required to make an immoral threat permissible.

And what of the second limitation – the temporary character of the threat? Our three cases do not differ significantly in this regard. Such threats are not emergency measures desperately put forward to ride out a crisis but, rather, standing elements of a nation's military policy. On this score, then, once again we find that none of the three nuclear threats qualifies as morally permissible.

Suppose that a nuclear power seriously committed itself to nuclear disarmament, in practice and policy alike, and yet chose to maintain a nuclear deterrent solely as a temporary measure to prevent the political instability which might result from sudden disarament, whether unilateral or multilateral. It was with this possibility in mind that the United States Conference of Catholic Bishops, having condemned the use of nuclear weapons in any form, granted their provisional approval to the maintenance of a nuclear deterrent force solely as a means to orderly and complete disarmament.[24] Clearly, the motives which maintain present nuclear arsenals are far from those recommended by the bishops. At the same time, it is not inconceivable, even if it is unlikely, that the future government of the United States or another nuclear power might follow precisely the course which the Bishops recommend. Were that to occur, we might then regard the remaining nuclear threat as an emergency measure of limited duration, and the second of the conditions set out might then be satisfied.

Third, we must consider the credibility of nuclear threats of these three kinds, for a threat which is obviously a bluff cannot benefit anyone. Credibility is an especially troublesome requirement in the case of threats of massive retaliation, for it is widely recognized that the enormity and the immorality of the consequences threatened undermine the threat's credibility. Bernard Brodie wrote in 1959 that "one of the first things wrong with the doctrine [of massive retaliation] is that in many instances the enemy may find it hard to believe that we mean it."[25] For this reason Albert Wohlstetter, who helped shape the nuclear strategy of the 1960s, now urges the repudiation of threats of large-scale counterattack: "Informed realists in foreign-policy

---

[24] "The Challenge of Peace: God's Promise and Our Response," the Pastoral Letter of the U.S. Bishops on War and Peace, published in full in *Origins*, a publication of the National Catholic News Service, 1312 Massachusetts Ave. N.W., Washington, D.C. 20005, (1983). The issue of the morality of threats and intentions seems to me to be one of the issues which is least satisfactorily dealt with in this insightful and provocative discussion.

[25] Bernard Brodie, *Strategy in the Missile Age*, p.273. Compare Secretary of State Caspar Weinberger's statement in the *Annual Report to Congress, Fiscal Year 1984*, p.52: "If our threatened response is perceived as inadequate *or contrary to our national interest*, it will be perceived as a bluff" (italics added).

establishments as well as pacifists should oppose aiming to kill bystanders with nuclear or conventional weapons," he writes, because "indiscriminate Western threats paralyze the West, not the East."[26]

The incredibility of the threat of massive nuclear counterattack not only undermines its effectiveness but constitutes a further strike against its moral standing as well. Extreme measures such as immoral threats are justified only when they promise to avert catastrophe; but when the threatened sanction would only compound the catastrophe, the threat lacks both practical effect and moral plausibility.

The threat of a limited first strike has considerably greater credibility than the threat of massive retaliation. It is for precisely this reason that such threats have come to be a central element in the military posture of the United States and its European allies. But it is noteworthy that several leading figures in the formulation of United States nuclear policy have recently argued that first-use threats in Europe, and specifically the US-NATO doctrine of "flexible response" at any nuclear or nonnuclear level, should be rejected for political and strategic as well as moral reasons.[27]

Limited retaliatory threats, finally, appear more credible than threats of the other two types, and for this reason such threats are more likely to have a significant effect in restraining nuclear attack. At least one of the three conditions for justified immoral threats, then, seems to be met by limited nuclear threats.

But there is a further difficulty which undercuts any moral defense of counterforce nuclear threats. It is a problem which arises from the nature of the weapons themselves. Counterforce weapons, by design, provide a highly effective means of destroying an adversary's offensive capability. Their stated purpose – in the case we are considering here – is limited to a retaliatory strike, a strike launched in response to a presumably limited first strike in order to reduce the damage that may be done by further exchanges of weapons. But declared policies do not have the power to restrain weapons themselves, and the same weapons which threaten a retaliatory counterforce attack could equally well be employed in a preemptive counterforce attack.

---

[26] Wohlstetter, p.15. Wohlstetter argues on this basis for modernization and refinement of both nuclear and nonnuclear weapons. His article and the exchange of letters which followed it ("Letters from Readers: Morality and Deterrence," *Commentary*, vol. 76 (Dec. 1983), pp.4–22), provide a clear and vigorous statement of the case for a major redirection of U.S. defense policy toward more discriminate targeting.

[27] See especially the article by McGeorge Bundy, George F. Kennan, Robert F. McNamara, and Gerard Smith, "Nuclear Weapons and the Atlantic Alliance," *Foreign Affairs*, vol. 60 (Spring 1982), pp.753–768; and McNamara's later article, "The Military Role of Nuclear Weapons: Perceptions and Misperceptions," *Foreign Affairs*, vol. 62 (Fall 1983), pp.59–80. McNamara's contentions are vigorously disputed by Wohlstetter in the article cited above.

The difference between first-strike and second-strike doctrines, in other words, is a difference of words but not of weapons.

The weapons of massive retaliation pose no such ambiguity, since no meaningful advantage can be gained by using them first. Any temptation which might arise to launch a large-scale attack before one's own weapons are destroyed is balanced by the certainty that such an attack can only be suicidal. To use counterforce weapons first, however, might appear an irresistibly attractive way of preventing large-scale nuclear war. Thus, as soon as one nation declares an intention to retaliate using counterforce weapons and builds suitable weapons and delivery systems, its adversaries cannot dismiss the possibility that the weapons may be used for a crippling first strike.

Thus far in this discussion I have avoided consideration of particular weapons sytems, but a concrete example will help to illuminate the point I am making here. The MX missile has been defended in political discussion as an effective means of limited retaliation, and hence a weapon which strengthens the credibility of the United States nuclear deterrent force. The basing mode finally approved for the MX, however, undermines deterrence and exacerbates Soviet fears because of the ambiguity just noted. The MX belongs to a new generation of high-precision warheads capable of destroying Soviet missiles in their silos, according to military authorities. But its placement in existing missile silos which are vulnerable (or so it is claimed) to Soviet attack makes it an unreliable retaliatory weapon. In Soviet eyes, therefore, this addition to the United States nuclear arsenal, introduced with the purpose of stabilizing nuclear deterrence by posing a more credible threat of limited retaliation, is both a tempting target for attack and a threat to Soviet deterrent capabilities.

Thus, even though the nuclear threat may be a credible threat, particularly if the stated intention is to launch only a limited retaliatory attack, the ambiguous nature of the weapons themselves ensures that the first two conditions for justified wrongful threats – that such threats be limited in scope and duration – are not satisfied. To be sure, it is possible that, as a result of future developments in weapons technology, nuclear weapons will no longer pose as severe a danger as they now do to the lives and well-being of civilian populations. If such development are accompanied by multilateral disarmament, including destruction of all but a limited number of low-yield nuclear weapons, then the specter of global devastation will no longer hang so heavily upon us. Perhaps, then, a generation from now, a more plausible case will present itself for condoning the threat of nuclear counterattack. But we do not live in such a world. Today, every nuclear threat is at least potentially the threat of great devastation. Even if we may hope that this will no longer be true a generation or a century from now, we must make our moral choices in the present and not in an imagined future.[28]

VIII. *Further Conditions for Justified Threats*

There remain two conditions, suggested by the example of the terrorist, which must also obtain if an immoral threat is to be justified, and I turn to them now. First, is the nuclear threat directed against an adversary relevantly like the terrorist of our example – a dangerously deranged fanatic who cannot be influenced except by such dire threats? This claim would not merit serious consideration in the international context, were it not regularly advanced by some commentators for whom patriotism takes precedence over sober realism. If the Soviet Union is, as some would have it, "the focus of evil in the modern world," and if Soviet leaders will trample on the lives and welfare of the citizens of their own nation and every other nation besides in the fanatical pursuit of Marxist ideology, then perhaps we would be justified in treating them as we would treat the terrorist of our example.

In a certain sense this fanatical view of the global situation undercuts the policy it supports: for if Soviet leaders are indeed bent on ideological conquest whatever the cost, they are unlikely to be deterred by threats against their people or territory. But this picture is, of course, wildly inaccurate, and it cannot be supported from the actual behavior of Soviet leaders, who behave in foreign affairs rather like their counterparts in the West – protecting vital economic and military interests by carefully calculated, if sometimes violent, means. In this regard, the case of the terrorist is altogether different.

We must consider, finally, whether nuclear threats represent a last and desperate resort to avert catastrophe, all less immoral means having been proven ineffectual. If nuclear deterrence is morally justified, in other words, it must be shown, first, that it provides an effective means of securing its ends – national security and global peace – and, second, that no equally effective and less morally problematic means to the same ends can be found. Are these claims true? The evidence is mixed. It is likely that the existence of nuclear weapons has helped, in some situations, to deter attack and to

---

[28] The context of discussion of nuclear deterrence has been altered significantly by President Reagan's open endorsement of the goal of defensive measures against nuclear attack employing high technology nuclear and nonnuclear weapons. Such measures, referred to by the President as the "Strategic Defense Initiative" and by critics as "Star Wars", pose formidable and, in the judgment of many experts, insurmountable technical difficulties; but they deserve careful consideration from a moral standpoint, since they are motivated at least in part by recognition of the immoral character of nuclear threats. The cautions voiced in the text about making moral decisions in the present need to be emphasized in this context as well: the dim possibility of future technologies which may provide an effective defense against nuclear attack has little relevance to the urgent task of orderly and effective disarmament which is our present responsibility.

prevent international rivalry and regional conflict from exploding into large-scale war. Yet the nature of nuclear weapons casts doubt on the claim that nuclear deterrence is the most effective means of preserving peace. For the very magnitude of the destruction threatened by nuclear weapons makes them remarkably poor means to the ends they purport to secure. In regional conflicts, in economic crises, in periods of heightened hostility between superpowers, the sheer scale of the destruction which would be wrought by the use of nuclear weapons makes them virtually useless as weapons. Hence, the threat of their use, though it can never be entirely disregarded, is seldom credible enough decisively to influence behavior. In George F. Kennan's words:

> I deny that the nuclear weapon is a proper weapon . . . It can serve no useful purpose. It cannot be used without bringing disaster upon everyone concerned.[29]

In a certain sense, there are no alternatives to nuclear threats: nothing but nuclear explosives can effectively threaten destruction and death on a scale which even approaches the probable results of a large-scale nuclear exchange. But in another sense, there are many alternatives to such threats, since their ultimate purpose is not destruction but the preservation of peace and order. The relevant alternatives to nuclear deterrence, in this broad sense, include not only conventional military means but also economic and diplomatic policies. In a still larger sense, programs of international development, which build other nations' self-reliance while at the same time fostering cooperation, must also be counted among alternative means to national security. Many of these alternatives are less expensive and less dangerous than the maintenance of a large nuclear arsenal. Several represent steps away from international competition and toward a closer community of nations. More important still, some go beyond the mere restraint of violence to alleviate its causes.

A dissenter might grant all that has been said about the need to explore alternatives to nuclear deterrence and yet hold that, if one's own nation is threatened by the nuclear weapons of a hostile power, one has no choice but to maintain a nuclear arsenal as a deterrent. Morality must not lead us to abandon realism and prudence, and the presence of a threat from others, it may be argued, justifies us in continuing to pose a threat which we would otherwise gladly abandon.

A moment's consideration reveals the inadequacy of such a response. The threat posed by others is an entirely acceptable reason for countermeasures

---

[29] George F. Kennan, "Two Views of the Soviet Problem," in *The Nuclear Delusion* (New York: Pantheon Books, 1982), p.158.

of one's own; but there is no reason why such countermeasures need mimic an adversary's immoral means. Consider the parallel case of chemical and biological weapons. When one nation develops and uses such weapons, its adversaries have the right and the obligation to defend themselves and to dissuade the offending nation by any means which fall within the range of morality. But to develop equally immoral weapons of one's own is wrong, whatever the provocation.

Similarly, should one nation threaten nuclear attack, the nations threatened may and should combine legitimate military countermeasures with any international measures which promise to persuade the offending nation to dismantle its nuclear arsenal. But to develop – or, once having developed, to retain – one's own nuclear arsenal is neither an adequate nor a necessary response. It is not adequate, since nuclear weapons offer no means of defense against a threat but only a means of retaliation which would be immoral and ineffective if it should ever be used. Nor is the nuclear threat necessary, since other military measures may create an effective deterrent to attack.

A widely dispersed force of several thousand highly accurate conventional weapons, for example, can effectively threaten an enemy's cities and military bases. Nuclear strategist Albert Wohlstetter has observed that "improving accuracy by a factor of 100 improves blast effectiveness against a small, hard military target about as much as multiplying the energy released about a million times."[30] As long-range targeting achieves accuracies which can be measured not in miles but in yards, the deterrent effect of a conventional threat against military targets may approach that of the present threat to use nuclear weapons. Equally important, the threat of such an attack, which would be more limited and more subject to control than a nuclear attack, has far greater credibility than a nuclear threat.

An adversary's nuclear threat, therefore, does not decisively affect the moral status of deterrence. Because the nuclear threat is a threat to do the immoral, we may not make such a threat unless the conditions noted above, including the exhaustion of all other alternatives to the ends sought, are satisfied. But few, if any, of these conditions are satisfied.

IX. *Conclusions*

The moral case for threatening nuclear attack, I conclude – whether first-strike or second-strike, directed against cities or against military targets only – must inevitably fail. There are decisive moral objections to the employment of nuclear threats as a means of preserving peace. These objections are not quite so straightforward as they may at first appear: the immorality of

[30] Wohlstetter, p.22.

deterrence is not entailed simply by the fact that it would be immoral to carry out a threat of nuclear retaliation, for example. The example of the terrorist offers a counterexample to the general claim that it is always wrong to threaten what it would be wrong to do. But deterrence through the threat of nuclear attack is not a temporary expedient in a single crisis; it is a permanent underpinning of a nation's foreign policy, and it is not warranted either by the supposed dangerous irrationality of the Soviets against whom it is directed or by the exhaustion of every other available means of achieving the same end.

To claim that nuclear deterrence is conceptually incoherent would be too strong a claim. Certainly the threat of force can be an effective deterrent to the use of force, and there is no reason in principle why this effect should not obtain in reference to nuclear weapons as well as other means of force. But nuclear weapons have such an awesome capacity to destroy that their actual use cannot be justified even by the principles which have been appealed to in defense of the use of conventional weapons of war.

It is possible that, if both nuclear weapons and international realities should change significantly in the future, conditions like those which obtain in the terrorist example may someday be present among nations. We cannot categorically exclude the possibility, therefore, that in some future state of the world nuclear threats might be justifiable measures to avert imminent catastrophe. In the world in which we presently live, however, such conditions do not obtain. In our world, therefore, the threat of nuclear attack or counterattack is unavoidably immoral.

Philosophy, University of Delaware

Social Philosophy & Policy 3:1 Autumn 1985 ISSN 0265–0525 $2.00

OPTIMAL DETERRENCE*

STEVEN J. BRAMS AND D. MARC KILGOUR

1. *Introduction*

The policy of deterrence, at least to avert nuclear war between the superpowers, has been a controversial one. The main controversy arises from the threat of each side to visit destruction on the other in response to an initial attack. This threat would seem irrational if carrying it out would lead to a nuclear holocaust – the worst outcome for both sides. Instead, it would seem better for the side attacked to suffer some destruction rather than to retaliate in kind and, in the process of devastating the other side, seal its own doom in an all-out nuclear exchange.

Yet, the superpowers persist in their adherence to *deterrence*, by which we mean a policy of threatening to retaliate to an attack by the other side in order to deter such an attack in the first place. To be sure, nuclear doctrine for implementing deterrence has evolved over the years, with such appellations as "massive retaliation," "flexible response," "mutual assured destruction" (MAD), and "counterforce" giving some flavor of the changes in United States strategic thinking.

All such doctrines, however, entail some kind of response to a Soviet nuclear attack. They are operationalized in terms of preselected targets to be hit, depending on the perceived nature and magnitude of the attack. Thus, whether U.S. strategic policy at any time stresses a retaliatory attack on cities and industrial centers (countervalue) or on weapons systems and armed forces (counterforce), the certainty of a response of some kind to an attack is not the issue. The issue is, rather, what kind of threatened response, or *second strike*, in the parlance of deterrence theory, is most efficacious in deterring an initial attack, or *first strike*.

This is the issue we address in this paper, though not in the usual way. Instead of trying to evaluate the relative merits of concrete nuclear retaliatory doctrines, we shall define these doctrines somewhat more abstractly in terms of "probabilistic threats." More specifically, by letting threats vary along a

*Steven J. Brams gratefully acknowledges the financial support of the Ford Foundation under Grant No. 845–0354 and the National Science Foundation under Grant No. SES84–08505. D. Marc Kilgour gratefully acknowledges the financial support of the Natural Sciences and Engineering Research Council of Canada under Grand No.A8974.

single continuous dimension from certain retaliation to no retaliation, we can compare different levels of threats in terms of the expected payoffs that they yield in a game. Additionally, by introducing probabilities of a first strike (or preemption) by both sides, we can analyze the relationship between preemption and retaliation probabilities and game outcomes.

Because the expected payoffs of probabilistic preemption and retaliation have certain equivalents, in that a player would be indifferent between choosing a lottery (over nonpreemption/preemption or nonretaliation/ retaliation) and a sure thing (a reduced level of preemption or retaliation), they can be interpreted in terms of *levels* of preemption and retaliation short of full-fledged first and second strikes. The first question we seek to answer is what levels render certain outcomes stable, in a sense to be specified later.

In the game we use to model deterrence, which is derived from the game of Chicken but is not Chicken itself, we identify four stable outcomes, or equilibria, three of which correspond to those in Chicken. The new equilibrium, which emerges when we incorporate the possibility of (probabilistic) preemption and retaliation into Chicken, we call the "deterrence equilibrium." It corresponds to the cooperative outcome in Chicken (never preempt), which by itself is unstable; in the new (deterrence) game, this outcome is rendered stable by the threat of retaliation above a calculable threshold, which makes preemption irrational.

But a threshold alone does not specify what level of threat (above this threshold) is optimal. Accordingly, we suggest a theoretical calculation of "robust threats" that makes retaliatory threats as invulnerable as possible to misperceptions or miscalculations by the players. We also indicate how precommitments to carry out these threats are in fact made credible, at least on a probabilistic basis, by the superpowers.

We think the deterrence equilibrium – and the robust threats that support it – is superior to any other equilibrium in the game we postulate as a model of deterrence. To be sure, this equilibrium is imperfect in the sense that it is irrational to carry out one's threats; however, because it renders preemption irrational, even when one thinks one's opponent might preempt, it is hard to see why retaliation would ever be necessary, at least in theory. This theoretical rationale for a particular kind of deterrence, *coupling a no-first-use policy with robust threats, appears to us the best one can do in a world that seems to make superpower confrontations unavoidable.*

The challenge facing the policy maker is to prevent such confrontations from escalating into nuclear war. As deleterious as threats are to the development of trust and good will, we conclude that they are inescapable for deterrence to be effective. It is far less clear whether the threats the superpowers hurl at each other today, and their concomitant actions to indicate the threats are not empty, are at an optimal level.

2. *Deterrence and the Game of Chicken*

There is a large literature on deterrence, but little of it is explicitly game-theoretic. That which is, or is pertinent to game-theoretic formulations, is discussed by Brams from both a theoretical and empirical perspective, so we shall not review it here.[1] Suffice it to say that we believe game theory not only provides a framework uniquely suited to capturing the interdependent strategic calculations of players but also that it can be adapted to modelling the threats necessary to deter an opponent from taking untoward action against oneself.

To incorporate threats into the structure of a game, we shall assume that players can precommit themselves to carrying out their threats with a given probability. Exactly how they do so will be considered later, but for now we shall assume precommitments are allowed by the rules of the game.

Because a game is defined by the rules that describe it, there is no problem in permitting precommitments as long as they are not inconsistent with other rules. In fact, as we shall show, the major issue precommitments raise is the rationality of holding to them in the play of a game. We shall discuss this issue after deriving the equilibria of the so-called Deterrence Game and analyzing their properties.

The Deterrence Game is based on the two-person game of Chicken, which we shall define and analyze in this section. In Chicken, each player can choose between two strategies: cooperate (C) and not cooperate($\bar{C}$), which in the context of deterrence may be thought of as "not attack" and "attack," respectively. These strategies lead to four possible outcomes, which the players are assumed to rank from best (4) to worst (1). These rankings are shown as ordered pairs in the outcome matrix of Figure 1, with the first number indicating the rank assigned by the row player and the second number indicating the rank assigned by the column player. Chicken is defined by the following outcome rankings of the strategy combinations of the two players:

1. Both players cooperate (CC) – next-best outcome for both players: (3,3).
2. One player cooperates and the other does not (C$\bar{C}$ and $\bar{C}$C) – best outcome for the player who does not cooperate and next-worst outcome for the player who does (2,4) and (4.2).
3. Both players do not cooperate ($\bar{C}\bar{C}$) – worst outcome for both players: (1,1).

[1] Steven J. Brams, *Superpower Games: Applying Game Theory to Superpower Conflict* (New Haven, CT: Yale University Press, 1985), chaps. 1 and 2.

	Cooperate (C)	Do not cooperate ($\overline{C}$)
Cooperate (C)	(3,3) Compromise	⟨2,4⟩ Column "wins", Row "loses"
Do not cooperate ($\overline{C}$)	⟨4,2⟩ Row "wins", Column "loses"	(1,1) Disaster

Row

Key: (x,y) = (rank of Row, rank of Column)
    4 = best; 3 = next best; 2 = next worst; 1 = worst
    Circled outcomes are Nash equilibria

Figure 1   Outcome Matrix of Chicken

Outcomes (2,4) and (4,2) in Figure 1 are circled to indicate that they are *Nash equilibria*: neither player (Row or Column) would have an incentive to depart from these outcomes because he would do worse if he did. For example, from (2,4) Row would do worse if he moved to (1,1), and Column would do worse if he moved to (3,3). By contrast, from (3,3) Row would do better if he moved to (4,2), and Column would do better if he moved to (2,4).

There is a third Nash equilibrium in Chicken, but it is not in *pure strategies*, or specific strategies that players would choose with certainty. Rather, it is in *mixed strategies*, which are defined by a probability distribution over a player's pure strategies. Because the calculation of equilibria involving mixed strategies requires that payoffs be given in cardinal utilities – not just ordinal ranks – we will postpone discussion of these strategies and the third equilibrium until the development of the Deterrence Game in Section 3.

The shorthand verbal descriptions given for each outcome in Figure 1 suggest the vexing problem that the players confront in choosing between C and $\overline{C}$: by choosing $\overline{C}$, each can "win" but risks disaster; by choosing C, each can benefit from compromise, but also can "lose." Each of the Nash equilibria shown in Figure 1 favors one player over the other, and the stability of these equilibria as such says nothing about which of the two – if either – will be chosen.

Other concepts of equilibrium distinguish (3,3) as the unique stable outcome, but the rules of play that render compromise stable presume that the players (1) act nonmyopically or farsightedly and (2) cannot threaten each other.[2] If threats are possible in repeated play of Chicken under still different rules, the stability of (3,3) is undermined.[3]

The effect that threats may have in Chicken is not hard to grasp. If one player (say, Row) threatens the other player (Column) with the choice of C̄, and this threat is regarded as credible, Column's best response is C, leading to (4,2).

Clearly, the player with the credible threat – if there is one – can force the other player to back down in order to avoid (1,1). Although Row would "win" in this case by getting his best outcome, Column would not "lose" in the usual sense by getting his worst outcome, but instead his next-worst. This is because Chicken is not a *constant-sum* game, in which what one player wins the other player loses. That is why we have put "win" and "lose" in quotation marks here and in Figure 1. In nonconstant-sum games like Chicken, the sum of the players' payoffs at each outcome (if measured cardinally by utilities rather than ordinally by ranks) is not constant but variable. This means that *both* players may do better at some outcomes [e.g., (3,3)] than others [e.g., (1,1)]. Outcomes, such as (1,1) in Chicken, which are inferior for *both* players to some other outcomes in a game, are called *Pareto-inferior*; those outcomes which are not Pareto-inferior are *Pareto-superior*, as are the other three outcomes in Chicken.

We have shown that Chicken is vulnerable to the use of threats, by which we mean precommitment (before the play of the game) to the choice of a strategy by one player in order to force the other player to choose a strategy, and hence an outcome (defined by a pair of strategy choices), favorable to the threatener. For a threat to be *effective* (i.e., force the threatened player to choose the strategy the threatener prefers), it must be *credible* – the threatened player must believe that the threatener will in fact carry out his threat.

Thus, for example, if Column did not believe that Row would actually choose C̄ in Chicken (e.g., because he himself also threatened to choose C̄), Column presumably would choose C̄ in the belief that Row would back down and choose C, leading to Column's best outcome of (2,4). Of course, if Column's belief were mistaken, the outcome for both players would be disastrous. In the Deterrence Game, we shall explore how mutual threats in Chicken may induce compromise rather than push the players toward the precipice.

[2] Steven J. Brams and Donald Wittman, "Nonmyopic Equilibria in 2 x 2 Games," *Conflict Management and Peace Science*, vol.6 (Fall 1981), pp.39–62; D. Marc Kilgour, "Equilibria for Far-sighted Players," *Theory and Decision*, vol.16 (March 1984), pp.135–157; see also Frank C. Zagare, "Limited-Move Equilibria in 2 x 2 Games," *Theory and Decision*, vol.16 (January 1984), pp.1–10.
[3] Steven J. Brams and Marek P. Hessel, "Threat Power in Sequential Games," *International Studies Quarterly*, vol.28 (March 1984), pp.15–36.

Chicken is not the only game vulnerable to threats. There are 78 distinct strict ordinal 2 x 2 games in which two players, each with two strategies, can strictly rank the four outcomes from best to worst. In 46 of them, one or both players has "threat power" of either a "compellent" or "deterrent" kind.[4] Chicken, however, is the only one of the 78 games that satisfies the following four conditions:

1. *Symmetry*: the players rank the outcomes along the main diagonal (CC and C̄C̄) the same; their rankings of the off-diagonal outcomes (CC̄ and C̄C) are mirror images of each other.

2. *Cooperation is preferable to noncooperation*: both players prefer CC to C̄C̄.

3. *Unilateral noncooperation helps the noncooperator and hurts the cooperator*: Row prefers C̄C to CC to CC̄, and Column prefers CC̄ to CC to C̄C.

4. *Retaliation for noncooperation is irrational*: if one player does not cooperate (i.e., the initial outcome is C̄C or CC̄), retaliation by the other player (to C̄C̄) is worse for the retaliator (as well as the player whom he retaliates against).

It is evident that all except Condition 1, which we assume in order to pose the same strategic dilemma for each player,[5] conspire to make Chicken a harrowing game to play. Cooperation is at the same time desirable (condition 2) and undesirable (condition 3). But the crux of the dilemma is that if one player is intransigent (i.e., noncooperative), the other player has good reason not to be intransigent (condition 4). If condition 4 does not obtain, but instead C̄C̄ is better than C̄C and CC̄ for the cooperative player, then the resulting game is a Prisoners' Dilemma, which presents the players with a very different kind of strategic problem.

We believe, however, that the heart of the problem with deterrence, especially of the nuclear kind, is the apparent irrationality of retaliating against a first strike by an opponent.[6] What sort of threats (if any) are

---

[4] *ibid.*; the original distinction between compellent and deterrent threats is due to Thomas C. Schelling, *Arms and Influence* (New Haven, CT: Yale University Press, 1966).

[5] The validity of the symmetry condition in the context of Soviet-American conflict is supported by the following statement of an authority on Soviet defense policy: "The answers [to the problems posed by nuclear war and nuclear weapons] the Soviet leaders have arrived at are not very different from those given by Western governments . . . The Soviet Union has not been able to escape from the threat of nuclear annihilation. Its leaders and its people share our predicament." David Holloway, *The Soviet Union and the Arms Race* (New Haven, CT: Yale University Press, 1983), p.182.

[6] For debate on this point, see Frank C. Zagare, "Toward a Reformulation of the Theory of Mutual Deterrence," *International Studies Quarterly*, vol. 29 (June 1985); Brams and Hessel, "Threat Power in Sequential Games"; and Brams, *Superpower Games*, Chap.1.

credible and will deter a first strike, so as not to put one in the unenviable position of having to decide whether to retaliate and court mutual annihilation? When is a policy of deterrence involving mutual threats of retaliation stable? How can players make their precommitments to retaliate compelling? We shall explore these and other questions in our analysis of the Deterrence Game, which permits the players to choose both levels of preemption and levels of retaliation.

3. *The Deterrence Game (with Preemption and Retaliation Probabilities)*
The Deterrence Game is defined by the following rules:

1. The final outcome will be one of the four outcomes of Chicken. The payoffs are the same as those of Chicken, except that cardinal utilities replace ordinal rankings. Thus r_4 and c_4 signify the highest payoffs for Row and Column, respectively, r_1 and c_1 the lowest, etc.
2. The players do not choose initially between C and $\bar{C}$, as in Chicken, but instead choose (unspecified) actions that have associated with them a nonpreemption probability (s for Row and t for Column) and a complementary preemption probability (1-s for Row and 1-t for Column). With these probabilities, the actions will be interpreted as cooperative (C) and noncooperative ($\bar{C}$) strategy choices, respectively.
3. If *both* players' initial choices are perceived as the same, the game ends at that position (i.e., CC or $\bar{C}\bar{C}$). If one player's choice is perceived as C and the other's as $\bar{C}$, the former player then chooses *subsequent* actions with an associated nonretaliation probability (p for Column and q for Row) and a complementary retaliation probability (1-p for Column and 1-q for Row). With the retaliation probability, the conflict is escalated to the final outcome $\bar{C}\bar{C}$; otherwise it remains (at $C\bar{C}$ or $\bar{C}C$).
4. The players choose their preemption probabilities and retaliation probabilities before play of the game. Play commences when each player simultaneously chooses initial actions that may be interpreted as either C or $\bar{C}$, with associated preemption probabilities. One player may then choose subsequent actions, according to rule 3, with the associated retaliation probability specified at the beginning of play.

The Deterrence Game is represented in Figure 2. Note that besides the fact that the initial strategy choices of the two players are probabilities (with assumed underlying actions), rather than actions (C and $\bar{C}$) themselves, this

Column

	t	$1-t$
s	(r_3, c_3)	$q(r_2, c_4)+(1-q)(r_1, c_1)$ $= (qr_2, q)$
1-s	$p(r_4, c_2)+(1-p)(r_1, c_1)$ $= (p, pc_2)$	$(r_1, c_1) = (0,0)$

Row

Key: $(r_i, c_i) = $ (payoff to Row, payoff to Column)
$r_4, c_4 = $ best; $r_3, c_3 = $ next best; $r_2, c_2 = $ next worst; $r_1, c_1 = $ worst
$s, t = $ probabilities of nonpreemption; $p, q = $ probabilities of nonretaliation
Normalization: $0 = r_1 < r_2 < r_3 < r_4 = 1$; $0 = c_1 < c_2 < c_3 < c_4 = 1$

Figure 2   Payoff Matrix of Deterrence Game

payoff matrix differs from the Figure 1 outcome matrix in having expected payoffs rather than (certain) payoffs in its off-diagonal entries. This is because we assume that if one player is perceived to preempt, the other player's (probabilistic) retaliation will be virtually instantaneous, so it is proper to include in the off-diagonal entries a combination of payoffs – reflecting both possible retaliation and possible nonretaliation – by means of an expected value.

We assume, of course, that $0 \leq s, t, p, q \leq 1$ because they represent probabilities. To simplify subsequent calculations, we normalize the payoffs of the players so that the best and worst payoffs are 1 and 0, respectively. Hence,

$$0 = r_1 < r_2 < r_3 < r_4 = 1$$
$$0 = c_1 < c_2 < c_3 < c_4 = 1$$

Because we assume the preemption and retaliation probabilities are chosen independently by the players, the expected payoffs for Row and Column are simply the sums of the four payoffs (expected payoffs) in the Figure 2 matrix, each multiplied by the probability of its occurrence:

$$E_R(s,q;t,p) = str_3 + (1-s)tp + s(1-t)qr_2;$$
$$E_C(t,p;s,q) = stc_3 + s(1-t)q + (1-s)tpc_2.$$

In the Appendix we show that there are effectively four Nash equilibria in the Deterrence Game, and that they can be grouped into three classes:

I. *Deterrence Equilibrium*: $s=1$, $q \leq c_3$; $t=1$, $p \leq r_3$. This equilibrium is one in which the players never preempt ($s = t = 1$), but Row retaliates with probability $1-p \geq 1-r_3$ and Column retaliates with probability $1-q \geq 1-c_3$. Essentially, these inequalities ensure that a player's expected payoff as the sole preemptor – p for Row and q for Column, as shown in the off-diagonal entries in Figure 2 – is not greater than what is obtained from the cooperative outcome of the underlying Chicken game, with payoffs (r_3, c_3).

II. *Preemption Equilibria*: (1) $s = 1$, $q = 1$; $t = 0$, p arbitrary; (2) $s = 0$, q arbitrary; $t = 1$, $p = 1$. The first equilibrium is certain preemption by Column and no retaliation by Row, because Row is deterred by Column's initiative; Column's retaliation probability is arbitrary since it never comes into play. The second equilibrium is analogous, with the roles of Column and Row switched. At these equilibria, the outcomes of the Deterrence Game are the outcomes of the underlying Chicken game associated with wins for Column and Row (discussed in section 2), with payoffs $(r_2, 1)$ and $(1, c_2)$, respectively.

III. *Naive Equilibrium*:

$$s = \frac{c_2}{1 - c_3 + c_2}, q = 1; t = \frac{r_2}{1 - r_3 + r_2}, p = 1.$$

At this equilibrium, each player preempts with some nonzero probability (which depends on the other player's payoffs and is always less than one) but never retaliates. Each of these preemption probabilities in fact (see Appendix) makes the opponent indifferent as to his level of preemption; in other words, a player's expected payoff depends only on his opponent's, and not his own, level of preemption. Because retaliation would only degrade these expected payoffs, it is suboptimal. As shown in the Appendix, however, the Naive Equilibrium is Pareto-inferior to the Deterrence Equilibrium, which is the reason for our nomenclature. It corresponds to the mixed-strategy equilibrium of the underlying Chicken game (discussed but not given in Section 2), which is similarly deficient, as well as difficult to interpret as a one-shot choice of rational players in this game.

4. *Rational Play in the Deterrence Game*

Of the four Nash equilibria, only the Deterrence Equilibrium in class I depends on the possibility of retaliation – specifically, precommitted threats to respond (at least probabilistically) to a provocation when it is viewed as equivalent to the choice of $\bar{C}$. Such threats distinguish the Deterrence Game from the underlying game of Chicken, in which retaliation against the choice of $\bar{C}$ is not permitted.

Note that the two Preemption Equilibria in class II, and the one Naive Equilibrium in class III, occur only when retaliatory threats are never used (p = 1 or q = 1 or both). They correspond precisely to the three Nash equilibria in Chicken and so introduce no new element into the analysis of deterrence beyond what was earlier provided by Chicken. However, when a threat structure is added to Chicken to give the Deterrence Game, a qualitatively different equilibrium (the Deterrence Equilibrium) emerges in the latter game that demonstrates how threats can work to the advantage of both players to stabilize the Pareto-superior cooperative outcome (r_3, c_3), which is unstable in Chicken without the possibility of retaliation.

Because the Deterrence Equilibrium depends fundamentally on threats, it is not surprising that it is neither perfect nor subgame-perfect in Selten's sense.[7] Nevertheless, the Deterrence Equilibrium possesses a dynamic-stability property that should, once the equilibrium forms, contribute to its persistence in repeated play. That is to say, given that the players are at the Deterrence Equilibrium, if one player (say, Column) for any reason suspects that the other player (Row) may contemplate preemption, thereby rendering s < 1, Row can do no better than continue to choose t = 1.

In other words, even should Row think he might be preempted, he should still continue to refuse to preempt, in order to keep his expected payoff at its maximum. This obviates the problem that Schelling called "the reciprocal fear of surprise attack" that leads inexorably to preemption.[8]

We prove this dynamic-stability property of the Deterrence Equilibrium in the Appendix, which shows, in effect, that any perceived departures of sort from 1 will not initiate an escalatory process whereby the players are motivated to move closer and closer toward certain preemption. The fact that the Deterrence Equilibrium is impervious to perturbations in s or t means that the players, instead of being induced to move up the escalation ladder, will have an incentive to move down should one player deviate from s = t = 1.[9]

---

[7] Reinhard Selten, "Reexamination of the Perfectness Concept for Equilibrium Points in Extensive Games," *International Journal of Game Theory*, vol.4 (1975), pp.25–55; see also Martin Shubik, *Game Theory in the Social Sciences: Concepts and Solutions* (Cambridge, MA: MIT Press, 1982), pp.265–270.

[8] Thomas C. Schelling, *The Strategy of Conflict* (Cambridge, MA: Harvard University Press, 1960), chap.9.

[9] In a more complete dynamic analysis, we show that there is a trajectory or path from either of the Preemption Equilibria to the Deterrence Equilibrium that the player who is preempted can trigger by threatening to move – with a probability above a particular threshold – to the mutually worst outcome. Although this player incurs a temporary cost in making this threat, the rational response of the preemptor is to move to the Deterrence Equilibrium, whose dynamic stability would then preclude a rational move away from it. See Steven J. Brams and

The restoration of the Deterrence Equilibrium depends on probabilistic threats of retaliation that satisfy

$$0 < q < c_3, 0 < p < r_3. \tag{1}$$

But note that if deterrence should fail for any reason, it is irrational to retaliate, even on a probabilistic basis, because retaliation leads to a worse outcome for the threatener – having to carry out his threat – as well as for the player who preempted and thereby provoked retaliation.

The apparent irrationality of retaliating in the Deterrence Game is, as we indicated earlier, precisely what makes the Deterrence Equilibrium imperfect. Despite its imperfectness, we believe there are at least two ways in which it may be strengthened, one theoretical and one practical.

In theory, all threats which satisfy inequalities (1), given that $s = t = 1$, define a Deterrence Equilibrium. But in the intervals defined by (1), which values of p and q should be used? One of us proposed, as most insensitive to misperceptions or miscalculations by the players, *robust threats*,

$$q = \frac{c_3 - c_2 r_3}{1 - c_2 r_2}, p = \frac{r_3 - r_2 c_3}{1 - c_2 r_2},$$

which are easily shown to satisfy (1).[10] Such threats, when carried out, are equally damaging to the preemptor, and equally costly to the retaliator, whichever strategy (preempt or not) either player perceives the other might choose at the start. This property makes each player's preemption decision independent of his reading of his opponent's choice – the damage or cost will be the same whatever he chooses – and should serve to enhance the stability of the Deterrence Equilibrium.

A by-product of robust threats is that they render nonpreemption (strategies s and t in the Figure 2 Deterrence Game) *strictly dominant* – better for each player whatever his opponent does – and hence unconditionally best. This, of course, is not true of the C strategies in Chicken, which are *undominated* – sometimes best (when the opponent chooses $\bar{C}$) and sometimes not (when he chooses C).

In practice, the Deterrence Equilibrium depends on the credibility of

D. Marc Kilgour, "The Path to Stable Deterrence," *Dynamic Models of International Relations*, Urs Luterbacher and Michael D. Ward, eds., (Boulder, CO: Lynne Rienner, 1985). A game analogous to the Deterrence Game, but based on Prisoners' Dilemma rather than Chicken, permits the players to move from the Pareto-inferior "Escalation Equilibrium" to the Pareto-superior "Deescalation Equilibrium," that is costless to the player who initiates a move from the Escalation to the Deescalation Equilibrium. See Steven J. Brams and D. Marc Kilgour, "Rational Deescalation" (mimeographed, 1985).

[10] Brams, *Superpower Games*, chap.1.

threats satisfying (1). But how does a player persuade his opponent that he will retaliate if attacked, even though retaliation would be irrational at the time it is undertaken?

In the case of the superpowers, both the United States and the Soviet Union have institutionalized detailed procedures for responding to a nuclear attack that are designed to ensure – insofar as possible – that retaliation will occur, even if communication, command, control, and intelligence (C^3I) capabilities are damaged by the attack.[11] However, although each side promises that a first strike will inevitably be met by a second strike, there is significant uncertainty about each side's likely response

> because of a number of operational factors, including problems related to identifying the attacker, identifying the magnitude of the attack, failures of weapons being used for the first time on a massive scale, problems of communication and control, lack of resolve, and the like. In light of these difficulties, both sides have, not surprisingly, resorted less to making probabilistic threats and more to employing their certain equivalents – usually controlled steps up the escalation ladder.
>
> These . . . may be thought of as probabilistic threats insofar as they give an opponent a better idea of how close each side is moving toward full-scale retaliation – that is, they indicate more palpably the probability that the opponent will carry out a threat and what its expected damage will be. So far, fortunately, these probabilistic threats have been sufficient to persuade the two sides to back off, beyond a certain point, from continued escalation.[12]

We conclude that: (1) the deterministic threats proclaimed by the superpowers today are, in truth, probabilistic (as we have modeled them); and (2) they have in fact deterred nuclear war. Moreover, there seems little doubt that both sides have precommitted themselves to retaliating, even if the resulting doomsday machines have built-in uncertainties because of possible failures in C^3I – some of which may be irremediable – and other factors (e.g., lack of will to order a second strike).

---

[11] Paul Bracken, *The Command and Control of Nuclear Weapons* (New Haven, CT: Yale University Press, 1983). Gauthier claims that such precommitments are not necessary to deter aggression, but threats which are not credible are empty, and empty threats invite attack. His calculus of deterrence, we believe, is sensible only when his retaliator's threats will assuredly be implemented because of precommitments. See David Gauthier, "Deterrence, Maximization, and Rationality," *Ethics*, vol.94 (April 1984), pp.474–495.

[12] Brams, *Superpower Games*, pp.45–46.

5. *Conclusions*

Deterrence means threatening to retaliate against an attack in order to prevent it from occurring in the first place. It is widely held that only through continuing mutual deterrence has a nuclear confrontation of the superpowers been avoided. Yet the central problem with a policy of deterrence is that the threat of retaliation may not be credible if retaliation leads to a worse outcome – perhaps a nuclear holocaust – than a side would suffer from absorbing a limited first strike and not retaliating.

We analyzed the optimality of mutual deterrence by means of a Deterrence Game, in which each player chooses a probability (or level) of preemption, and of retaliation if preempted. The Nash equilibria, or stable outcomes, in this game duplicate those in the game of Chicken, on which it is based, except for a Deterrence Equilibrium, at which the players never preempt but are always prepared to retaliate with a probability above a calculable threshold. This equilibrium is Pareto-superior, dynamically stable, and – when supported by robust threats – as invulnerable as possible to misperceptions or miscalculations by the players.

How do these results accord with the strategic doctrine of MAD? First, MAD is not only an acronym for "mutual assured destruction" but also for "mutual assured deterrence." In its former incarnation, MAD is more of an epithet than a statement of policy, except insofar as it implies that to save the world each side must be willing to destroy it.

Second, our Deterrence Equilibrium suggests that this is only partially true: there is not, and need not be, "assured destruction," but only a probabilistic threat of such to induce "assured deterrence." If the threat of retaliation is sufficiently great, and perceived to be credible, neither side will find it advantageous to preempt.

Credibility depends on precommitments by both sides to implement a (probabilistic) threat. Such precommitments, backed up by the formidable second strike capability of the superpower's largely invulnerable submarine-launched missiles, certainly seem to characterize the nuclear retaliatory policies of the superpowers. As we indicated earlier, however, probabilistic threats of full-fledged retaliation may be interpreted as diminished responses to a provocation, but carried out with certainty. Such responses in repeated play of a game would, it seems, drive one up the escalation ladder. Fortunately, the nuclear rung has never been reached in any superpower confrontation, which seems at least partially explained by the dynamic stability of the Deterrence Equilibrium – after any perturbation in a player's preemption probability, that probability tends to be restored to zero. Thus, equilibrium is maintained by a powerful force.

This self-restoring quality of the Deterrence Equilibrium will be reinforced by robust threats, which are always above the threshold level necessary to deter but never commit a player to certain retaliation. Because these threats are both equally damaging and equally costly whatever one side thinks the other might do, they would, we believe, enhance the stability of the Deterrence Equilibrium in a game of incomplete information.

The difficult question to answer is what, operationally, constitutes a robust threat. We argued earlier that the present nuclear doctrines of the superpowers seem to preclude a certain response except, perhaps, to a massive nuclear attack wherein all signs are unambiguous. On the other hand, they would seem to imply probabilities above the (minimal) threshold values. But are these threats, and the actions to make them credible, as nonprovocative as practicable?

If false signals should trigger an unprovoked attack, the consequences surely would be deadly. It therefore seems better to err on the side of not being responsive enough – having "only" a probabilistic threat, which our model indicates is quite sufficient if a doomsday machine largely beyond human control undergirds it – rather than making one's retaliation too automatic or too sensitive to provocation.

If it is hard to say exactly what constitutes a robust threat today, there is no ambiguity in our model about the undesirability of preemption. It is *never* optimal unless one can rest assured that the other wide will never retaliate. Since this presumption seems hopelessly naive, there seems no good reason ever to contemplate preemption, given at least threshold threats of retaliation by both sides.

Yet this is not necessarily to commend "no first use" at levels below that of superpower confrontation. In response to conventional attacks, it is conceivable that holding out the possibility of introducing nuclear weapons into a conventional conflict may help to deter an attack in the first place. But then this benefit must be weighed against the increased risk of nuclear escalation should the attack actually occur and, once initiated, there were no self-imposed restraint on the first use of nuclear weapons.

This and other instances of potentially apocalyptic conflict that deterrence may prevent from erupting seem capable of game-theoretic modelling. At least in the case of the Deterrence Game, the effects of threats that under-lie nuclear deterrence seem salutary. But when threats themselves become provocative and severely undermine trust, one must ask whether their deterrent value outweighs the costs of creating an inflammatory situation.

Appendix

In this appendix we shall conduct an exhaustive search for Nash equilibria in the Deterrence Game and analyze their properties. The rules of this game, along with payoff and strategy definitions, are given in Section 3. The game is depicted in Figure 2.

The expected payoffs of Row (R) and Column (C) are repeated below:

$$E_R(s,q;t,p) = str_3 + (1-s)tp + s(1-t)qr_2; \qquad (2)$$
$$E_C(t,p;s,q) = stc_3 + s(1-t)q + (1-s)tpc_2; \qquad (3)$$

Our search will be broken down according to the values of s and t at the equilibrium.

Case 1: s = t = 1.

From (2), if t = 1 then $\dfrac{\partial E_R}{\partial s}$ = r_3 – p. Since s = 1 at equilibrium only if

$\dfrac{\partial E_R}{\partial s} \geq 0$, p $\leq r_3$ is necessary. Analogous consideration of (3) shows that q $\leq c_3$ at any equilibrium with s = 1. Now suppose that t = 1 and p $\leq r_3$. From (2), R's expected payoff is

$$E_R(s,q;1,p) = p + s(r_3-p),$$

so that R can never do better than to choose s = 1 and q $\leq c_3$. Similarly, t = 1, p $\leq r_3$ is C's best response to s = 1, q $\leq c_3$.

Therefore, the only equilibria consistent with Case 1 are

$$s = 1, q \leq c_c; t = 1, p \leq r_3. \qquad (4)$$

The family (4) is called the *Deterrence Equilibrium*, since every strategy combination in the family leads to the same outcome – the cooperative outcome of the underlying Chicken game, with payoffs (r_3,c_3). Properties of the Deterrence Equilibrium will be adduced below.

Case 2: t = 0.
From (2), if t = 0 then

$$E_R(s,q;0,p) = sqr_2,$$

so that R can maximize his expected value only by choosing s = q = 1. If s = q = 1, then (3) shows that

$$E_C(t,p;1,1) = 1 - t(1-c_3),$$

so that C's best choice is t = 0, and his payoff does not depend on p.

Therefore, the only equilibria consistent with Case 2 are

$$s = 1, q = 1; t = 0, p \text{ arbitrary},$$

which we call the *Preemption by C Equilibrium*. At this equilibrium, the outcome of the Deterrence Game is always the outcome of the underlying Chicken game associated with a "win" for C – the outcome with payoffs $(r_2,1)$.

Case 3: $s = 0$.
This case is analogous to Case 2, and reduces to the *Preemption by R Equilibrium*:

$$s = 0, q \text{ arbitrary}; t = 1, p = 1.$$

The outcome corresponds, in Chicken, to a "win" for R, and has payoffs $(1,c_2)$.

Case 4: $0 < s < 1, t = 1$.

If $0 < s < 1$, (3) implies that $\dfrac{\partial F_C}{\partial p} = (1-s)tc_2 > 0$ provided $t > 0$. Thus, at any equilibrium with $0 < s < 1$ and $t = 1, p = 1$ also since E_C is increasing in p. Now if $t = 1$ and $p = 1$,

$$E_R(s,q;1,1) = 1 - s(1-r_3)$$

by (2), so that R's expected payoff is maximized only when $s = 0$. This contradiction shows that there are no equilibria consistent with case 4.

Case 5: $s = 1, 0 < t < 1$.
This case contains no equilibria, by an argument analogous to that for Case 4.

Case 6: $0 < s < 1, 0 < t < 1$.

Equation (2) shows that $\dfrac{\partial E_R}{\partial q} = s(1-t)r_2$ so that, for an equilibrium with $0 < s < 1$ and $0 < t < 1$, $q = 1$ is a necessary condition since E_R is increasing in q. Analogously, so is $p = 1$. Now suppose that $0 < t < 1$ and $p = 1$ are fixed. To maximize

$$E_R(s,q;t,1) = t + s[tr_3 - t + (1-t)qr_2],$$

it is clear that R must choose either $s = 0$ or $s > 0$ and $q = 1$. We discard $s = 0$ since it is not consistent with Case 6. Now in order that some s satisfying $0 < s < 1$ maximize E_R, it must be that $\dfrac{\partial E_R}{\partial s} = 0$, i.e.,

$$tr_3 - t + (1-t)r_2 = 0.$$

This equation implies that

$$t = t^* = \frac{r_2}{1 - r_3 + r_2}.$$

Note that $0 < t^* < 1$. Analogously, for fixed s and q satisfying $0 < s < 1$ and $q = 1$, $p = 1$ and some t satisfying $0 < t < 1$ maximize E_C only if

$$s = s^* = \frac{c_2}{1 - c_3 + c_2},$$

where, again, $0 < s^* < 1$. Finally, one can verify directly that

$$s = s^*, q = 1; t = t^*, p = 1 \tag{5}$$

is an equilibrium. We refer to this equilibrium as the *Naive Equilibrium*.

It is easy to show that, at the Naive Equilibrium, the players' expected payoffs are

$$E_R^* = \frac{r_2}{1 - r_3 + r_2}, \quad E_C^* = \frac{c_2}{1 - c_3 + c_2},$$

and that $r_2 < E_R^* < r_3$ and $c_2 < E_C^* < c_3$. Thus, the Deterrence Equilibrium (4), with payoffs (r_3, c_3), is Pareto-superior to the Naive Equilibrium (5).

The Deterrence Equilibrium possesses a dynamic-stability property which, once it forms, will (in repeated play) contribute to its persistence. To see this, assume that the Deterrence Equilibrium (4) has become established, and, further, that

$$0 < q < c_3, 0 < p < r_3 \tag{6}$$

holds. Suppose that player C is concerned that there is some chance that R will preempt, i.e., that $s < 1$, and that C is therefore contemplating whether he should preempt with some positive probability. In other words, C is no longer sure that s = 1, and is reconsidering his choice of t = 1. But now differentiation of (3) yields

$$\frac{\partial E_C}{\partial t} = s(c_3 - q) + (1-s)pc_2,$$

so that, if (6) holds, $\frac{\partial E_C}{\partial t} > 0$ for every value of s satisfying $0 \leq s \leq 1$. Therefore, C is motivated to choose t = 1, despite his doubts about the value of s, since E_C is increasing in t. A similar calculation shows that R is motivated to choose s = 1 regardless of his perception of the value of t, providing (6) holds. Thus, probabilistic threats of retaliation which are more than minimal (q = c_3, p = r_3) but less than certain (p = 0, q = 0) will tend to restore the Deterrence Equilibrium if it is perturbed.

Politics, New York University;
Mathematics, Wilfrid Laurier University

Social Philosophy & Policy 3:1 Autumn 1985 ISSN 0265–0525 $2.00

MORALITY AND PARADOXICAL DETERRENCE*

STEVEN LEE

Nuclear deterrence is paradoxical. One paradox of nuclear deterrence we may call the rationality paradox:

> (RP) (1) While it is a rational policy to threaten nuclear retaliation against an opponent armed with nuclear weapons, it would not be rational to carry out the retaliation should the threat fail to deter; and (2) what would not be rational to do is not, in the circumstances characteristic of nuclear deterrence, rational to threaten to do.

This is a paradox in the standard sense that it involves contradictory claims, for it implies that adopting a policy of nuclear deterrence is both rational and not rational, yet we have strong reason to believe that each of the claims is true. Claim (1) is a recognition that, though we believe nuclear deterrence works, there would seem to be no reason to carry out the threat if it were to fail. Claim (2) is part of the logic of all forms of deterrence, military and nonmilitary, and it relates to the important notion of *credibility*: if an opponent knows that one has no reason to carry out a threat, the threat would not be credible and so one would have no reason to make it. Further, it is characteristic of a state of nuclear deterrence that the opponent would recognize that one would have no reason to carry out the threat.

The rationality paradox is but one of the paradoxes raised by nuclear deterrence. Some other of the paradoxes of nuclear deterrence have the same form as the rationality paradox: for a certain set of predicates x,

> (PND) (1) the act of threatening nuclear retaliation (against an opponent with nuclear weapons) is x, while the act of carrying out the threat would be not-x; and (2) if it is not-x to perform some action, then, in the circumstances generally characteristic of a situation of nuclear deterrence, it is not-x to threaten to perform that action.

Since "rationality" in the context of nuclear strategy, as in other contexts, concerns the means of promoting one's (national) interests, the rationality

*My thanks to Scott Brophy, Gregory Kavka, and John Ahrens, who provided many valuable comments on an earlier version of this essay.

paradox is a *prudential* paradox. But nuclear deterrence also gives rise to *moral* paradoxes. One of these paradoxes, which has the same form as the rationality paradox, is generated by substituting "morally justifiable" for "x" in (PND). Under this paradox, nuclear deterrence is seen as being both morally justifiable and not morally justifiable. I plan to examine this moral paradox, in part through a study of the parallel features of the rationality paradox. Moral paradoxes of nuclear deterrence have received only a small amount of attention in comparison with the rationality paradox.[1] To begin, I will offer some observations on the source of paradox in nuclear deterrence.

I

Why is nuclear deterrence paradoxical?[2] Deterrence in general is not a paradoxical policy. In the context of the criminal justice system, *both* threatening punishment for lawbreaking and carrying out the threat in those cases where it fails to deter are regarded as rational actions. The situation is the same in the case of military deterrence not involving nuclear weapons: not only is it rational to threaten war to seek to deter hostile powers from actions harmful to one's national interests, it is also sometimes rational to go to war to protect those interests if the threat fails. How is nuclear deterrence different from these other forms of deterrence?

Carrying out the deterrent threat in the case of legal-punishment deterrence or nonnuclear military deterrence can be an effective means of serving the ends of the policy, just as making the threat can. Punishing lawbreakers usually increases the effectiveness of the general deterrent by increasing the credibility of the threat of punishment in the eyes of potential lawbreakers. Going to war, where nuclear weapons are not involved, can also serve to increase the credibility of the military deterrent in the eyes of other powers who would be inclined to encroach on one's national interests. More importantly, nonnuclear war can serve to halt or to reverse the harm to national interests inflicted by the nation with which one goes to war. Britain's war with Argentina over the Falkland/Malvinas Islands served not only, presumably, to increase the future deterrent value of British military power, but also to resecure the lost territory.

But there are a number of enduring features of the present military reality which combine to make nuclear weapons fundamentally different from nonnuclear weapons in regard to their military usefulness. These features include not only the increase in magnitude of destructive power that nuclear

---

[1] One person who has given attention to the moral paradox is Gregory Kavka; see his "Some Paradoxes of Deterrence," *Journal of Philosophy*, vol.75 (June, 1978), pp.285–302.

[2] For a further development of some of the themes in this section, see the essay by myself and Avner Cohen, "The Nuclear Predicament," in A. Cohen and S. Lee, eds., *Nuclear Weapons and the Future of Humanity* (Totowa, N.J.: Rowman and Allenheld, 1985).

weapons represent, but also their existence in large numbers, their distribution in the hands of hostile powers, the ineffectiveness of defensive measures against them, and their ability to survive in large numbers a surprise nuclear attack. Taken together, these features mean that each of the nuclear superpowers can completely destroy the other's society, and that each cannot be prevented from doing this if it so chooses. Moreover, these features are likely to characterize our military reality for the foreseeable future: societies will remain effectively defenseless and their nuclear arsenals will remain substantially invulnerable to a first-strike.[3] This makes the weapons unusable in war, in the sense that such use could not be expected to serve national interests, since any use of nuclear weapons in battle seriously risks escalation leading to national destruction. This is a familiar point. We have learned from Clausewitz* that war is an extension of politics; but there are no political purposes that the use of nuclear weapons in battle are likely to be able to achieve. So any use of nuclear weapons, even in retaliation against a nuclear attack, could not be expected to serve national interests.

But while nuclear weapons have no purpose in war, the threat to use them is strongly believed to serve the political purpose of avoiding nuclear war. It is the policy of nuclear deterrence that is widely thought to have kept the great powers from war with each other over the past forty years (1945–1985). Robert Jervis points to "the conflicts between the destructive power of the weapons, which makes them unusable, and the need to make them serve political goals. Nuclear weapons are simultaneously crucial to and set apart from normal politics."[4] Nuclear weapons are valuable as a deterrent but irrelevant if deterrence fails. Hence, the first half of the paradox: nuclear retaliation would not be rational, since any use of nuclear weapons would not serve national interests; yet nuclear deterrence is rational, because (we strongly believe) it is effective in avoiding war.

The second half of the paradox concerns the way in which nuclear weapons undercut the traditional logic of deterrence. The effectiveness of deterrence depends on the threats being credible, and the credibility of the threat depends on the perception that the threat would be carried out. Other forms of deterrence are effective in this way because carrying out the threat can promote one's interests, either by reversing the immediate harm to those interests or by lessening the likelihood of future harms. But the capacity to

---

[3] The kinds of ballistic-missile defenses proposed by the present administration would have to be virtually 100 percent effective in order to provide real protection for cities, and such perfection is not to be expected. Even proponents of the plan have begun to speak of the purpose of the defenses as protecting missiles only.

[4] Robert Jervis, *The Illogic of American Nuclear Strategy* (Ithaca, N.Y.: Cornell University Press, 1984), p.48.

*Karl von Clausewitz (1780–1831), the influential Prussian writer on military strategy.

carry out the nuclear threat is *not* seen as potentially effective in either of these ways. Unlike carrying out a nonnuclear military threat, it would succeed only in punishing the opponent, not in reversing the immediate harm to national interests by denying the opponent the gain from its aggression.[5] And unlike carrying out the threat of legal punishment, it could not be counted on to promote one's future interests because it would carry the serious possibility of national destruction (or occur in a situation in which national destruction had already occurred). If nuclear retaliation would not promote one's interests, then it would not be rational, and so the credibility of the threat to retaliate, and hence its rationality, is called into question.

II

The state of paradox is uncomfortable. One does not like to have to hold contradictory claims, however true each may seem to be. Many strategic theorists over the past twenty-five years have sought ways to escape from the rationality paradox. The intellectual battlelines between contending strategic camps may be understood in terms of the reaction of the theorists to this paradox. In general, the paradox has been accepted as an inevitable feature of deterrence policy by proponents of *countervalue strategy*, while those who have rejected or sought escape from the paradox have advocated, instead, *counterforce strategy*. A brief survey of this debate will lead to a better understanding of the rationality paradox and will be valuable for our later discussion of the moral paradox. I will argue for a particular position in this debate. My purpose, however, is not to add anything new to the debate, but to use the position I outline to make some points about the moral paradox.

Under countervalue strategy, the main targets of one's nuclear warheads are the population centers and economic assets of the opponent. Counter-value strategy involves a capacity for "assured destruction," the ability to destroy the opponent's society in retaliation, even after a massive surprise attack. When both sides have such a capacity, the situation is one of "mutual assured destruction" (or MAD). The characteristics of this strategy, in the words of Fred Iklé, are:

> One: our nuclear forces must be designed almost exclusively for "retaliation" in response to a Soviet nuclear attack – particularly an attempt to disarm us through a sudden strike.
> Two: our forces must be designed and operated in such a way that this "retaliation" can be swift, inflicted through a single, massive and – above all – prompt strike. What would happen after this strike

---

[5] Glenn Snyder has emphasized the point that nuclear deterrence is deterrence by punishment rather than denial; see his *Deterrence and Defense* (Princeton, N.J.: Princeton University Press, 1961), pp.14ff.

is of little concern for strategic planning.

Three: the threatened "retaliation" must be the killing of a major fraction of the Soviet population; moreover, the same ability to kill our population must be guaranteed the Soviet government in order to eliminate its main incentive for increasing Soviet forces. Thus, deterrence is "stablized" by keeping it mutual.[6]

This shows how countervalue strategy is based on an explicit recognition of the rationality paradox. The use of nuclear weapons is irrational due to their society-destroying potential, and countervalue strategy emphasizes this by threatening this destruction directly. What better way is there to guarantee their nonuse than by making such a threat?

But, of course, this is paradoxical. The deterrent effect requires that the opponent's use of nuclear weapons would be irrational, and thus depends on the guarantee that such use would result in retaliation. But how can there be such a guarantee (i.e., how can the threat be credible) when the irrationality of using the weapons applies as well to one's own retaliatory use? To consider the irrationality of retaliation in greater detail, we should distinguish two kinds of cases in which the need for it might arise: retaliation in response to a massive nuclear first-strike and retaliation in response to a limited nuclear first-strike.

If an opponent launched a massive nuclear first-strike, one's society would be in ruins, though one's retaliatory capacity would be largely intact. Retaliation could not serve national interests in this case because the national interests would have already been destroyed along with the society. Thus, retaliation would not be rational, in the sense that it would not further one's national interest.[7] However, though retaliation would not be rational in this sense, this does not guarantee that it would not occur. If one's society had been destroyed, retaliation would not promote one's interests, but neither would it harm them, and it might be done out of mere revenge. The threat might be carried out despite its irrationality. But credibility here is much more problematic than it would be if retaliation were clearly perceived to promote national interests. In this light, proposals to shore up the credibility of this kind of threat have ranged from the building of a "doomsday machine" to the cultivation of the appearance of madness in one's leaders. The credibility of the threat to retaliate against a massive first-strike cannot be completely secured by the possibility that such retaliation may occur out of nonrational motivation.

[6] Fred Iklé, "Can Nuclear Deterrence Last Out the Century?" *Foreign Affairs*, vol.51 (January, 1973), p.268.

[7] This is what Jonathan Schell calls the "monumental logical mistake" on which deterrence is based: in *The Fate of the Earth* (New York: Avon, 1982), p.202.

Consider, now, the irrationality of retaliation for a limited nuclear first-strike. If the opponent launches a limited attack, it would have sufficient reserves to destroy one's society in subsequent attacks. Hence, retaliation would not be rational because it would initiate an escalatory process that would be likely to bring on the complete destruction of one's society. It is said that the threat to retaliate against a limited attack is a threat to commit suicide, and, as Albert Wohlstetter observes, "Suicidal threats are *in general* not a reliable means of dissuasion."[8] While individuals may at times be able credibly to threaten acts leading to their own self-destruction, nations cannot do this.

How do the counterforce critics of countervalue strategy respond to these arguments? They reject the rationality paradox by asserting, in denial of claim (1), that nuclear retaliation may in some cases be rational. Specifically, they take issue with the argument in the preceding paragraph that retaliation against a limited nuclear attack would never be rational. The way to make such retaliation rational is to adopt a different kind of target for the nuclear warheads. In counterforce targeting the warheads are aimed at military rather than civilian targets. It is argued that this can make nuclear retaliation rational (i.e., subservient to political purposes) by creating the possibility of *limited* nuclear war. Nuclear war fought only against military targets would be limited in the sense that cities would not be intentionally hit. If nuclear war could be kept limited, it need not lead to the destruction of one's society, and so it might serve national interests. There could be a rational retaliatory response to a limited nuclear first-strike, viz., a limited retaliation aimed at military targets. Destroying the opponent's military machine, and hence its ability to maintain political control, while avoiding destruction of one's society through deterring the opponent from escalating the conflict further, would be a form of victory in a nuclear war that could make such war, like nonnuclear war, a rational instrument of national policy.

The paradox is overcome because nuclear retaliation, at least in the case of a limited first-strike, can be made rational. Thus, the rationality of the threat is no longer called into question in every case by the irrationality of carrying out the threat. The paradox inheres not in nuclear deterrence itself but in a particular doctrine: countervalue strategy. With the adoption of counterforce strategy the paradox dissolves. So the argument goes.

What the proponents of counterforce strategy have done in this argument is to treat nuclear weapons like nonnuclear weapons. That is how they think that the rationality paradox can be overcome: if nuclear weapons are like nonnuclear weapons, the traditional nonparadoxical logic of deterrence, as it applies in the case of nonnuclear military deterrence, is restored. The way to

---

[8] Albert Wohlstetter, "Bishops, Statesmen, and Other Strategists on the Bombing on Innocents," *Commentary*, vol.72 (June, 1983), p.30.

treat nuclear weapons like nonnuclear weapons is to give nuclear weapons the same kinds of targets that nonnuclear weapons have traditionally had: the opponent's military forces. The practice of treating nuclear weapons like nonnuclear weapons is referred to by Robert Jervis as "conventionalization," which is "to apply the same way of thinking to them that applied to araments in the prenuclear era."[9] If the same way of thinking is applied to nuclear weapons, the traditional logic of deterrence applies nonparadoxically.

But they should not be treated in the same way. Given the features of contemporary nuclear weapons sytems, a large-scale nuclear war between the superpowers would inevitably involve the destruction of both societies. This destructive capacity is unique to nuclear weapons, and it casts a long shadow over any use of these weapons on a lesser scale. Under this shadow, traditional military concepts or ways of thinking simply do not apply. While it is recognized that a counterforce capacity cannot effectively remove the society-destroying retaliatory capacity of the opponent, it is thought that a superior counterforce capacity can be pressed to advantage on the battlefield (thus making counterforce retaliation rational). But when each side can completely destroy the other, a relative military advantage cannot be pressed to achieve victory as it can in nonnuclear contexts.[10] The threat that one's superior counterforce capacity poses to the opponent would always be far less than what the opponent can threaten in countervalue retaliation. One need not argue that it is impossible that a nuclear war would be limited, only that we could never have enough assurance that a war once started would stay limited to make the risk a rational one, given the ultimacy of what is at stake. Thus, the paradox of nuclear deterrence reasserts itself. The paradox is not a function of this or that strategic doctrine, but rather, it inheres in the society-destroying potential of contemporary nuclear-weapons systems.

Because the paradox remains independently of strategic doctrine, the threat of counterforce strategy cannot have the great gain in deterrent credibility claimed by its proponents. Against a limited nuclear attack, the threat of counterforce retaliation may be somewhat more credible than countervalue retaliation, since there is at least the possibility that the resulting nuclear war could be kept limited. But this does not make counterforce retaliation rational, since the expectations that the nuclear war would remain limited would never be sufficient to make rational the risk of one's own destruction. This may lead one to think that there is little to choose between the two strategies. Michael Walzer observes that "given the existence of large numbers of nuclear weapons and their relative invulnerability, and barring major technological breakthroughs, *any imagin-able strategy* is likely to deter a 'central war' between the great powers."

[9] Jervis, p.56. Jervis adopts the term "conventionalization" from Hans Morganthau.
[10] ibid., pp.59–63. Jervis points out that what is important in the case of nuclear weapons is absolute rather than relative military capability.

Walzer goes on to note that once "the strategists helped us to understand" that any strategy would deter, "it became unnecessary to adopt any of their strategies – or at least, any particular one of them"[11] But there is reason to question this assertion.

Though counterforce strategy may provide a small gain in credibility over countervalue strategy, credibility is not the only factor to consider in assessing the likelihood that a strategy will avoid nuclear war. The credibility of the retaliatory threat may be the most important factor in deterring a coolly premeditated surprise attack, a "bolt from the blue." But in a situation of crisis, another factor comes more prominently into play: the extent to which each side can be assured that the other side is not planning to strike first. When such assurances are lacking, war is much more likely, because fear that the other side is about to strike first might lead one side to launch a preemptive attack in an attempt to limit the damage from the other's attack by destroying some of its nuclear forces. The extent of these assurances is the degree of crisis stability. Countervalue strategy has a high degree of crisis stability, but counterforce strategy does not. Under countervalue strategy, each side can have assurance that the other side is not planning a first strike because such a strike would be tantamount to committing national suicide: not only does the fact of assured destruction guarantee that one's own society is likely to be destroyed in response, but since the targeting is not counterforce, a preemptive attack would do nothing to lessen the retaliatory damage.

But under counterforce strategy, because a first-strike would lessen the damage from an attack by the other side, each side might be tempted to strike first, and the other side, knowing and fearing this, might launch a preemptive attack. The pressures for launching first in a crisis would be much greater because there are apparent advantages from doing so and apparent disadvantages from holding back. This is true even though, given the fact of assured destruction, these advantages are more apparent than real. Because counterforce strategy is thought, however mistakenly, to make nuclear war a rational instrument of policy, each side has some inclination to initiate such a war, and is even more likely to do so because it perceives that the other side is so inclined and believes that if there is to be war the advantage would lie in striking first. Under countervalue strategy, a first-strike in a crisis is not only in fact irrational, but is perceived to be irrational: each side can afford to hold back, secure in the integrity of its retaliatory capacity and the perception that the other side would see no advantage in a first-strike.

One proposal to overcome the lack of crisis stability of counterforce strategy is a policy of launch-on-warning, but this would in fact make the risk

---

[11] Michael Walzer, *Just and Unjust Wars* (New York: Basic Books, 1976), p.278.

of war even greater. Seeking to discourage preemptive attacks by planning to launch one's missiles in the brief time between the launching and impact of the opponent's missiles, greatly increases the likelihood of war by accident or mistake.

The perceived trade-off in adopting a counterforce strategy between what is thought to be a significant advantage in credibility and what is a significant disadvantage in crisis stability may be referred to as "the usability paradox."[12] If one makes nuclear weapons more usable, they are more likely to be used: if, in an attempt to increase credibility, one tries to make nuclear weapons more usable (i.e., one tries to create, through counterforce targeting, rational uses for them), then in the process one makes it more likely that they will be used (due to lessened crisis stability). But there is, in fact, no real trade-off: *in the switch to a counterforce strategy, crisis stability is sacrificed with little gain in credibility.* Counterforce strategy carries little of the prudential advantage claimed for it, but it does carry a serious prudential liability. We will find a parallel to this in the case of the moral paradox.

III

The moral paradox (MP) of nuclear deterrence, which results from substituting "morally justifiable" for "x" in (PND), is this:

> (MP) (1) The act of threatening nuclear retaliation (against an opponent with nuclear weapons) is morally justifiable, while the act of carrying out the threat would not be morally justifiable; and (2) if it is not morally justifiable to perform some action, then, in the circumstances generally characteristic of a situation of nuclear deterrence, it is not morally justifiable to threaten to perform that action.

In regard to claim (1), the reason that the act of threatening retaliation is morally justifiable is that it provides the great social benefit of simultaneously lessening significantly the likelihood of nuclear war and preserving one's national interests against aggression. The reason that it would not be morally justifiable to carry out the threat is, primarily, that a large number of innocent persons would be killed.

What makes the paradox is claim (2). This claim is based on the moral principle that what is wrong to do is wrong to intend to do. What makes this principle relevent to the moral assessment of nuclear policy is that in the

---

[12] This term is used by the Harvard Nuclear Study Group, *Living with Nuclear Weapons* (New York: Bantam, 1983), p.34; but I am using it in a different sense.

circumstances in which nuclear deterrence occurs, the threat of retaliation must involve an intention to carry out the threat should the threat fail. Some threats are bluffs, and so do not involve the intention to carry out the threat, but there are good reasons to hold that the threat of nuclear retaliation cannot, in practice, be a bluff. Those seeking an effective deterrence policy at the institutional level would certainly adopt the intention to retaliate, i.e., plan to retaliate; for if the threat were mere bluff, institutional provisions or plans would have to be made not to retaliate, and these might be discovered by the opponent, destroying the threat's credibility.

The moral principle that what is wrong to do is wrong to intend to do is a characteristic feature of deontological ethical theory, where the intention with which an action is done is often a crucial moral consideration. Gregory Kavka refers to this principle as the Wrongful Intentions Principle ("To intend to do what one knows to be wrong is itself wrong").[13] It is, he claims, "significant and widely accepted," and it "seems so obvious that, although philosophers never call it into question, they rarely bother to assert it or argue for it."[14] In addition, and especially relevant in the context of the moral assessment of nuclear deterrence, this principle is central to just war theory. Just war theorist Paul Ramsey states the general principle and then applies it to the nuclear context:

> Whatever is wrong to do is wrong to threaten, if the latter means 'mean to do.' If aiming indiscriminately in actual acts of war (or in fight-the-war policies) is wrong, so also is threatening indiscriminately aimed actions wrong to adopt in deter-the-war policies.[15]

The paradox is, then, that nuclear deterrence is morally justifiable despite this principle. As an aspect of just war theory, this principle is part of our traditional understanding of the moral logic of military matters, just as claim (2) of the rationality paradox is part of our traditional understanding of deterrence logic.

In his presentation of the moral paradox, Kavka argues that, in what he calls "special deterrent situations," of which he believes nuclear deterrence

---

[13] Kavka, p.289 (emphasis removed). The epistemological feature Kavka includes is important to the principle. This feature, I believe, applies as well in the case of nuclear deterrence. Despite the moral blindness often characteristic of policymakers, it is hard to imagine that such indiscriminate slaughter is not known by them to be wrong.

[14] ibid., pp.286, 289.

[15] Paul Ramsey, "A Political Ethics Context for Strategic Thinking, " in Morton Kaplan, ed., *Strategic Thinking and Its Moral Implications* (Chicago: University of Chicago Center for Policy Study, 1973), pp.134–135.

may be an example,

> it would be wrong for the defender to apply the sanction if the
> wrongdoer were to commit the offense, but it is right for the
> defender to form the (conditional) intention to apply the sanction if
> the wrongdoer commits the offense.[16]

Kavka's account of the paradox brings out the conflict between the utilitarian
and deontological considerations involved. The Wrongful Intentions Principle is a deontological principle. But what decides the case in favor of the
moral justifiability of threatening, are the consequences. "The assumption
that produces the paradoxes of deterrence concerns the role of utilitarian
considerations in determing one's moral duty in a narrowly limited class of
situations." The assumption is that "the most useful act should be
performed whenever a great deal of utility is at stake."[17]

But it would be trivializing the moral paradox to regard it as just another
example of the sort where a great deal of utility can be secured only by
violating deontological constraints. For most such examples work only
because they are individual, isolated cases: maybe hanging this innocent
person can save many lives, but an institution of punishing the innocent
would surely not have utilitarian value overall. Nuclear deterrence,
however, is a rare, if not unique, example where institutionalized, deontological rule-violation (holding hostage an entire population) apparently has
great utilitarian value.[18]

The moral paradox, like the rationality paradox, has its source in the
immensely greater destructive power of nuclear weapons. These weapons
not only have local effects, like blast and heat, much greater than nonnuclear
explosives; they also have unique, geographically widespread effects, such as
radiation. The geographically widespread effects guarantee that the use of
nuclear weapons will result in the deaths of a large number of innocent
persons. This would be a violation of another basic moral rule, characteristic
of deontological moral theories in general and just war theory in particular:
the principle of discrimination. Violence is morally justifiable in war only
when it is not used against persons who are innocent, in the sense that they
are not responsible for the aggressive acts which justify the defensive
violence. Nonnuclear weapons, because of their lesser effects, can be used
discriminately; but nuclear weapons cannot. Nuclear weapons are *inherently*

---

[16] Kavka, p.290.
[17] ibid., p.287.
[18] For a development of this point, see my "The Morality of Nuclear Deterrence: Hostage-
Holding and Consequences," *Ethics*, vol.95 (April, 1985).

indiscriminate. Thus, nuclear retaliation would not be morally justifiable, and we have the paradox.

But this paradox, like the rationality paradox, has been challenged by those who argue for counterforce strategy. Wohlstetter criticizes the "moralists who have chosen to emphasize the shallow paradoxes associated with deterrence by immoral threats against population."[19] Counterforce strategists argue, as they do in the case of the rationality paradox, that the moral paradox is not inherent in nuclear deterrence, but is a function of the adoption of a countervalue strategy. The relativity of the moral paradox to a particular strategy is presumably what Wohlstetter has in mind in referring to the paradox as shallow. A counterforce strategy would avoid the moral paradox. Counterforce targeting's promise of limited nuclear war would not only save the rationality of retaliation, it would save its morality as well.

One of the strongest advocates of the moral argument in favor of counterforce strategy is Paul Ramsey. Ramsey regards MAD as "the most politically immoral nuclear posture imaginable," and favors counterforce strategy, which is "just according to the principle of discrimination."[20] Counterforce strategy satisfies the principle of discrimination because it does not involve the intention to kill innocent persons, since the nuclear warheads are aimed at military targets. The deaths of the innocent persons killed in the retaliation would be foreseen but unintended consequences of the retaliatory act, hence the act would not violate the principle of discrimination. By focusing only on what is intended, inherently indiscriminate weapons can be used in a discriminate way. Counterforce deterrence is morally justifiable because it would be morally justifiable to carry out the threat. Claim (1) in the moral paradox is false and the moral paradox is dissolved.

Ramsey gives much of his attention to the problem of whether counterforce strategy could be an adequate deterrent: the "question of how what is morally right in war and deterrence can be made feasible."[21]

> The question, therefore, of the ethical justification of deterrence depends crucially on a question of fact, or of plannable policy: namely, whether the only *effective* deterrent must be suspended from the meant mutual threat of ultimate indiscriminate destruction.[22]

[19] Wohlstetter, p.29.
[20] Ramsey, pp.136, 142.
[21] ibid., p.139.
[22] ibid., p.135.

Ramsey argues that there is a feasible, effective counterforce alternative to the deterrence that is suspended from a countervalue threat. This is "graduated deterrence," which is

> deterrence from a shared anticipation of collateral damage that is unavoidable, unintended, in no measure enlarged; deterrence from the ambiguity inherent in weapons that *could* be used against populations indiscriminately, or ambiguity in how an opponent *perceives* these weapons may be used.[23]

In other words, for a counterforce strategy to be effective as a deterrent, it must still rely on the countervalue damage retaliation would do or might do. But whatever countervalue damage counterforce retaliation would do would not be intended. So a morally justifiable deterrent could in fact deter. This is the casuistry of effective counterforce deterrence.

Before considering whether this argument succeeds in avoiding the moral paradox, I would like to consider a curious inconsistency between Ramsey's argument and the argument of those who advocate counterforce strategy on strategic grounds. Ramsey puts a great deal of effort into arguing that counterforce strategy could be almost as effective in deterring as counter-value strategy. But the strategic theorists do not seem at all concerned that counterforce strategy might not be as effective as countervalue strategy; on the contrary, as we have seen, their main argument for counterforce strategy is that it is a *more* effective deterrent than countervalue strategy. Why this inconsistency? The reason, I believe, is that the strategic theorists arguing for the abandonment of countervalue strategy are not advocates of a genuine counterforce strategy. Rather, they want to *add* counterforce capability to existing countervalue capability. This mix characterizes current American deterrence strategy – countervailing strategy – which requires the capacity to threaten effectively the use of nuclear weapons at every potential level of nuclear conflict, including, at the extreme, attacks on cities. This is what Ramsey calls "suspended deterrence," and it is in contrast with genuine counterforce deterrence which he advocates, where there is no plan to retaliate against cities. Countervailing strategy, including as it does an intended countervalue threat, does not even have the apparent moral advantage that Ramsey sees in counterforce strategy. It is, thus, hypocritical of proponents of countervailing strategy to defend this strategy by charging that countervalue strategy violates the principle of discrimination.

But does a genuine counterforce strategy in fact have the moral advantage Ramsey claims for it? Does it avoid the moral paradox? Ramsey's argument

---

[23] ibid., p.142.

amounts to the claim that, however many innocent persons a counterforce retaliation would kill, it would not kill them intentionally, and so the killings might be morally justifiable. The number of innocent persons killed is not what is morally relevant; rather, it is the intention of the act whereby they are killed. According to Ramsey, "it is *not* possible to violate the principle of discrimination by numbers or amount of destruction."[24] Ramsey's point, we might say, is that nuclear war can be kept *morally limited*. A morally limited nuclear war is not the same as the kind of prudentially limited nuclear war considered earlier. A nuclear war is characterized as morally limited in terms of the quality of the intention with which it is fought, not the amount of destruction that results. While the question to be asked is the same as before – Can a nuclear war be limited? – what is at issue is moral limitation.

Can nuclear war be fought (and so deterred) with a discriminate intention? There is reason to think that it cannot. In judging the quality of the intention, one cannot ignore the fact that any user of nuclear weapons must know that, inevitability, a large number of innocent persons will be killed. A weapon that is known by its user to be inherently indiscriminate cannot be used with a discriminate intention. But even if the intention could be regarded as discriminate, this would not allow for the moral justifiability of the use of nuclear weapons, as Ramsey maintains. Before this argument is presented, however, more should be said regarding the inherent indiscriminateness of nuclear weapons.

Because the widespread effects of radiation from nuclear explosions would cause the deaths of a large number of persons at a great distance from the sight of the explosion, innocent persons will be killed regardless of how the weapons are targeted. This is what is meant by claiming that nuclear weapons are inherently indiscriminate: they cannot be used in such a way that their effects discriminate between innocent and noninnocent persons. Two kinds of exceptions to this claim may be granted: (1) nuclear weapons used on extremely isolated military targets, such as ships on the high seas or orbiting satellites and (2) special types of nuclear weapons, e.g., the neutron bomb, which create little wind-borne radiation and are meant for special kinds of targets, such as troop concentrations. But these uses of nuclear weapons, which in any case would be exceptional, are indiscriminate in the following extended sense. Given the present distribution of nuclear weapons in the hands of hostile powers, the use of a neutron bomb or a nuclear attack on ships or satellites would surely lead to escalation to the more standard sorts of uses of nuclear weapons. Even if the resulting nuclear war were kept limited in the sense that cities were not attacked, the loss of innocent life would be very great. Counting this escalation as an effect, then, the use of

[24] ibid., p.133.

nuclear weapons in these two exceptional categories would also be indiscriminate. Indiscrimateness is an invariable feature of the use of nuclear weapons.

If nuclear weapons are inherently indiscriminate, then how could someone who uses them with this knowledge be said to do so with a discriminate intention? What one is properly said to intend is not the product of an unconstrained psychological act; it is dependent not only on what one desires or thinks ought to be done, but also on what one knows about the action situation, including the instrument of action. The content of the intention cannot be indifferent to what the agent knows to be the nature of the instrument. If, for example, A injects B with a poison that A knows to be uniformly lethal, A cannot be said not to have a lethal intention towards B. Similarly, if an agent uses on a population weapons the agent knows are invariably indiscriminate, that agent cannot be said not to have an indiscriminate intention towards that population. This argument, however, runs counter to the implications of the doctrine of double effect, which is a central feature of just war thinking.[25] The doctrine of double effect holds that an action is morally evaluated more stringently in regard to its intended effects than in regard to its merely forseen effects.

Thus, according to the doctrine of double effect, the principle of discrimination applies only to an action's intended effects. If a user of nuclear weapons knows them to be inherently indiscriminate, this is to say only that this agent foresees that innocent people will be killed; but the intention behind the agent's use may nonetheless be discriminate, if it is directed at other of the weapon's effects. If a military facility is struck with a nuclear weapon, for example, one effect would be the deaths of military personnel and another would be the deaths of innocent persons from windborne radiation. Nuclear weapons are indiscriminate because they have the second kind of effect. But if the intention in this case is to destroy the military facility, that intention is directed only at the first effect, and so is discriminate. This use of nuclear weapons may, then, be morally justifiable despite the foreseen deaths of innocent persons. But this response to the argument does not succeed: the inherent indiscriminateness of nuclear weapons undercuts the claim that the kind of distinction between effects the doctrine of double effect draws has the moral implications the doctrine claims.

The point of the doctrine of double effect is that the moral assessment of actions requires a form of selective attention to the action's foreseen effects. The most serious attention is given to the effects that the doctrine regards as

---

[25] For a discussion of the doctrine of double effect, see William May, *Encyclopedia of Bioethics*, ed. Warren T. Reich (New York: Free Press, 1978), pp.317–320.

intended (including those effects that are the means to the action's end), and less serious attention is given to the other foreseen effects. In just war theory, for example, the intended effects of a military action must satisfy the principle of discrimination, while the merely foreseen effects must satisfy only the less stringent principle of proportionality. The issue, then, is one of whether the different effects distinguished by the doctrine should be treated differently in the moral assessment of an action. The question at hand is this: Is there adequate reason in the case of nuclear weapons used against military targets to regard the foreseen indiscriminate effects as being of lesser concern in the moral assessment of the action than those effects regarded by the doctrine as intended? But it is not clear that the reason that should be given here is the one offered by the doctrine – that the latter effects are intended and the former are not. Rather, the variety of proposals that have come from philosophy, law, and ordinary discourse for how the intended/ unintended distinction should be drawn among an action's foreseen effects suggests that the drawing of this distinction is partly a matter of stipulative definition and partly a matter of whether there is independent reason to treat the foreseen effects differently in the moral assessment. The question of which effects should be treated morally differently does not seem to be properly dependent on how the distinction is drawn, as the doctrine would have it; instead, it seems to be the other way around.

What other reason could be given, then, for treating these different effects differently in the moral assessment? The mere fact that the effects are in different positions in the causal chains, some preceding others, does not by itself seem to be a difference with any moral relevance. Nor can the distinction between desired and undesired effects be used by a defender of the doctrine to mark a moral difference, since some of the effects that the doctrine regards as intended, specifically the means to the intended end, may be as undesired as the effects that it regards as the merely foreseen. The only difference with any moral relevance, it seems, is a difference in likelihoods: the effects the doctrine regards as intended are certain to occur (if the actions succeeds), while the other foreseen effects, in most situations in which the doctrine applies, are not certain to occur. For example, if a nonnuclear bomb is used on a military facility, the deaths of military personnel are certain, while the deaths of innocent persons are usually only more or less likely, depending on whether they happen to be in the vacinity. If one aims nonnuclear weapons at noncivilian areas, there is usually some chance that innocents will not be killed. Such a difference in likelihoods would justify different treatment in the moral assessment of an action: other things being equal, we would hold agents more to account for those effects of their actions that are certain than for those that are only probable.

The implications of this are that in those situations in which this difference in likelihoods does not hold, the doctrine of double effect does not apply. This difference never holds for the use of nuclear weapons: innocent persons are certain to die even when civilian areas are not targeted. There is, then, no reason not to treat these different effects of the use of nuclear weapons alike in our moral assessment. Thus, all use of nuclear weapons stands in violation of the principle of discrimination. If it is the question of whether an action's forseen effects should be treated morally differently which determines how the intended/unintended distinction should be drawn, our earlier claim can be reasserted: the intention in the use of nuclear weapons is always indiscriminate. In any case, there is no use of nuclear weapons that is morally justifiable. *The conclusion is that counterforce strategy no more avoids the moral paradox than it avoids the rationality paradox.*

Ironically, this position is suggested by Ramsey's own argument. In claiming that the effectiveness of a counterforce strategy would depend on the countervalue damage that would inevitably result from counterforce retaliation, he makes the threat of such damage part of the means by which the deterrent end is achieved. Thus, such damage is conditionally intended in the terms of the doctrine of double effects itself, making the intention behind the counterforce deterrent threat indiscriminate. If this conditional intention were carried out in counterforce retaliation, the deaths of the innocent persons would be regarded by the doctrine as intended.

Thus, counterforce strategy lacks the moral advantage claimed for it. But in addition, it carries a serious moral liability in comparison with counter-value strategy. The moral advantage that it lacks is conformity with the principle of discrimination, and this is a deontological principle. Its moral liability is utilitarian. Counterforce strategy, as we saw above, is more likely to lead to nuclear war, because it has a low degree of crisis stability. In terms of its consequences, then, counterforce strategy is morally unacceptable, given the increased chances of avoiding nuclear war offered by countervalue strategy. If counterforce strategy had the moral advantage Ramsey claims it does, we would then be forced in choosing between the two strategies to think in terms of a trade-off between the deontological advantage of one and the utilitarian advantage of the other. But even in such a case, it seems clear that, given the enormity of the consequences at stake, the utilitarian concerns of the likelihood of avoiding nuclear war would be overriding, and we would still choose countervalue strategy.[26]

---

[26] On the riskiness of counterforce elements in present U.S. deterrence policy and the overriding nature of consequentialist considerations, see Russel Hardin, "Risking Armageddon," in Cohen and Lee.

IV

The tenacity of these paradoxes indicates that they are rooted in something that cannot be altered by choice of strategy: the unique features of nuclear weapons. Counterforce strategy fails to avoid the paradoxes because it denies this uniqueness by treating nuclear weapons, militarily and morally, like other weapons. Precisely because of their uniqueness, however, nuclear weapons have raised the hope, if it is not perverse to call it a hope, that we could permanently put an end to war between the great powers. Countervalue strategy is the embodiment of this hope that we can banish war by terrible threat. The way to avoid war is to make it too costly to be perceived as a rational instrument of policy. But the hope has faded as a result of the inexorable movement toward counterforce (more precisely, countervailing) strategy. This movement has shown that the uniqueness of the weapons has not been sufficiently recognized to halt the age-old pursuit of military advantage. If nuclear war is perceived as a rational instrument of policy, there is no reason to think that the threat of it will be any more successful at indefinitely avoiding great-power wars than was military deterrence prior to 1945. If we are led by this fading hope again to seek to avoid the paradox of nuclear deterrence, it would have to be in a different way: not by denying the uniqueness of the weapon, as counterforce strategy does, but by rejecting nuclear deterrence itself, the logic of which the weapons have undercut; not through a change in deterrence strategy, but through nuclear disarmament.

Philosophy, Hobart and William Smith Colleges

Social Philosophy & Policy 3:1 Autumn 1985 ISSN 0265–0525 $2.00

IMMORAL RISKS:
A DEONTOLOGICAL CRITIQUE OF NUCLEAR
DETERRENCE

Douglas P. Lackey

I. BEYOND UTILITARIANISM

In the summer of 1982, I published an article called "Missiles and Morals," in which I argued on utilitarian grounds that nuclear deterrence in its present form is not morally justifiable.[1] The argument of "Missiles and Morals" compared the most likely sort of nuclear war to develop under nuclear deterrence (DET) with the most likely sort of nuclear war to develop under American unilateral nuclear disaramament (UND). For a variety of reasons, I claimed that the number of casualties in a two-sided nuclear war developing under DET would be at least fifteen times greater than the number of casualties in a one-sided nuclear attack developing under UND. If one assumes that human lives lost or saved is the principal criterion by which nuclear weapons policies should be measured, it follows that DET is morally superior to UND on utilitarian grounds only if the chance of a two-sided nuclear war under DET is more than fifteen times less than the chance of a one-sided nuclear attack under UND. Since I did not believe that the chance of nuclear war under deterrence is fifteen times less than the chance of nuclear war under unilateral nuclear disarmament, I inferred that utilitaranism failed to justify DET. Indeed, on utilitarian grounds, DET stood condemned.

In the years since, "Missiles and Morals" has been variously reprinted and variously condemned.[2] Some critics reject the assumption that the number of

---

[1] Douglas P. Lackey, "Missiles and Morals: A Utilitarian Critique of Nuclear Deterrence," *Philosophy and Public Affairs*, vol.11 (Summer 1982), pp.182–231.

[2] For criticisms, see, for example, Russell Hardin "Unilateral and Bilateral Disarmament," *Philosophy and Public Affairs*, Vol. 12 (Summer 1983), pp.236–254; and Gregory Kavka "Doubts About Unilateral Disarmament," *Philosophy and Public Affairs*, vol. 12 (Summer 1983), pp.255–260. The reprints include Jan Narveson, *Moral Issues* (Oxford: Oxford University Press 1983) and Richard Wasserstrom, *Today's Moral Problems* (New York: Macmillian, 1985). As given here, the consequences of DET and UND are stated entirely in terms of lives saved and lost. Though I consider these the primary effects to be considered in evaluating nuclear weapons policies, many are concerned with such effects as the increased chance of nuclear blackmail that might result from unilateral nuclear disarmament. These and many other consequences of nuclear weapons policies relevant to the utilitarian calculation are considered in "Missiles and Morals" and in D. Lackey, *Moral Principles and Nuclear Weapons* (Totowa, NJ: Rowman and Allanheld, 1984).

casualties in a one-sided nuclear attack will be fifteen times less than the number of casualties in an all-out nuclear war. Perhaps a greater number reject the view that the chance of nuclear war under UND is not more than fifteen times greater than the chance of nuclear war under DET. Many seem to feel that the chance of nuclear war under UND is *nearly certain*, while the chance of nuclear war under DET is *quite slight*. In general, the empirical estimates of casualties and chances of war given in that article have not won wide acceptance. Obviously, if the empirical estimates presented in "Missiles and Morals" can be challenged, the moral conclusions can be challenged as well.

For my part, I stand by the empirical estimates given in "Missiles and Morals." Indeed, if the hypothesis that nuclear wars can generate nuclear winters is correct,[3] the empirical side of "Missiles and Morals" is considerably strengthened. Suppose that the United States were to give up its nuclear weapons unilaterally. Then, in the event of war, the Soviet Union would take precautions to avoid a nuclear winter, since such a winter would destroy the Soviet Union as well as the United States. (This presumes that the Soviets are rational, but deterrence presumes this as well.) On the other hand, suppose that the United States retains nuclear weapons. Then, in the event of war, there would be a two-sided nuclear exchange which, in all probability, would generate a nuclear winter. Given the nuclear winter hypothesis, the number of casualties to be expected from a one-sided nuclear attack on the United States (10,000,000) is at least twenty times less than the minimum number of casualties expected from a nuclear winter (at least 200,000,000). If the number of casualties resulting from a nuclear winter reaches two billion, then the number of casualties resulting from a one-sided nuclear attack on the United States would be two hundred times less than the number of casualties resulting from a two-sided nuclear exchange. It would follow that DET is superior to UND on utilitarian grounds only if the chance of two-sided nuclear war under DET is two hundred times less than the chance of a one-sided nuclear attack under UND, a proposition that I find completely untenable.

Nevertheless, I am sure that many critics will reject these new empirical estimates, just as they rejected the old ones. They may argue that the nuclear

---

[3] For an account of the nuclear winter hypothesis, see Richard P. Turco, Owen B. Toon, Thomas A. Ackerman, James B. Pollack, and Carl Sagan, "Nuclear Winter: Global Consequences of Multiple Nuclear Explosions," *Science*, vol. 222 (23 December 1983), pp.1283–92; Paul Ehrlich *et. al.*, "Long Term Biological Consequences of Nuclear War," *Science*, vol. 222 (23 December 1983), pp.1293–1900; Carl Sagan, "Nuclear War and Climatic Catastrophe," *Foreign Affairs*, vol. 62 (Winter 1983/84), pp.257–292; Curt Covey, Stephen Schneider, and Stanley Thompson, "Global Atmospheric Effects of Massive Smoke Injections from a Nuclear War," *Nature*, vol. 307 (1 March 1984), pp.21–25; and Richard P. Turco, *et. al.* "The Climatic Effects of Nuclear War," *Scientific American*, vol. 251 (August 1984), pp.33–43.

winter hypothesis is unsupported conjecture. Or they may argue that the chance of a one-sided nuclear attack under UND is *thousands* of times greater than the chance of a two-sided exchange under DET and, thus, that the number of expected deaths under UND is greater than the number of expected deaths under DET even if DET generates a nuclear winter and UND does not. (An "expected death" is a death multiplied by the probability that it will occur.) Estimating the probabilities of singular future events is a subjective business, highly sensitive to the prejudices of the estimators. If one feels that 1985 is rather like 1938, one will feel that unilateral nuclear disarmament will encourage aggressors and bring war. If one feels – as I do – that 1985 is rather like 1913, then one will feel that the delicate balancing act of deterrence is sure to break down and that a two-sided nuclear holocaust is bound to ensue if anything like the *status quo* is maintained.

Thus, the utilitarian critique of nuclear weapons policies ends in a stalemate, with each side rejecting the empirical estimates and, therefore, the moral conclusions of the other. This sort of dead-end leads one to hope that there might be some intuitively acceptable nonutilitarian moral system which can pass judgment on nuclear weapons policies without becoming hopelessly entangled in empirical considerations.

Nonutilitarian criticisms of nuclear deterrence are, of course, nothing new. Indeed, many of the moral charges made against nuclear deterrence in the first great wave of writing about nuclear weapons policies (1958–1963) were of a nonutilitarian sort.[4] Perhaps the most common criticism of nuclear deterrence in those years was the argument that nuclear deterrence required a conditional commitment to a direct attack on millions of noncombatants, a commitment often interpreted by deontologists as a commitment to mass murder.[5] This argument from "immoral intentions," still popular with the anti-nuclear public, is no longer commonly endorsed by moral philosophers.[6] Some of its original proponents have abandoned it because of the

---

[4] The "first wave" of writing about nuclear weapons policies was provoked by (a) the development of thermonuclear weapons, which convinced many unbelievers that nuclear weapons were fundamentally different in kind from nonnuclear weapons, (b) the public announcement of a policy of "massive retaliation" by John Foster Dulles in 1954 (that is, a policy of nonminimal, nonfinite nuclear deterrence), and (c) the development of new delivery systems which provided a variety of new strategic options. Exemplary moral writing about nuclear weapons in those years can be found in Bertrand Russell, *Common Sense and Nuclear Warfare* (New York: Simon and Schuster, 1959) and Philip Toynbee, *The Fearful Choice* (Detroit: Wayne State University Press, 1959). For examples of criticism with a distinctly nonutilitarian slant, see the essays by G.E.M. Anscombe and others in Walter Stein, ed., *Nuclear Weapons: A Catholic Response* (London: Merlin, 1961).

[5] This is generally assumed by the authors in the Stein volume, cited above, and is especially evident in the appendix by Anthony Kenny in the hard-to-locate second edition of the Stein volume that was published in 1965.

[6] One philosophical critic who does continue to press the critique of nuclear deterrence because of its "immoral threats" is Michael Walzer, *Just and Unjust Wars* (New York: Basic Books, 1977, Chapter 17.

development of so-called "counterforce" targeting, in which nuclear weapons are directed towards military targets. With such targeting, the deaths of civilians result from "indirect" killing, and the indirect killing of civilians is sanctioned by the traditional theory of just war, provided that such killings are kept to a minimum and provided that they are militarily necessary.[7] An even greater number of moral philosophers have become persuaded that the argument from "immoral intentions" depends on the principle that it is wrong to intend to do what it is wrong to do (dubbed by Gregory Kavka the "wrongful intentions principle") and that this wrongful intentions principle is in fact false.[8] If the wrongful intentions principle is false, one cannot infer the immorality of conditionally intending to launch a nuclear second strike from the immorality of actually launching a nuclear second-strike, and one cannot infer the immorality of nuclear deterrence from the immorality of nuclear war.[9] I am not prepared to reject the wrongful intentions principle, but I am ready to admit that the moral analysis of conditional intentions is complicated, and that moral philosophers have not achieved a consensus about how to evaluate them.[10] And even if we retained the wrongful intentions principle, we would still have the problem of developing a procedure for determining what a nation's nuclear intentions are, if, indeed, one can speak of the "intentions" of nations at all. It would be an advantage, then, to have a nonutilitarian, deontological critique of nuclear weapons policies which does not rely on the moral analysis of conditional intentions.

II. DETERRENCE AND RISK

In this essay, I propose to avoid the snares of outcome-estimation and the analysis of conditional intentions by construing nuclear deterrence as a risk management procedure. The procedure works as follows: the United States attempts to reduce the risk of nuclear attack on itself by increasing the risk of American nuclear attack on others. The "increased risk" of attack on other nations is an increased risk relative to the policy of American unilateral

---

[7] The swing from denunciations of the "countervalue" form of deterrence to applause for the "counterforce" variety is exhibited in the difference between Paul Ramsey's *War and the Christian Conscience* (Durham, NC: Duke University Press, 1961) and *The Just War* (New York: Scribner's, 1968).

[8] The most forceful attack on the "wrongful intentions principle" is Gregory Kavka, "Some Paradoxes of Deterrence," *Journal of Philosophy*, vol. 75 (June 1978).

[9] This conclusion is drawn by several authors; see, for example, William H. Shaw, "Nuclear Deterrence and Deontology," *Ethics*, vol. 94 (January 1984).

[10] Some of the ambiguities and complexities in the notion of conditional intentions concerning nuclear weapons are discussed in Douglas P. Lackey, "The Intentions of Deterrence," Avner Cohen and Steven Lee, ed., *Nuclear Weapons and the Future of Humanity* (Totowa, N.J.: Rowman and Allanheld, 1985).

nuclear disarmament. If the United States had no nuclear weapons, the risk of an American nuclear attack on other nations would be zero. If the United States retains nuclear weapons for purposes of deterring nuclear first strikes, then the chance of an American nuclear attack is (approximately) the chance of a first strike against the United States, multiplied by the chance that the United States will strike back if attacked, plus the chance of an accidental, unintentional, or unauthorized American first strike. Since this chance is greater than zero, deterrence so defined involves an increased risk of American nuclear attack.

Notice that nuclear deterrence defined as a risk management procedure corresponds to what in the strategic literature is defined as "finite" deterrence, as opposed to "extended" deterrence. A nation which practices finite deterrence commits itself to using nuclear weapons only in response to a nuclear first strike or first use.[11] A nation which practices extended deterrence is prepared to use nuclear weapons even in the absence of a nuclear first strike or first use by opponents. Since current American nuclear policy is a policy of extended deterrence, deterrence as evaluated here differs from the nuclear policy actually in force. But I agree with the many critics of extended deterrence that it is inferior to finite deterrence on both prudential and moral grounds.[12] Thus, if finite deterrrence is immoral, extended deterrence must be immoral as well.

At first sight, it might seem that the problems of risk evaluation are no different from the problems of outcome estimation and the analysis of conditional intentions. For how can we measure the gravity of risks except by considering the probability and severity of the results that come when the risk is realized? How can we measure the deontic quality of risks raised except by considering the acts that will be done if worst comes to worst? But first appearances deceive. In considering the badness of risks, we make a moral judgment about the gravity of the risk of *each* outcome of a policy; we do not take a sum of the expected values of all the outcomes, nor do we compare the quantity of expected value generated by one policy with the quantities of expected values generated by its rivals. In fact, the only quantitative judgment relevant to the deontological evaluation of risk is the judgment about whether the risk of a possible outcome is a negligible risk or

[11] "First use" refers to any first use of nuclear weapons, tactical or strategic. "First strike" refers to a first use of *strategic* nuclear weapons. A first strike need not be a first use need not be a first strike.

[12] For criticisms of extended deterrence, see McGeorge Bundy *et. al.*, "NATO and the Atlantic Alliance," *Foreign Affairs*, vol. 60 (Spring 1982), pp.753–768; and Robert S. McNamara, "The Military Role of Nuclear Weapons: Perceptions and Misperceptions," *Foreign Affairs*, vol. 61 (Summer 1983), pp.59–80. Notice that if finite deterrence is permissible, extended deterrence need not be permissible. Thus, the failure of the arguments against finite deterrence given in this article would provide no justification for extended deterrence.

a nonnegligible risk. (If the risk is negligible, then the deontological analysis does not proceed.) In assessing the qualitative character of risks, we do not consider only the deontological quality of the acts done if worse comes to worst; we consider the act of risk creation itself. This shift of attention from an act risked to the creation of the risk simplifies the evaluation of the intentional characteristics of the act being assessed. For when we consider the act that is risked, we are considering a conditionally intended act, an act that someone intends to perform if, and only if, worst comes to worst. But when we consider the act of risk creation, we consider a directly intended act, an act which is a means to a desired end. The moral assessment of risk creation is logically distinct from the moral assessment of risked outcomes or risked acts.

III. ARE DETERRENT RISKS NEGLIBLE

In *Anarchy, State, and Utopia*, Robert Nozick suggests various rules for the permissible infliction of risks, and of these the first is that it is permissible to inflict a risk if the risk is "negligible."[13] Nozick does not spell out what is meant by "negligible," but when Institutional Review Boards struggle with the moral permissibility of experiments on human subjects it is generally assumed that a "negligible" risk is one no larger than the risks of normal life; that is, the risks experienced by the subject during the experiment are not appreciably greater than the risks he would be experiencing if he chose not to participate. Are the risks of deterrence no larger than the everyday risks of life?

To me, at any rate, it seems practically self-evident that the risks of nuclear deterrence are *not* everyday risks and, therefore, that they cannot be dismissed as negligible. (Likewise, the risks of unilateral nuclear disarmament in a world of armed nuclear powers are admittedly not negligible.) Nevertheless, to my surprise, I have heard distinguished strategists and philosophers maintain that the risks of deterrence as currently practiced are quite small, that present arrangements are exceedingly stable, and that the main threats to peace come from tampering with the *status quo*.[14] For example, in the course of a public lecture in 1983, George Mavrodes likened the risks of deterrence to the risks of highway driving: innocent people may be killed as a result of driving but, Mavrodes claims, the numbers are small relative to total miles driven, the advantages of driving are great, and so the risks of normal driving relative to the advantages are negligible. When it

[13] Robert Nozick, *Anarchy, State, and Utopia* (New York: Basic Books, 1974), Chapter 4.
[14] On the strategic side, see Bernard Brodie, "The Development of Nuclear Strategy," *International Security*, vol. 3 (Spring 1978), pp.65–83.

comes to driving, the impermissible risks are not the risks inflicted by the average driver, but the risks inflicted by the minority of reckless drivers. Similarly, when it comes to deterrence, the impermissible risks are not the risks inflicted by the average type of deterrence, but the risks inflicted by reckless forms of nuclear deterrence. Just as there are good and bad drivers, so there are good and bad forms of deterrence.

The analogy between the risks posed by a nuclear nation and the risks posed by an automobile driver is certainly worth exploring. There are about 44,000 automobile fatalities per year in the United States, and each year Americans travel about 2,100 billion passenger miles by car. Now, since the morally significant risks of deterrence are the risks inflicted by each nuclear nation on the populations of *other* countries, the relevant fatalities for the Highway Analogy are the fatalities inflicted by drivers on *other* persons. If we assume that half of the 44,000 fatalities are fatalities inflicted by drivers on others, and that the average car on the roads carries two passengers, we get 22,000 fatalities per 1,100 billion driver miles, or about one driver-inflicted fatality per 100 million miles driven. Since the average American driver drives about 20,000 miles per year, it follows that the average driver will cause the death of some other person about once every 5,000 years. If the risks of nuclear deterrence are of the same magnitude as the risks inflicted by drivers on persons other than themselves, nuclear deterrence will cause a fatality only once every 5,000 years. I leave it to the reader to judge whether or not nuclear deterrence in its present form or some approximation thereof will break down less than once every 5,000 years. If you believe that breakdowns will occur more frequently, you will not believe that the risks of deterrence are like the risks of driving an automobile.[15]

Those who believe that something like the present system of deterrence cannot last for 5,000 years without catastrophe should conclude that the risks of deterrence are not negligible risks. But before we end discussion of the Highway Analogy, it is worth noting four other points at which the Highway Analogy breaks down. First, the risks of American automobile driving are regulated by laws, laws adopted in a putatively democratic society. So automobile driving in American is a socially sanctioned activity, and the risks of automobile driving are, in some sense, risks inflicted by all Americans on all Americans. Since (at least some of) the risks of deterrence are inflicted by nuclear nations on nonnuclear nations, it is not possible to

[15] There is another way to make the comparison. Suppose that a nuclear winter will take 200,000,000 lives outside the United States, and that there are 20,000 driver-inflicted fatalities in the United States each year. Then, automobile driving will inflict in 10,000 years the number of deaths that a nuclear winter will inflict in one year. Can anyone honestly believe that something like the present system of superpower deterrence, given the usual swings between rationality and irrationality exhibited in the history of nations, can last more than 10,000 years without producing a catastrophe?

describe deterrent risks as self-inflicted risks. Second, even if we dismiss the "self-inflicted" character of American driving risks as an holistic metaphor inappropriate to proper social analysis, and if we consider only the separate risks inflicted by particular Americans on particular Americans, it is still the case that a substantial majority of Americans (152 million out of 234 million) possess driver's licenses, while only a minority of the world's peoples live in nations that possess nuclear weapons and practice deterrence (1.617 billion out of 4.889 billion)[16] There is, then, a reciprocity in the risks that American drivers inflict on other Americans that is not exhibited in the risks that nuclear nations inflict on other nations.[17] Third, one of the risks associated with nuclear deterrence is the risk of human annihilation, and this is not an outcome that can be generated by automobile driving. I do not consider the annihilation of the human race an infinitely bad outcome, but I do think that we ought to consider the annihilation of the human race to be qualitatively distinct from any accumulation of deaths accruing under any other policy that does not threaten the survival of the human species. Thus, even if a million years of driving at current death rates will produce more deaths (44 billion killed) than the annihilation of the human species by nuclear war in 1985 (5 billion killed), the risks of nuclear deterrence are morally different from the risks of automobile driving. Finally, the risks of highway driving are avoidable; persons who wish to avoid them can stay out of cars and move away from roads. But the risks of nuclear war are unavoidable; there is no place to which one can move to avoid a nuclear winter.

IV. ARE DETERRENT RISKS FREELY ACCEPTED?

A second Nozickian principle for the evaluation of risks is the rule that *risks are permissible if they are freely accepted*. In the usual case, the rule is invoked to show the permissibility of self-inflicted risks, but it is easy to imagine circumstances in which a risk is freely accepted by some target of

---

[16] The nations practicing deterrence are China (one billion), the U.S.S.R. (272 million), the U.S. (234 million), the United Kingdom (56 million) and France (54 million), for a total of 1.617 billion, or 33% of the world's population of 4.889 billion people. I exclude India, which exploded a nuclear device in 1974 but which probably has no nuclear weapons and certainly has no delivery capability.

[17] George Fletcher has argued that fair risk infliction is essentially reciprocal risk infliction, and that risk infliction is unfair if the victim of the risk cannot reciprocate ("Fairness and Utility in Tort Law," *Harvard Law Review*, vol. 85 (January 1972), pp.537–73). Not only can non-nuclear nations not reciprocate the risks of deterrence presently inflicted on them, the nuclear nations are making every effort to keep the nonnuclear nations from reciprocating in the future. For an argument that lack of willingness to share nuclear weapons violates the Categorical Imperative, see Douglas P. Lackey, "Ethics and Nuclear Deterrence," James Rachels, ed., *Moral Problems* (New York: Harper and Row, 1975).

risk: as a favor to the risk producer; or as a moral duty; or in return for some sort of compensation; or in return for consent to the infliction of a reciprocal risk; or for some other reason. Can the risks inflicted by American deterrent capacities be justified as risks to which the subjects of risk have consented? In considering this problem, it is helpful to consider: (a) risks inflicted on America's allies; (b) risks inflicted on the U.S.S.R.; and (c) risks inflicted on other nations.

(a) It might be argued that America's allies have freely accepted the risks that American strategic weapons inflict on them. Leaders in these nations view themselves as somewhat sheltered by the American strategic umbrella, and many of them prefer the risks posed by American strategic weapons – for example, the risk that a nuclear war will be initiated by the United States, the risk that American weapons may accidentally trigger a nuclear war, or the risk that an American second strike might produce a nuclear winter – to the risks posed by Soviet nuclear weapons if the use of those weapons were undeterred by American strategic power. This argument, however, is unsound because the consent of the Allies is not truly voluntary. All these national leaders know that the United States will retain its strategic forces whether they consent to them or not. Consent to the infliction of risk is truly voluntary only if the victim has some confidence that if he refuses his consent, the risk will not be imposed. Apart from some fraction of the German population, many of the people living in nations allied with the United States, if they were given a choice between American deterrence or American unilateral nuclear disarmament, would probably choose the latter on the grounds that the world would be safer if there were fewer nuclear weapons in it. I doubt that, outside of Germany, there are very many people in the world who believe that the Soviets will attack them if the United States gives up its nuclear weapons, and that the Soviets will not attack them if the United States keeps its nuclear weapons.[18] (They may fear Soviet attack in either case, or neither case, but that is another matter.)

(b) It might be argued that the U.S.S.R. has consented to the imposition of deterrent risks by the United States in return for the right to inflict deterrent risks of its own, an agreement formalized by the SALT I and ABM treaties of 1972. In those treaties, each side agreed to limit offensive forces

[18] For evidence about attitudes among NATO allies, consider that the independent development of strategic nuclear forces by Great Britain and France, and the de-coupling of French strategic forces from NATO in 1966, indicates that these nations do not base their security expectations on the American deterrent; on the contrary, the reigning strategic fear in these countries is that the superpowers will initiate nuclear war over British or French territory, even when Britain and France are not committed to the conflict. As of this writing (April 1985), increasing public and official opposition exists to the placement of NATO cruise missiles in Belgium and the Netherlands; in Greece, the administration is actively considering leaving the Alliance, and the easy placement of missiles in Italy is more a result of political disorganization than a sign of popular support. Of course, in Germany, a substantial, vocal minority opposes placement.

and not to undertake strategic defense; each side allegedly gave up the search for first strike capacity in return for a secure second strike capacity; each side agreed to accept the risks of the possession of strategic forces by the other side in return for a guarantee that these strategic forces would be deployed in a second-strike mode, at least insofar as such a deployment mode could be devised. If so, then the risks imposed on the Soviets by American weapons are morally justified risks, and the risks imposed on Americans by Soviet weapons are morally justified risks.

But I cannot agree that the two treaties of 1972 support the view that each superpower has consented to deterrent risks imposed by its opponent. It is true that each side agreed to build small ABM systems rather than large ones. But it cannot be said that each side agreed to give up strategic defense, since in fact no ABM system in 1972 had any chance of providing a genuine strategic defense. (Indeed, no system in 1985 can provide a genuine chance.) The U.S. and the U.S.S.R. could not "agree" to give up strategic defenses because they did not have them to give up, nor did they have any prospect of obtaining them. This "agreement" to forego strategic defenses was like an agreement to pay off a creditor when one knows that one has only counterfeit money.

But what about the other agreement, the agreement to limit offensive forces? Did each superpower signify by *this* agreement its consent to the deterrent risks imposed by its opponent in return for retention of its ability to inflict its own deterrent risks? Once again, it can be argued that the superpowers only agreed to give up what they did not have and probably could not obtain – first strike capacity against the opponent. Given the growth of the Soviet strategic submarine fleet, there was no technical route to American first strike capacity for at least several decades, and the same was even more true for the Soviet Union.

Several other points also demonstrate that SALT I did not and does not signify consent to deterrent risks. (1) The agreement by the United States to keep the number of launchers within a given limit was hardly a burden since the United States had no intention of building beyond this limit, agreement or no agreement. Secretary of Defense Robert McNamara's cost-effectiveness studies in the mid-60s had indicated that little additional destructive capacity would be obtained by building more launchers, and the favored cost effective numbers – about 1000 ICBMs and 650 SLBMs – had been reached years before SALT I.[19] (2) Given the degree of overkill in existence by 1972, it was clear that developments in offensive capacity in the 1970s would consist not in adding new launchers, but in improving launcher accuracy, launcher lethality, and warhead quality; and through the 1970s,

[19] Alain Enthoven and Wayne Smith, *How Much Is Enough?* (New York: Harper and Row, 1971).

the United States did improve launcher lethality by the installation of MIRV on the Minuteman and Poseidon, the insertion of Mk12a warheads on the Minuteman, and so forth. In addition, subsequent to the SALT I agreements, the United States began a substantial improvement of its strategic bomber force through the installation of air-launched cruise missiles. It is difficult to find any technically and economically viable improvement in offensive capacity that was foresworn by the United States in the wake of SALT I.[20] (3) Even if the SALT I treaty *had* signified consent to deterrent risks, the treaty has now expired with no new agreement having been consummated extending the alleged past consent. (4) The March 1983 announcement by President Reagan of new plans for strategic defenses – the socalled "Star Wars" announcement – certified that at least in the present administration there is no desire to continue to accept the risks of mutual deterrence. From all this, we should conclude that Mutual Assured Destruction was never a condition to which the citizens of the superpowers, or even their leaders, freely consented: it was a fact of life from which each superpower sought to extricate itself by whatever technical means were available, affordable, and politically possible.

(c) If the nations with which the United States has forged alliances or signed treaties have not "consented" to the risks imposed by America's nuclear deterrent, then the nations that have not joined in alliances or signed treaties have consented even less. On occasions when the nonaligned nations have had an opportunity to express their views, they have not considered the maintenance of a second strike capacity to be part of the normal mechanisms of national defense. On the contrary, in 1961 the United Nations General Assembly condemned the mere possession of nuclear weapons as a threat to peace and a violation of international law. The direct risks of deterrence, then, are not risks to which anyone has freely consented.

V. CAN THE MERE INFLICTION OF RISKS BE A WRONGFUL ACT?

Thus far, my argument has presumed the moral impermissibility of inflicting risks (with the exceptions previously noted). The preceding sections have sought excuses for inflicting deterrent risks, and the search for

---

[20] In various places in the late 1970s, members of the Committee on the Present Danger claimed that the United States had set self-imposed limits on missile accuracy in the early 1970s, allegedly because increased accuracy was thought by those in power to be destabilizing. I have not been able to verify the existence of these self-imposed limits, and I tend to doubt that the United States ever set out deliberately to build less accurate missiles than it possibly could. If indeed the United States had built less-than-maximally accurate missiles, I am confident that the reasons for the choice were economic and not derived from any strategic doctrine. My reason for this confidence is that the United States has never formally adopted a strategic doctrine from which such decisions could be deduced.

excuses presumes that a wrong has been done. One might develop three counter-arguments to the effect that such excuses are unnecessary, since the mere infliction of risk is not a wrong. The first is that the mere infliction of risk cannot be a wrong, because no harm is done: the wrong is done only when the risk is realized. The second argument is that the mere infliction of risk is not a wrong, but only the infliction of risk that passes above a certain threshold; above the threshold we call the risk infliction "reckless," and, therefore, wrong. The third is that risk infliction as such cannot be wrong because it is impossible to do anything at all without inflicting some risks on some persons, and what cannot be avoided cannot be blamed.

These three counterarguments, however, are all unsound. It is generally acknowledged that the reckless infliction of risks is a wrong, and remains a wrong even if worst does not come to worst. (The widespread contemporary excoriation of drunk driving properly assumes that drunk driving is a wrong even if the drunk driver gets safely home.) As for the distinction between "reckless" risks and "nonreckless" risks (assuming that this distinction is different from the distinction between "negligible" and "nonnegligible" risks), it is obviously the result of social convention; in tort cases, this is a matter to be decided by juries, with some small guidance by the judge regarding precedents. Since there is no substantial equivalent to domestic tort law in the relations of nations, there is no established convention that separates reckless risks from nonreckless risks. But if reckless risks cannot be excused when they produce no harm, the argument that risks as such are excusable *because* they do no harm must be rejected.

But it is the third argument, the argument from unavoidability, that deserves the most consideration. The argument from unavoidability is *not* an argument that *nuclear* risks are unavoidable. The United States has the power to avoid inflicting nuclear risks simply by giving up its nuclear weapons. The argument is that no nation can avoid inflicting *some* risks on other nations, and that the United States has chosen to make these risks nuclear risks.

Stated this way, the argument from unavoidability is rather like Charles Fried's argument for a "risk pool," raised to the level of nations. In 1970, Fried suggested that societies, recognizing that social life cannot proceed without some infliction of risks on innocent bystanders, subliminally decide on some total of risk as socially tolerable. From this "risk pool," individuals draw allotments of permissible risk.[21] Fried did not generalize his notion of a "risk pool" to international affairs, but it is clear that if the living of normal individual lives inevitably generates risks, the living out of a normal national life might generate risks for other nations as well: factories in England may

---

[21] Charles Fried, *An Anatomy Of Value* (Cambridge, MA: Harvard University Press, 1970),

cause acid rain in Germany, and so forth. Are the risks of nuclear deterrence legitimate American withdrawals from an international "risk pool"?

For three reasons, it seems to me that the sort of risk imposed by American nuclear deterrence could not qualify as a morally acceptable withdrawal. First, the United States has *already* made numerous withdrawals from the international risk pool. The United States was the first to develop nuclear weapons, the first to use them in war, the first to explode a thermonuclear device, the first to develop a strategic delivery capacity, the first to deploy MIRV, and so forth. It is difficult to find risks *accepted* by the United States to compensate for all these impositions since 1945. And it is hardly sensible to postulate a "risk pool" which extends infinite credit to a nation that never stoops to make a deposit.[22] Second, the notion of a "risk pool" implies a certain reciprocity; each member of the pool inflicts risks on others and accepts risks from others. But the risks of nuclear deterrence are special, and only other nuclear powers can reciprocate. As I have already noted, the United States has taken many precautions to prevent the imposition of nuclear risks by nations that do not have nuclear weapons but might wish to acquire them. Third, it seems wrong to compare the risks individuals inflict on each other in a highly industrialized society with the risks contemporary nations must "unavoidably" inflict on each other. Certainly, there are many nations in the world which inflict few risks on their neighbors, and there could be many more if national governments set a high priority on the mitigation of risks. In particular, the risks of nuclear deterrence imposed by the United States (and other nuclear nations) on nonnuclear nations have been extraordinary risks, far beyond anything in the previous historical experience of nations. In magnitude, they would swamp any pool constructed to contain them. Aside from nuclear risks, those risks that do present problems (e.g., the risks of acid rain) can and should be rectified by a proper system of international tort action, not by acquiescence to some vaguely specified level of acceptable risk. Whatever validity there might be in Fried's notion of a social "risk pool," it breaks down generally

---

[22] I reject as frivolous the suggestion that the American contribution to the "risk pool" consists in its decision since 1945 not to wage preventive war with opposing superpowers. True, the United States contemplated preventive war with the Soviet Union in 1948 and 1954, and with China in 1964, but in all three cases the dominant reasons for deciding not to launch preventive wars were military, not moral. Even if the reasons had been moral, to argue that the United States has contributed to international safety by not launching preventive wars is like saying that a driver makes a positive contribution to public safety by not driving drunk. But not driving drunk is a moral duty, and one cannot claim special credit for doing what one is required to do. (For the preventive war of 1948, suggested by Bertrand Russell and others, see D. Lackey, "Russell's Contribution to the Study of Nuclear Weapons Policy," *Russell*, vol. 5 (Spring 1985); for 1954, see David Alan Rosenberg, "The Origins of Overkill," *International Security*, vol. 6 (Spring 1983), pp.3–71; for 1964, see Daniel Ellsberg, "A Call to Mutiny," E.P. Thomson, ed., *Protest and Survive* (New York: Monthly Review Press, 1981.

for the intercourse of nations and specifically for the risks of nuclear deterrence.

VI. BRIDGING THE GAP BETWEEN POSSIBLE AND ACTUAL HARMS: THE PRINCIPLE OF PARALLELISM

The risks of deterrence, then, cannot be dismissed as negligible, voluntary, or unavoidable. But I have characterized deterrent risks as an attempt to reduce the risks of first strikes on the United States by increasing the risks of second strikes on opponents. Can we justify the increase in one risk by the decrease in another?

For the utilitarian, this is a simple problem. If the increased risk is smaller than the decreased risk, the increase is justified. But the utilitarian calculation is controversial, and I will not rely on it in this essay.

We might make our judgment contingent upon how things turn out. If worst does not come to worst, then we might say that the risks of deterrence are justified. But this is not a good approach. We want our moral system to tell us which policy to choose; we want it to tell us if we are morally required to accept the risks of disarmament or morally permitted to inflict the risks of deterrence. If we must wait to see how things turn out, our moral system necessarily fails to guide our acts and choices.

What we need is some concept or principle that bridges the gap between acts risked and acts done. In the case of risks of death, one candidate might be the concept of a "statistical death," which is any combination of probable and actual deaths equal to 1. For example, we could construe the creation of a 10 percent risk of 100 deaths as "causing 10 statistical deaths," and so forth. We then might go on to say that, from the moral point of view, a statistical death is equal in disvalue to an actual death, and that any policy which sacrifices X number of statistical lives could only be permissible if it were permissible to take X actual lives in pursuit of the policy, and so forth.

I feel great sympathy for the suggested equivalence of statistical deaths and actual deaths. At the same time, I have discovered that most people (that is, at least, most people in the audiences to whom I deliver talks on the subject of nuclear war) vehemently reject the equivalance of statistical deaths and actual deaths. I have yet to find an audience of which a substantial fraction believes that it is as morally culpable to inflict a one percent risk of death on 100 persons as it is to inflict a 100 percent risk of death on one person, even if it is carefully explained that all other factors – especially the factor of intent – are equal. ("If you inflict a 100 percent risk of death on someone, you have a corpse on your hands," someone always says, "but if you inflict a one percent risk of death, you have good odds that no one will be hurt.") I have suggested to these audiences that they are not paying sufficient attention to the differences between the size of the losses in the two cases, and that they are not taking the one percent probability of the loss of 100 lives seriously, perhaps even treating a one percent chance as "negligible," as really no larger than "one in a million." But my efforts have not met with success.[23]

Fortunately, for the moral evaluation of the risks of nuclear weapons policies, we do not have to assume any equivalence of statistical deaths and actual deaths. Since worst has not come to worst and there has been no nuclear war, the risks of deterrence have only taken statistical lives, not actual lives. Likewise, unilateral nuclear disarmament has not taken any actual lives; we need only consider its cost in statistical lives if, *per impossibile*, it were ever implemented. Thus, we are considering statistical lives versus statistical lives or, more precisely, the taking of certain statistical lives *by* the United States versus the taking of certain statistical lives *in* the United States. What we need is not a bridge principle connecting actual lives with statistical lives, but a bridge principle connecting moral views about the taking of actual lives with moral views about the taking of statistical lives. The correct bridge principle, I suggest, is this:

> It is morally permissible to take X statistical lives in order to save Y statistical lives in circumstances C if, and only if, it is morally permissible to take X actual lives in order to save Y actual lives in circumstances C.

Notice that this bridge principle makes no attempt to equate actual and statistical life. But it insists that the moral principles used to assess trade-offs between some *statistical* lives and others should be the same moral principles as are used to assess trade-offs between some *actual* lives and others. Because this principle insists on parallelism between the moral structure of the actual and the moral structure of the possible, we might call it the *Principle of Parallelism*. According to this principle, it is morally permissible to reduce the risk of a Soviet first strike by increasing the risk of an

[23] To see the equivalence of a 100 percent chance of one death and a one percent chance of 100 deaths, suppose that you are in a group of 100 people confronted by a sadistic dictator who presents the group with the following options: (a) everyone's name will be put in a hat; one name will be drawn out, and that person will be executed; or (b) the numbers 0 to 99 will be written on slips of paper and put in a hat, and if the number 54 is drawn all 100 people in the group will be executed. From the prudential standpoint, there is little to choose between (a) and (b). Each gives you a one percent chance of being killed. For discussions of actual versus statistical lives, see Fried, "An Anatomy of Value," pp.207–210; and Thomas Schelling, "The Life You Save May Be Your Own," T. Schelling, ed., *Choice and Consequence*, (Cambridge, MA: Harvard University Press, 1974), pp.113–146.

American second strike if, and only if, it would be permissible in similar circumstances to kill a certain number of Russians in order to save a certain number of Americans.

VII. APPLYING THE PRINCIPLE OF PARALLELISM

If the principle of parallelism is correct, then the problem of assessing nuclear deterrence reduces to the more familiar problem of assessing the taking of lives in order to save lives. We proceed as follows: we consider circumstances C in which, at least according to moral rule R, it is permissible to take lives in order to save lives. Then we ask whether these circumstances are similar, in the morally relevent respects, to the circumstances in which the United States practices deterrence. If the circumstances are similar, then the risks of deterrence are permissible, provided that R is acceptable. We will consider six candidates for circumstances C.

(a) All those except strict pacifists believe that it is permissible to take a life to save a life, if the circumstances constitute "self-defense," and many people do believe that nuclear deterrence is a kind of self-defense. But the circumstances of deterrence are not similar to the circumstances of self-defense. In the case of justified self-defense, the victim must (i) have good reason to believe that his life and limb are in immediate peril, (ii) have done nothing to provoke the attack to which he is subjected, and (iii) use deadly force only against those who cause the threat to his life and limb. American nuclear deterrence fails as self-defense on all three counts. First, the United States is not in immediate peril of Soviet attack, nor would it be if it gave up its nuclear weapons. (Not even the hardiest Russian can eat radioactive wheat!) Second, it could be argued that the threat emanating from the Soviet Union is a threat largely provoked by the United States. The United States had nuclear weapons when the Soviet Union had none, and we are now aware of numerous plans for the use of those weapons against the Soviet Union during the period when the Soviets had no capacity to inflict a nuclear strike on the United States.[24] Third, the risks of deterrence fall on innocent bystanders as well as potential aggressors: the innocent people of the nonnuclear nations who might be enveloped in a nuclear winter caused by an American second strike; and, for that matter, the innocent people in the Soviet Union who have no say in what threats the Soviet leadership makes or

[24] Good sources for early American nuclear war-fighting plans are Anthony Cave Brown, *Dropshot: the [1949] United States Plan for War with the Soviet Union in 1957* (New York: Dial Press, 1978); David Alan Rosenberg, "A Smoking Radiating Ruin at the End of Two Hours, *International Security*, vol. 4 (Winter 1981), pp.3–38; Rosenberg, "The Origins of Overkill;" and Desmond Ball, *Targeting for Strategic Deterrence* (London: Institute for Strategic Studies, 1983).

does not make vis-à-vis the United States. Directing deterrent risks at these people is the statistical equivalent of shooting through an innocent bystander to get at a gunman who is threatening one's life, and shooting bystanders never qualifies as self-defense.

(b) It is sometimes suggested that it is morally permissible to take a life in order to save a life, if the life taken is "already threatened with death."[25] For example, most people and even many Catholics believe that in the case of life-threatening pregnancy it is permissible to kill the fetus to save the mother, if the fetus is sure to die whether an abortion is performed or not. From the Principle of Parallellism, it follows that it is permissible to inflict deterrent risks on people in other nations, provided that they will be threatened with deterrent risks regardless of what the United States does. But it would be difficult to argue that other nations would experience the same deterrent risks even if the United States gave up nuclear weapons. True, even if the United States gave up its weapons, there would be nuclear weapons and deterrent risks. But obviously the level of risk would be different, and different populations would be targets of the risk, or more susceptible to the long-term effects of nuclear explosions. Different statistical lives would be at stake, and it could not be said of any particular person that the presence or absence of American nuclear weapons made no difference to the chances that he would die from nuclear explosions.

(c) Defenders of traditional Catholic moral theology believe that it is permissible to kill one innocent person in order to save other innocent persons provided that (i) at least some innocent lives are saved on balance, (ii) the death of the innocent persons is not desired as an end, and (iii) the death of the innocent person is not a means by which a desired end is obtained.[26] Given this *principle of double effect*, plus the Principle of Parallellism, nuclear deterrence would be morally justified if it saved statistical lives on balance, provided that the taking of statistical lives is not desired as an end and provided that the taking of statistical lives is not a means by which a desired end is obtained. Let us assume, contrary to my argument in "Missiles and Morals," that nuclear deterrence saves statistical lives on balance, and let us assume further that the risks of deterrence inflicted on innocent parties are not desired as ends of American policy. It would still be the case that the taking of statistical lives is the means by which American ends are obtained because, if the lives of Soviet citizens were not placed at risk, the chance of a Soviet first strike against the United States would not be reduced.

[25] See, for example, James A. Montmarquet, "On Doing Good: the Right way and the Wrong Way," *Journal of Philosophy*, vol. 79 (August 1982), p.170.
[26] See, for example, the article "Double Effect, Principle of" by F.J. O'Connell in the *New Catholic Encyclopedia*; and J.T. Mangan, "An Historical Analysis of the Principle of Double Effect" *Theological Studies*, vol. 10 (1949).

Against this, it might be contested that the United States does not seek to endanger innocent people in the Soviet Union, that since McNamara's Ann Arbor speech in 1962 the United States has desired to target Soviet military installations rather than the civilian population, that the Schlesinger reforms of 1974 placed civilian population centers on "withold" in American targeting plans, and that the Reagan administration has reaffirmed that it is not American policy to target cities "as such."[27] But all that these repeated commitments to "counterforce" rather than "countervalue" targeting show is that the risk of killing Soviet civilians is not a desired end of American policy. They do not show that the risk of killing Soviet civilians is not a means to the achievement of American ends. The primary end of American deterrent policy is a reduction in the probability of a Soviet first strike. It so happens that the possession by America of strategic weapons puts the Soviet population at risk, and it so happens that putting the Soviet population at risk from an American second strike reduces (so the story goes) the chance of a Soviet first strike. This makes the risk to Soviet civilians a means to an American end, even if it is a means the existence of which the United States happens to regret.

(d) Few people are willing to grant that it is permissible to kill whenever killing will produce a net balance of lives saved, for example, when killing 99 persons will save 100 others. But the majority of people reverse themselves if the net balance of lives saved is great enough. Most of my students, for example, think that it is morally permissible to kill an innocent human being if killing him is the only way, and a sure way, to save 10,000 other innocent people. (10,000 seems to be the "break point:" there is considerable wavering as to whether it is permissible to kill 1 to save 1,000, and most reject the proposition that it is permissible to kill 1 to save 100.) Thus, if deterrence takes only a small number of statistical lives while saving a great number of statistical lives, then, by the Principle of Parallellism, deterrence would be morally justified. But, as I have indicated, it is controversial whether or not deterrence saves *any* statistical lives on balance, and I doubt if even the most vigorous supporters of the present system of deterrence could marshall any evidence to show that deterrence saves statistical lives at a ratio of 100 to 1, much less anything like 10,000 to 1.

(e) In my discussions of nuclear weapons policies with people in or near the national security establishment, I have found that they often infer the permissibility of deterrence from the obligatoriness of deterrence, and the

---

[27] For McNamara's position, see Morton Halperin, "The No-Cities Strategy," *New Republic*, (8 October 1962), and W.W. Kaufman, *The McNamara Strategy* (New York: Harper and Row, 1964). For Schlesinger's position, see Desmond Ball, *Targeting for Strategic Deterrence*. For targeting policy in the Reagan era, see letter by (then) National Security Advisor William Clark to the National Council of Catholic Bishops, reprinted in *Origins*, vol. 8 (October 1982).

obligatoriness of deterrence from the special duty of American leaders to "preserve, protect, and defend" the security of the United States. Thus, if the Principle of Parallelism indicates that practicing deterrence is like killing Russians to save Americans, the argument is that American leaders have a special moral duty to save Americans, even if the only way to save them is by killing Russians. (Some of the more warm-blooded advocates of this view have said to me that it is a moral duty of American leaders to kill 100 Russians to save 1 American, if that is the only way that the American can be saved.)

Now, I agree that, given a choice between saving some Americans and saving some Russians, there would be something remiss in American leaders if they preferred to save the Russians, even if the number of Russians saved was greater than the number of Americans left to die. But the decision represented by nuclear deterrence is not a decision to save one group rather than another; it is a decision to kill one group in order to save a different group, and this is an entirely different moral situation, at least from the deontological point of view.[28] If we bluntly describe the killing of Russians as murder by the United States and the killing of Americans as murder by the Soviet Union, then deterrence is the policy of murdering Russians in order to prevent the murder of Americans. It is a standard feature of deontological systems that it is not permissible to commit murder to prevent murder, nor to commit murder to prevent a greater number of murders. For it is part of the deontological thrust in moral thinking that there are agent-centered restrictions, for example, that each moral agent must take special pains that *he* not be a murderer, even if by so doing he could prevent others from becoming murderers. Since this is a core feature of deontological thinking, it cannot be overwhelmed by an agent-centered permission which justifies Americans preferring the welfare of Americans to that of Russians (or Russians preferring the welfare of Russians to that of Americans). Given the Principle of Parallellism, deterrence make murderers of us; but if we disarm, we let murder be done. For deontologists, this is not a difficult moral choice.

(f) In her analysis of deadly risks, Judith Thomson has suggested that it is impermissible to *create* a deadly risk, but permissible to *deflect* a deadly risk once it has already been created.[29] If a trolley is running loose down a track, it is, according to Thomson, morally permissible to switch the trolley on to a siding on which two people are standing rather than let it continue along the

[28] I take it that treating the distinction between killing and failing to save from death as morally relevant is an essential part of the deontological moral point of view, just as refusing to recognize the moral relevance of the distinction is an essential part of utilitarian morality. The complexities of this problem are canvassed in the articles collected in Bonnie Steinbock, ed., *Killing and Letting Die* (Albany, NY: SUNY Press, 1981.

[29] Judith Thomson, "Killing, Letting Die, and the Trolley Problem," *The Monist*, vol. 59 (April 1975).

main line on which five people are standing; but it is not permissible to throw a fat person in front of the trolley to make it stop before it hits the five. Likewise, it is permissible for the American President to use a magnetic tractor beam to deflect a Soviet missile heading for New York so that it lands on Worcester, Massachusetts, but it is not permissible for the President to explode a bomb that will simultaneously destroy Worcester *and* the missile as it flies towards New York. My experiences with students and audiences considering these examples is that most people believe that it is morally worse to throw the fat man than to throw the switch and morally worse to explode the bomb than to use a tractor beam, though a substantial fraction believe that both are permissible and a substantial fraction believe that both are impermissible. Now, we might construe deterrence as the deflection of risk from the American people to the Soviet people: if we disarmed, then all the threat of nuclear annihilation falls on ourselves, whereas if we deter, at least part of the risk is deflected back on the Soviet people. If Thomson is right that risk deflection is permissible, then it follows that deterrence is permissible.

This argument for permissibility can be attacked from two angles: the premise may be false, or the analogy may be unsound. Is it really the case *on deontological grounds* that it is bad to create risks but all right to deflect them? (What if we always choose to deflect risks from whites to blacks?) And even if it is much worse to create risks, can we really decide what qualifies as "risk deflection" and what qualifies as "risk creation?" It does seem to be splitting hairs to say that it is permissible to solve the problem of the runaway trolley by throwing the trolley against different people but not permissible to solve the problem by throwing different people against the trolley. At best, it seems that risk-deflection is permissible only in those cases in which it is already determined that the risk will be actualized, but not yet decided who the victims of the actualized risk will be. In that case, the risk deflector who chooses the victims of the risk is not choosing between killing some or failing to save others, but between saving some potential victims or saving some other potential victims.[30] But the risks of deterrence are not risks that we can now say are sure to be actualized.

Thus, it is the appropriateness of the deflection analogy which is the weak spot in this defense of deterrence. Is it really the case that the construction of the American apparatus of deterrence merely deflects Soviet risks rather than creating risks of its own? Thomson provides no analysis of the

---

[30] Perhaps another reason why people are more sympathetic to what they take to be risk deflection than they are to what they take to be risk creation, is that they assume that risk creation brings more evil into the world than risk deflection. But this assumption is false since, if risk deflection is permissible at all, it should be just as permissible to shift the risk from a group of two to a group of five as to shift it from a group of five to a group of two.

difference between "creating" and "deflecting," and it seems intuitively clear that if an American missile launched by the free decision of an American leader lands on a Soviet target, the risk to the target presented by that missile was a risk created by the missile and born in the U.S.A. In both the tractor beam case and the switched trolley case, what was deflected was a physical object, and without a physical object it is difficult to speak of deflection or to trace the difference between the deflection of risk and the creation of risk.

VIII. EXOTIC FORMS OF DETERRENCE

The reason that the standard forms of deterrence cannot count as risk deflection is that, with standard deterrence, American hardware lands on (or, at least, threatens) the Soviet Union. For the purpose of moral analysis, it is interesting to consider forms of deterrence which eliminate this feature. Suppose that the President did possess a tractor beam like the one Thomson describes or, better still, suppose that the United States built a defensive shield that invariably bounced incoming missiles back to their point of origin. And suppose, furthermore, that after building the shield the United States dismantled all of its offensive missiles. I think that almost everyone would agree that it would be morally permissible for the United States to erect such a shield, even if, due to population distribution and wind patterns, more people would be killed in the attacking country by the operation of the shield than would be killed if the United States allowed an attack to penetrate its defenses.[31] Were Soviet leaders (dismissing talk about the shield as imperialist propaganda) to launch an attack on the United States, responsibility for the resulting destruction in the Soviet Union would clearly fall on their heads, not on the American leaders who chose to erect the shield. This example shows that there is no *a priori* deontological argument against nuclear deterrence; there are only deontological arguments against some forms of deterrence. Unfortunately, the deontological arguments apply to the form of deterrence that is currently in force, the kind that does not bounce Soviet missiles back on the Soviets but, instead, commits the United States to launching its own missiles. It also applies to all systems of nuclear deterrence that might be constructed in the near or middle future.

[31] Interestingly, one of the few arguments against erecting the shield must be conceded by those who believe that deterrence is *obligatory*. If the United States retained an offensive nuclear capacity, then it would be wrong to erect the shield because it would deprive the Soviet Union of its deterrent capacity and prevent the Soviet leaders from doing what (according to the argument) is morally required.

IX. WHY PEOPLE IGNORE DETERRENT RISKS

It is more than obvious that the 25,000 or so nuclear weapons and the various delivery systems possessed by the United States pose substantial risks to people in the world. A large portion of the total of risk is the risk of deterrence: the risk caused specifically by the attempt to forestall a first strike with threats of a second strike. It is interesting and puzzling that when most people worry about nuclear war, they do not worry about the risk of deterrence as such, but focus instead on the risk that deterrence will break down and that the United States will be attacked by Soviet missiles. Similarly, the experts and strategists of the nuclear priesthood rarely consider the risk of deterrence as such, but conentrate instead on the relative risks of different forms of deterrence. Most consider the risks of current deterrence policy to be small and morally tolerable. I have often wondered how Americans can be so cavalier about the risks of deterrence, even given the mentally appealing feature that these risks are principally imposed on non-Americans. I conjecture that many find these risks morally tolerable because they resemble in size some of the life-threatening risks that their fellow Americans inflict on each other, risks that are sanctioned and mitigated by American law and custom. But there is a significant difference between the risks that people in a single society inflict on each other (risks the permissibility of which is certified by a social contract) and the risks that one society inflicts on the rest. Among societies, there is no social contract, and the risks that one society inflicts on another are inflicted without justification or consent.

If the present forms of deterrence are morally unacceptable, what nuclear weapons policy should the United States adopt? In particular, if deterrence is unacceptable, is it morally obligatory for the United States to develop strategic defenses along "Star Wars" lines? All that I can say here is "not necessarily." The moral analysis of strategic defense is complicated, and needs an article all its own. Enough has been said here, however, to show that if we are moral beings, we cannot rest easy with the nuclear *status quo*.

Philosophy, Baruch College and the Graduate Center,
City University of New York

Social Philosophy & Policy 3:1 Autumn 1985 ISSN 0265–0525 $2.00

NO WAR WITHOUT DICTATORSHIP, NO PEACE WITHOUT DEMOCRACY:
FOREIGN POLICY AS DOMESTIC POLITICS

AARON WILDAVSKY

I wish to consider the possibility that a good part of the opposition to the main lines of American foreign policy is based on deep-seated objections to the political and economic systems of the United States. This is not to say that existing policy is necessarily wise or that there may not be good and sufficient reasons for wishing to change it. Indeed, at any time and place, the United States might well be overestimating the threat from the Soviet Union or using too much force. What I wish to suggest is that across-the-board criticism of American policy as inherently aggressive and repressive, regardless of circumstance – a litany of criticism so constant that it does not alert us to the need for explanation – has a structural basis in the rise of a political culture that is opposed to existing authority.

To the extent that this criticism is structural, that is, inherent in domestic politics, the problem of fashioning foreign policies that can obtain widespread support is much more difficult than it is commonly perceived to be. For if the objection is to American ways of life and, therefore, "to the government for which it stands," only a transformation of power relationships at home, together with a vast redistribution of economic resources, would satisfy these critics. If the objection is not only to what we do but, more fundamentally, to who we are, looking to changes in foreign policy to shore up domestic support is radically to confuse the causal connections and, therefore, the order of priorities. Unless or until they face an overwhelming external threat, how people wish to live with one another must take precedence over how they relate to "foreigners." Foreign policy is forged at home.

SUSPICION OF AMERICAN MOTIVES

It is a commonplace to observe that foreign policy depends on domestic support. When such support declines, as it did during the war in Vietnam, the proposition becomes self-evident. However, as important as that war was (and is) in undermining governmental willingness to use troops and the credibility of its actions abroad, it has served to obfuscate the dramatic change that has taken place in the structure of American opinion in regard to foreign policy. It is worthwhile, therefore, to contrast the structure of this opinion from the end of the Second World War to the mid-1960s with what it has become afterwards, until this very day.

The lesson learned from the Second World War is that aggressive dictatorships have to be nipped in the bud before they become so dangerous and so strong that they are tempted to attack. After the war, elite opinion –interested members of Congress, the few foreign policy organizations, the press – was internationalist and interventionist (except for the most conservative Republicans). Mass opinion was uninterested or deferential. But only up to a point. When called upon to make sacrifices in remote places, viz. Korea, people were subject to rapid disenchantment.

Presidents and secretaries of state found the domestic scene loosely organized. Aside from Jews on Israel, the Irish on Ireland, and Catholics on the Papacy, the citizenry exhibited few strong commitments in the area of foreign policy. (Foreign economic policy was another matter, but it was the province of specialists and a few banks and corporations, which carried out their functions largely out of sight of the general public. After initial hesitation on the part of some Republicans, congressional leadership remained supportive of whatever foreign policy the executive branch set. There was, in a phrase, lots of leeway.

Gaining domestic support for foreign policy was always necessary, sometimes problematic, but rarely impossible. In the main, the difficulties were out there – a recalcitrant world – not in here – a generally pliable domestic opinion. Contrasted with the densely filled territory of domestic policy, the foreign scene was largely unoccupied. That is why presidents did so much better in gaining congressional support for their foreign (as opposed to domestic) initiatives; they had very few competitors.[1]

In sum, if foreign policy was successful abroad, it generated little trouble at home. Today, trouble at home precedes performance abroad.

What happened? Were Vietnam the explanation, we would expect the situation to have changed in the decade since the war ended. Instead, difficulty in gaining domestic support for foreign policy initiatives has intensified. Tiny appropriations for opposing Leninist forces in Central America, for instance, are bitterly resisted in Congress. Mass movements, e.g., Ground Zero, occur to force changes in policy. The sense that governmental officials cannot be trusted is pervasive.

One way of describing what has happened is to say that, while mass

---

[1] See Aaron Wildavsky, "The Two Presidencies," *Transaction*, vol. 4 (December 1966), pp.7–14.

opinion is slightly more skeptical, elite opinion has turned against the authorities who are formally in charge of foreign policy. Where before the formal decision makers had the benefit of the doubt, now they are guilty until proven innocent. The accusations against them, moreover, are of a single kind: they are too war-like. They overestimate the danger of communism; they use too much force; they spend too much on defense. It is America as well as the Soviet Union that poses a major threat to peace.

A related difference between the 1950s and the 1970s and 80s lies in what is missing. In the earlier times, a politician could be for welfare *and* for warfare. Henry Jackson and Hubert Humphrey exemplified the dual commitment to a strong defense and to provision for those in need. No longer is this true. There must be prominent politicians today who publicly espouse this dualism, but I cannot think of any. Indeed, the six major candidates for the Democratic Party presidential nomination in the 1984 election all specified conditions – completely containable consequences, impeccable moral character, Soviet acquiesence, etc. – for armed intervention that could never be met. And the Democrats, considering their representation in state government and Congress, and the loyalties of citizens, are still the majority party in the United States. What is more, Secretary of Defense Casper Weinberger's specification of the conditions required to justify military intervention is almost as stringent. The military does not want to fight without the full support that politicians and populace are now unwilling to give them.

ATTRIBUTING BENIGN INTENT TO THE SOVIET UNION

Suspicion of American motives is only one part of the theme: attributing benign intent to the Soviet Union is another. Their vast arms build-up is argued away as defensive; presumably, the more weapons they employ, the greater their fear of being attacked. The continuing Soviet invasion of Afghanistan is, amazingly, attributed to fear of encirclement. (After all, if a nation keeps expanding, it is bound to get closer to others who worry about it.) The entire Soviet military posture is rationalized as proportionate to the threats it faces, even though no such case can reasonably be made.

The disproportion of the Soviet defense effort to the military dangers it faces has not received sufficient attention. Instead, the usual task of relating resources to objectives in order to assess the reasonableness of a policy – the fit between means and ends – has been short-circuited by the use of ready-made explanations. The Soviets are fearful; they are paranoid. The Second World War, the allied expeditionary forces after the First World War, HISTORY, in short, is responsible for what is called "defensive" Soviet behavior. The trouble is that any Soviet behavior, including launching military attacks on those it deems its adversaries, fits this ample rationale. However disproportionate Soviet behavior may appear in the circumstances, it can be rationalized by invoking this defensiveness. What else, given Soviet history, could you expect?

But let us pierce this easy rationalization and examine the facts. If Soviet concern is supposed to be with military attack by the Peoples Republic of China, there is no need for the Soviets to keep two million troops on their border. The PRC is so weak compared to the Soviet Union – hopelessly outclassed in nuclear weapons, badly under-armed in conventional forces – that it would be suicidal for the PRC to launch an attack.

Who believes that any or all of the nations of Western Europe, with or without American troops, are likely to invade Eastern Europe or the Soviet Union? Who believes that any Eastern European nation, alone or in concert with others, will attack the Soviet Union? Why, then, does the U.S.S.R. keep so many troops (two million by current estimates[2]) on Western borders? Were there such a thing as a negative probability, I would assign a negative value to the likelihood that any nation will invade the U.S.S.R. Would the reader argue otherwise? How, then, is Soviet behavior to be explained?

The Kuril Islands, formerly part of Japan, were occupied by the Soviet Union at the end of the Second World War. The Soviets now have them fortified with naval facilities. Naturally, Japan would like them back. The U.S.S.R. is adamantly opposed. It threatens the Japanese with dreadful retaliation if they interfere with Soviet plans. Consequently, the U.S.S.R. faces an angry Japanese government when it could otherwise have had amicable relations. If the Soviets had relented on the islands, it would have been more difficult to convince the Japanese to rearm.

Nor is this all. The Soviet Union claims, quite rightly, that the Pershing missiles now placed in Western Europe significantly reduce the time required for nuclear explosives to reach its soil. While the presence of the Pershings does not enhance American defense beyond what is provided by its already substantial forces, it threatens the Soviets. Why, then, did they undertake the action – the deployment of their SS–20 multiple warhead missiles – that precipitated this predictable allied response?

There is little doubt in my mind that unilateral actions by the U.S.S.R., e.g., reduction of the number of conventional and nuclear weapons in Eastern Europe, could compel a reduction of defensive activities – including the deployment of the Pershings – in Western Europe. Why, then, does the Soviet Union, which claims to fear foreign attack, not take action reasonably calculated to achieve the objectives it espouses? Even if the SS–20s could

[2] International Institute for Strategic Studies, *The Military Balance*, 1984–1985, pp.18–19.

reasonably be regarded as replacements for older weapons, so that the U.S. need not have introduced the Pershings in response (as opponents of deployment claim) this still would not explain why the U.S.S.R. does not act in its own interest, i.e., to reduce the threat rather than to increase it. And even if the Soviet Union hoped that adverse public reaction would prohibit the placement of these missiles, why, once rebuffed, do they keep theirs in place when withdrawal could lead the Pershings to depart?

It is not one of these instances of Soviet overreaction that is troublesome but, rather, all of them taken together. Apparently, the Soviet Union is not expected to give a sensible accounting of its own actions. The nations of the democratic West do not seem to believe they are entitled to be given good reasons for Soviet behavior. Although they know that they have to deal with Soviet behavior, the nations of the West implicitly agree either to accept at face value Soviet explanations (i.e., that they are acting defensively) or to resign themselves to perpetual puzzlement over the mismatch between Soviet military resources and the stated objectives of Soviet foreign policy. This is bad for both sides. The Soviets are not required to give credible reasons for their behavior, and Western nations are not able to make sense of those they do give.

THE BEST CASE FOR THE U.S.S.R.
THE WORST CASE FOR THE U.S.A.

I maintain that Soviet military preparations are excessive. To argue otherwise is to argue that the force put in place by the Soviets is reasonably related to the threat they face. Who will stand up and say that China, Japan, or the Western and Eastern European nations pose military threats to the U.S.S.R.?

In an article in the May 1984 issue of *Commentary*, Owen Harries traces the "deeper roots" of such ("best case") thinking to the universalistic liberal tradition that denies "the reality of conflict in the name of a fundamental harmony of interest. . . ." Since "there are no real intractable conflicts of interest," it follows that enmity among nations "is illusory and unnecessary."[3]

But explaining one set of ideas by another separates them from their social context, as if they existed apart from the people who believed them. By asking a different kind of question, the tenacity with which these ideas are held and the immense challenge they pose to American foreign policy will become apparent. What sort of people, sharing which values and justifying what kind of practices, would act on these beliefs in order to shore up their way of life and tear down their opponents?

[3] Owen Harries, "Best-Case Thinking," *Commentary*, vol. 77 (May 1984), pp.23–28.

Does anybody actually believe in the universal harmony of interests? I think not. The idea is patently wrong-headed. In fact, the very people who argue the best-case thesis in foreign policy also argue the worst-case thesis in domestic policy. Harmony in domestic policy, they claim, is the ideology of the oppressor. There are irreconcilable conflicts between the haves and have-nots, conflicts which cannot be compromised but only overcome by struggle. Foreign policy, apparently, is different. Why?

No reasonable person believes in a worst case or a best case all the time in regard to everything. In fact, many of the people who hold a best-case belief about the Soviet Union hold a worst-case belief about capitalism. Indeed, I cannot think of a single committed environmentalist who is also a proponent of a strong national defense, or *vice versa*. There must be some, but they are few and far between.

Now I have a narrower and more interesting question to ask. Who sees harmony in international affairs and hostility in domestic politics? What else do the people believe who claim that the United States government vastly overstates the enmity of the Soviet Union? Many of these same people form the nucleus of other social movements borne out of frustration with the perceived injustice of their fellow citizens – the civil rights movement, the women's movement, the movements for children's rights, animal rights, the rights of the elderly, gay rights, and on and on.[4] Whereas a number of these movements began as proponents of equality of opportunity, they have rapidly turned into exponents of equality of condition.[5]

When I grew up, children could never do enough for their parents; now all we hear about is child abuse and the obvious need for the state to intervene to prevent parents from doing terrible things to their children. And this is not the only example of the belief in the domestic disharmony of interests;

[4] See Michael P. Hornsby-Smith and Elizabeth S. Cordingley, "Catholic Elites: A Study of the Delegates to the National Pastoral Congress," *Studies in English Catholicism No. 1*, Occasional Paper No. 3, Dept. of Sociology, University of Surrey; Michael Walzer, *The Revolution of the Saints: A Study in the Origins of Radical Politics* (Cambridge MA: Harvard University Press, 1965); James H. Kuklinski, Daniel S. Metlay, and W.D. Kay, "Citizen Knowledge and Choices on the Complex Issue of Nuclear Energy," *American Journal of Political Science*, vol. 26 (November 1982), pp.615–642; Stanley Rothman and S. Robert Lichter, "The Nuclear Energy Debate: Scientists, the Media, and the Public," *Public Opinion* (August/September 1982), pp.47–52; Robert Putnam, "Two Types of Democrats," Joel D. Aberbach, Robert D. Putnam, and Bert A. Rochman, eds., *Bureaucrats and Politicians in Western Democracies* (Cambridge, MA: Harvard University Press, 1981); Seymour Martin Lipset, "Why No Socialism in the United States?", Seweryn Bialer and Sophia Sluzar, eds., *Sources of Contemporary Radicalism* (Boulder, CO: Westview Press, 1977); Paul Hollander, "Reflections on Anti-Americanism in our Times," Hollander, eds., *The Many Faces of Socialism* (New Brunswick, NJ: Transaction Books, 1983); and Jack L. Walker, "The Origins and Maintenance of Interest Groups in America," *The American Political Science Review*, vol. 77 (June 1983), pp.390–406.
[5] William A. Donahue, *The Politics of the ACLU* (New Brunswick, NJ. Transaction Press, 1984); and Aaron Wildavsky, "The 'Reverse Sequence' in Civil Liberties," *The Public Interest*, number 78 (Winter 1985), pp.32–42.

virtually every identifiable subgroup in American society has its lobbyists. Harmony of interests, indeed!

How can harmony abroad be reconciled with fractiousness at home? The critics of America believe that the perpetrators of intolerable, unconscionable inequalities at home justify their behavior by invoking specious threats from far away places. It is not that they think the Soviet system is benevolent or that it provides a better way of life. They are not that dumb; they are not dumb at all. Nor are they, for the most part, Marxists. It is, rather, that they care almost exclusively about how people live with each other in the U.S., not in the U.S.S.R. It is their passion for equality of condition and their rage at inequality that leads them to a portrayal of an international heaven spoiled by people bent on maintaining a domestic hell. Acknowledging a Soviet threat would mean agreeing that: (a) the social system of the United States is worth defending; (b) other systems are worse; and (c) a morally legitimate government has the right to divert resources from domestic (i.e., egalitarian) to military (i.e., inegalitarian) purposes.

The debate throughout the Reagan Administration over whether the deficit should be reduced by cutting defense or domestic programs is instructive. To the extent that sacrifices are imposed, of course, sharing them among the beneficiaries of government programs makes sense. When civilian pensions are reduced, for instance, military pensions should follow suit. But there is more to it. Not only is defense treated as just another domestic special interest (as opposed to a *common* interest), it is also placed in a zero-sum relationship to welfare programs.

Precisely because those who adopt the best-case thesis abroad do so to support a vision of the worst-case at home, we should not be surprised at the tenacity with which they hold on to optimistic views of Soviet behavior. People who see themselves threatened by mobilization for war, under the aegis of a military hierarchy and capitalist competition run rampant, are not likely to accept the hypothesis that there is a genuine threat, at least not as long as there is some other explanation that will leave intact their dream of the good (i.e., egalitarian) life.

UNFAIRNESS AT HOME, EXPLOITATION ABROAD

Suppose that the United States government is, indeed, immoral (or perhaps even illegitimate) because it fails to provide social justice, understood as much greater equality of condition. (A current codeword is "fairness.") What follows from this assumption?

Unfairness at home is exported abroad as exploitation. The Third World serves as a surrogate proletariat; its poverty is a result of domination by multinational capital led by the United States. Inequalities within the United States thus spread their tentacles to the rest of the world. It follows that the United States owes redress to poorer nations, just as it owes reparations to its own poorer people. Assuming, further, a fixed limit to the world's goods (as advocates of this world-view generally do), more for arms means less for welfare. In brief, the industrial North exploits the Third World South; the United States rules the North; capitalists rule the United States. Hence, an end to inequality in the United States is necessary for social justice in the world.

Immoral does as immoral is. Any use of force by the United States is illegitimate. This perspective accounts for the exclusive emphasis by America's internal critics on negotiation for handling conflict. It also contains the answer to Secretary of State George Schultze's perplexity:

> From one side, we hear that negotiations alone are the answer. If we will only talk (the argument runs), we can have peace. If we will only talk, our differences will easily be resolved. It is as if negotiations were an end in themselves, as if the goal of American foreign policy were not primarily to protect the peace, or defend our values, or our people, or our allies, but to negotiate for its own sake.[6]

Negotiation is an end in itself, if one side is so morally tainted. Force is corrupting because it is coercive, and coercion is wrong because those doing the coercing are morally unworthy.

Now we know why arms control is so often viewed as desirable in itself, rather than as a means to an end. In much the same way, deterrence is said to depend on uncertainty about nuclear retaliation, rather than on the certainty that an aggressor will suffer defeat. Hence, America's war-fighting capability is said to be destabilizing, while its inability to carry on a nuclear exchange, except against cities and people, is considered to be stabilizing. But we have yet to understand the animus against measures that might defend the West against nuclear attack, such as anti-ballistic missiles (ABMs) or "star wars" satellites. On the face of it, ABMs are true defensive weapons, in that they cannot be used for aggressive purposes. Curiously, those who claim to speak for peace prefer the strategy of Mutual Assured Destruction (MAD), in which each of the superpowers holds the other's population hostage. Defensive measures are said to be destabilizing because they might give their possessors the idea that they could attack without being struck in return. It is all a bit Orwellian: weapons that defend against missiles are offensive and

---

[6] George Schultze, "Power and Diplomacy," address to the Veterans of Foreign Wars, Chicago, August 20, 1984 (U.S. Department of State, Bureau of Public Affairs, Current Policy No.606).

missiles that rein down destruction are defensive. What lies behind this "newspeak"?

The United States and the Soviet Union are considered to be (im)morally equivalent. They are now abstractions, divorced from behavior. If the United States would, given a momentary superiority, use its nuclear weapons against the Soviet Union, it must be restrained by fear of nuclear destruction. Here we have it: a MAD doctrine is supported because the United States is mad enough to destroy the world. Who believes this? And why?

WHO (DIS)TRUSTS AUTHORITY?

Among the various ways of life competing for power in America, three stand out most prominently: market; hierarchial; and sectarian. Only the latter, by its very definition, is distrustful of authority.

The social ideal of market cultures is self-regulation. Such systems favor bidding and bargaining in order to reduce the need for authority. They support equality of opportunity to compete in order to facilitate arrangements between consenting adults with a minimum of external interferences. They seek opportunity to be different, not equality of condition to be the same, for they recognize that the quest to directly diminish social differences would require a central, redistributive authority.

The social ideal of a hierarchial system is authority. Advocates of such a system justify inequality on grounds that specialization and division of labor enable people to live together with greater harmony and effectiveness than do alternative arrangements. Belief that hierarchy creates a caring collective, with rulers responsive to the ruled, is essential to its nature. Hence hierarchies (such as bureaucracies) are rationalized by a sacrificial ethic: the parts are supposed to sacrifice for the good of the whole.

Committed to a life of purely voluntary association, egalitarian (sometimes called sectarian) cultures reject authority. Sectarians wish to live a life without coercion or authority, a life exemplified by equality of condition. In the real world, sectarians attempt to reduce differences – between races, income levels, men and women, parents and children, teachers and students, or authorities and citizens. Translated into organizational terms, reducing differences means equalizing the status of different individuals and groups.

Let us suppose that, as often happens in life, things go wrong. Who is to blame? Sectarians blame "the system," the established authority that introduces unnatural inequality into society. Hierarchialists blame deviants who harm the collective by failing to follow its rules. Market advocates fault the individual for failing to be productive. Suppose a new development occurs. Without knowing much about it, those who identify with each political culture can guess whether its effect is to increase or decrease social distinctions, impose, avoid, or reject authority – guesses made more definitive by observing what like-minded individuals think. It does not take much, for example, for devotees of hierarchy to surmise that central financial control is better than fragmentation. Of course, people may be, and often are, mistaken. To seek is not necessarily to find a culturally rational course of action. Gramsci's would-be capitalists may try to establish hegemony over others[7] but they are often mistaken about which ideas and actions will in fact support their way of life. To be culturally rational, to support not merely one's material interest but one's preferred mode of social relationships, is the intention, but it is not always accomplished.

Consider the question of coping with external threats in the absence of definitive information, e.g., an invasion. Since motives cannot be known by any except those who have them, and even they may engage in self-deception, residual uncertainty about foreign danger cannot be resolved by anything short of experience. When we say the external threat is real and apparent, we mean there is widespread social agreement on its existence. Lacking such consensus, citizens use whatever preconceptions they have – call it theory or ideology – connecting how they would like to live (their values) with how they think the world works (the facts). The most general theories held by citizens are their political cultures. The more citizens support an existing regime, the more they will accept the desires of its leaders and be ready to pay for preparedness. If, on the other hand, they see their regime as unworthy, citizens are more likely to believe that it is a producer, rather than an alleviator of danger to national security, and hence they will not favor spending (or acting) in advance of immutable evidence: an attack.

DEFENSE AS A FUNCTION OF REGIME

Among our several political cultures, which would interpret events to support more defense spending, and which less: Hierarchialists believe in defense of the collective. Doubt about military spending implies that military experts and the civilian leadership are not trusted to appraise the situation, nor thought to be competent enough to know what to do about foreign dangers. Thus, hierarchialists are loathe to question military spending.

There is not much place for competitive individualism in war except, perhaps, for *prima donna* generals. Market cultures fear war for its disruption of trade and its subordination of individual economic motives. During wars

[7] See Raymond Geuss, *The Idea of a Critical Theory: Habermas and the Frankfurt School* (New York: Cambridge Univ. Press, 1982).

of mass mobilization, they give up their individualism in return for being
sheltered from competition. During peacetime, they grudgingly pay higher
taxes. Market regimes are reluctant warriors, especially when there is no
booty.

So long as it is in a minority, the sectarian culture is anti-military. Opposing
authority, seeing American society as the cause of immoral differences, fearing
subjugation by established institutions, egalitarians favor at most a small
volunteer army. Only by sustaining a belief that their cause is entirely
just, and their opponent's entirely evil, can they accept even minimal
subordination to authority. Hence, they respond to such unifying slogans as
"The war to end all wars," or "The war to make the world safe for
democracy," or "Unconditional surrender!".

The foreign policy of egalitarianism flows naturally from its commitment
to redistribution. First, there is redistribution from rich to poor countries.
Second, there is redistribution from defense to domestic welfare expendi-
ture. Third, there is redistribution of authority from government officials to
mass movements, from those now in power to those left out.

How, then, do egalitarians deal with Soviet aggression? By arguing it away
as a defensive response to offensive (i.e., inegalitarian) American behavior.
For it is inequalities in their own country, not outrages by others, that are
their chief concern. Since they are not in power – constituting, in their own
minds, a permanent opposition – they do what oppositions do: they oppose.

DEMOCRACY, MARXISM, AND MILITARISM

If the avoidance of nuclear war is an important moral value, we can ask
whether the egalitarian stance is well calculated to achieve that end. Here I
shall call on two bodies of research. One is the extensive corpus by Rudolph
Rummel, who demonstrates empirically that democracies do not make war
on each other. They may go to war but, if they do, there is far less violence
than when nondemocratic states engage in warfare. (Rummel, I should add,
distinguishes between democratic states based on consent and free elections,
and libertarian states that, besides being democratic, practice extensive self-
regulation. The less internally coercive a democratic government, in his
scheme, the more libertarian it is.) As he writes:

> Libertarian states have no violence between them. . . .
> *We have not had a real war between democracies in over a century and*
> *a half from 1816 to 1980. . . .*
> . . . A necessary condition of violence between two states is that at
> least one of them be partially or completely nonlibertarian. Or, to

turn this around, violence does not occur between libertarian states. Moreover, whether states are considered individually or dyadically, the less free – libertarian – a state, the more violence it engages in ... Whether having common borders or not, the less freedom in states, the more violence between them.[8]

From Rummel's powerful analysis, it is clear that democracy is the best inhibitor of violence and, conversely, that dictatorship is its greatest generator. Why?

The greater the diversity of interests that receive expression within a policy, the more each needs the other to form majority coalitions. These cross-cutting cleavages (agreeing on some issues, disagreeing on others) reduce the desire to wage war for religious or ethnic or other single-issue reasons. The more that government is involved in meeting domestic demands, the less interested it is in diverting resources to foreign affairs. And since, as Rummel says, wars involve considerable deprivation, which voters don't like, democracy restrains external aggression. The thread that runs through Rummel's substantial corpus of research is that external aggression is limited by internal nonaggression, i.e., by the consent of the governed.[9]

How, then, is the considerable armament of the United States justified? The United States is not alone in the world with the Soviet Union. Whether it wishes to be or not, America is one of the pillars in a bipolar international system. Without going into this subject, it suffices to say that as the democratic pole in an essentially anarchic world (dis)order, the United States has obligations thrust upon it that, even at a time when its people are

[8] Rudolph J. Rummel, "Libertarianism and International Violence," *The Journal of Conflict Resolution*, vol. 27 (March 1983), pp.27–71.

Wars, Democracies, and Opposing Dyads, 1816–1965[a]

	Dyads Engaged in War[a]		
Dyads	1816–1918	1919–1965	Total
Democracy vs. democracy[b]	(1)	(10)	(11)
Democracy vs. nondemocracy	37	99	136
Nondemocracy vs. nondemocracy	92	86	178
Totals	130	195	325

[a] Dyadic count based on Small and Singer (1976: 56–58)
[b] Democracy is defined by Small and Singer as "a rather crude dichotomy" based on "(a) ... periodically scheduled elections in which oposition parties were as free to run as government parties, and in which (b) at least ten percent of the adult population was allowed to vote either directly or indirectly for (c) a parliament that either controlled or enjoyed parity with the executive branch of government" (1976: 54–55). Wars represented in this row are put in parentheses because they are identified by Small and Singer as "marginal exceptions" for reasons given in note 13 of the text.

[9] Rudolph, J. Rummel, *conflict and War* (Beverly, CA: Sage Publications, 1975).

most interested in exploring their "inner space," limit the possibility of passivity. While the disinclination to attack others is part of the character of democratic society, the disinclination to defend oneself, except by the threat of mutual suicide, is something else again. The defensive posture of the United States is remarkable. For it has not merely rejected a defense of its population, or of its missiles, it has also spurned civil defense and air defense, stripping its people of even such protection as is available, and all with the purpose of proving its peaceful intentions. Resistance to President Reagan's effort to research a possible, partial defense as not merely infeasible but wrong in principle (defense is, after all, the first duty of government) suggests that the United States is not worth defending.

Next I turn to James L. Payne's "Marxism and Militarism," a careful comparison of the differential tendencies of Marxist and non-Marxist states to arm themselves.[10] His primary tool of comparison is the force ratio (the number of men under arms per capita): "Marxist regimes have a mean force ratio of over twice that of the non-Marxist countries." What happens, then, when a nation changes from non-Marxist to Marxist? "For the average non-Marxist country, . . ." Payne estimates, " this means that Marxism would more than double its force ratio." In order to keep constant a nation's history and traditions, Payne also makes "before" and "after" calculations of Marxist takeovers. He finds a four-fold increase in force levels. The policy implications, Payne argues, are profound, especially

> for those who oppose the growth of military establishments on the grounds that military forces represent a threat to peace and a waste of national resources. For example, suppose a Marxist regime comes to power in El Salvador. According to our best prediction equation, the force ratio for El Salvador under Marxist rule would be 11.0. This compares to the current (1980) force ratio of 1.7 under the non-Marxist regime. Forestalling Marxist victory in El Salvador, therefore, would avoid this sextuple increase in the Salvadorean armed forces. It is a point that opponents of militarism ought not to ignore.[11]

MARXISM AND MILITARISM GO HAND IN HAND

The war-like, militaristic character of Marxist-Leninist regimes cannot be explained, as James Payne rightly notes, by their desire for domestic repression. The police, the concentration camps, and other such devices are

[10] James L. Payne, "Marxism and Militarism," forthcoming in *Polity*.
[11] *ibid.*

more than adequate for that task. It is rather, I believe, that external militarism is the counterpart to the internal monopoly of power in these regimes. The implacable hostility of Marxist-Leninist governments to pluralism, to independent sources of domestic power, is mirrored by their determination to weaken potential foreign rivals. Marxist-Leninists cannot live with diversity. It is not so much how the United States acts, therefore, but that it exists as an independent entity that threatens the U.S.S.R.[12]

"WOULD IF COULD" OR "WON'T IF CAN"

Where does the safety of mankind reside? Is it in a monolithic political regime that would launch a nuclear attack if it thought it could do so without suffering fatal damage to itself, or in a pluralistic democracy that would not do so even if the opportunity appeared to present itself? To pose the question this way is to answer it. Yet we know that the United States is the only nation to have used nuclear weapons against a foe. We also know, however, that this use was limited to ending the war with Japan, despite the fact that the United States had a monopoly on nuclear weapons at that time. The United States did not, as it could have done, use or threaten to use these weapons to impose its will on the Soviet Union or any other nation. Under comparable conditions, there is little reason to believe that the Soviet Union would have restrained itself.

We also know (or, at least, we like to believe) that fear of reprisal prevents the Soviet Union from attacking the West. This belief, if true, is of vital importance. But that is all it can be, a hopefully well-founded belief. Life, as we are wont to say, is full of surprises.

Really, the question will not go away: can the world be secure in the face of a power that would attack if it could but (we hope) will not because it fears retaliation? Only by altering Soviet motivation from "would if it could" to "won't even if it could" can mankind be safe. And that requires, if not a democratization, then at least a pluralization of the Soviet Union, so that its inability to tolerate variety will not tempt it to destroy all differences in the world.

I have been arguing that external constraints, though essential, are insufficient in the absence of internal restraints. A moral vision of the future, therefore, looks to the pluralization of the Soviet Union, not to the weakening of democratic societies that constitute the only effective restraint on its behavior.

---

[12] See my "The Soviet System," in Wildavsky, ed. *Beyond Containment: Alternative American Policies Toward the Soviet Union* (San Francisco, CA: Institute for Contemporary Studies Press, 1983), pp.25–38.

A student of international law, Richard Falk, writes that there may be no way to secure a safe world order without "delegitimating the state in the area of national security." Falk argues that the existence of nuclear weapons leads to "the erosion of democratic governance," as governments resort to "repression at home" due to the "governmental need to frighten its own citizenry into subservience."[13] The question is: All states or just the United States? Since he and others who think like him are active in the U.S.A. and not the U.S.S.R., the only state likely to be delegitimated is the United States. The same sort of thing has happened as the nuclear freeze movement has turned "against defense spending in general."[14] In the words of Leon Wieseltier, "What began as a campaign against bombs has become a campaign against tanks. . . . The problem is not pacificism . . . [but] a much more serious proposition, which is that the use of force is not a legitimate instrument of national policy in the nuclear age."[15] True, the proponents of a freeze are here and not there, and they must do what they think right wherever they are. But the moral consequence is to weaken democracies, which will not initiate war, while leaving the Leninist monolith, which will, untouched.

In small doses, egalitarians are indispensible to democracy. They unmask the pretensions that governmental hierarchies are prone to. They attack the tendency to secretiveness and to shedding blame. By challenging existing presuppositions, they introduce new hypotheses into public policy. And by defending the rights of minorities, they extend civil liberties.

In large doses, however, egalitarians undermine existing authority. They increase its size and scope for redistributive purposes, while denying it legitimacy for purposes of defense. Where a nation is warlike, egalitarians, by attacking its authority, may mitigate militarism. But since they won't fight unless they can picture the enemy as a wholly evil creature, they may impose conditions, (such as unconditional surrender) that prolong hostilities. Their tendency toward black and white classifications makes them dangerous allies when in government. For they will deny defense until war is upon them, and then demand fearful punishment of the aggressor.

Democracy is a high moral value, and to it sectarianism is a mixed blessing: it both facilitates and undermines democracy. Because market cultures generate inequality, egalitarianism is mortally opposed to capitalism.

---

[13] Richard Falk, "Nuclear Weapons and the End of Democracy," The Swedish Institute of International Affairs Research Report.

[14] Wallace Earl Walker and Andrew F. Krepinevich, "No First Use and Conventional Deterrence: The Politics of Defense Policymaking." A version of this article entitled "Domestic Coalitions and Defense Policymaking" is published in Col. James R. Golden, LTC Asa A. Clark, IV, and Cpt. Bruce E. Arlinghaus, eds., Conventional Deterrence in NATO: Alternatives for European Defense (Lexington, MA: D.C. Heath, 1984).

[15] "The Great Nuclear Debate," The New Republic (January 17, 1983), p.14.

Yet there is no example of a democracy without significant market elements.

Curiously, egalitarian movements exist only in Western democracies. The egalitarian opposition in Russia, such as the social revolutionaries, was destroyed by Lenin's Communist Party soon after it took power and established the U.S.S.R. To the degree that egalitarians destabilize democracies while leaving the Soviet regime unchallenged, therefore, egalitarians are immoral by their own standards. They help bring about inequality instead of equality, repression instead of liberty, war instead of peace. For if it is peace they want, they should be shoring up instead of tearing down democracy. Indeed, their first aim should be democratizing or, more accurately, pluralizing the Soviet Union so it will become more peaceful.[16] Reducing the external threat will not work when the source of aggression is internal.

A dilemma of democracy is that what is good internally – democracies are not warlike – may be bad externally – democracies are unwilling to recognize external threats. The greater their devotion to equality of condition, the more democracies exaggerate their domestic defects and the more they minimize foreign aggression. All that can be done, since one cannot eliminate the difficulty except by abolishing democracy, is to recognize this tendency and guard against it.

If aphorisms are needed to sum up the relationship between political cultures and world order, I offer these two:

(1) Without dictatorship there is no war;
(2) Without democracy there is no peace.

Political Science, University of California, Berkeley

---

[16] See my "Containment Plus Pluralization," in *Beyond Containment*, pp.125–46.

Social Philosophy & Policy 3:1 Autumn 1985 ISSN 0265-0525 $2.00

MARXISM-LENINISM AND ITS STRATEGIC IMPLICATIONS FOR THE UNITED STATES

PAUL SEABURY

My central concern in this paper is with the implications of Marxist-Leninist ideology for Western defense policy and for United States strategic policy in particular. However, this is an extremely complex issue, and consideration of it will lead me to examine the ways in which ideas are related to interests, interests to strategy, and strategy to actions.

I

I begin with an important observation: Americans in general, and for various reasons, have not taken Marxism-Leninism seriously for a long time. This is true even of many experts who consider the Soviet challenge to be very serious, affecting our very survival as a free society. At the risk of oversimplification, I would claim that many quite well-informed Americans, hardened to the realities of the Soviet "empire" and its activities, have come around to the view that Marxist-Leninist ideology has simply degenerated into a rigid system of enforced belief administered by authorities who have no particular commitment to it other than to employ it in order to remain in power. In this regard, "Marxism" (like "God" in America in the 1960s) is deemed "dead," surviving only in the publicity offices of formal establishments as a means of maintaining their authority. Marxism-Leninism is thought to be no different from the moribund "divine right of kings," which undergirded the monarchical establishments of 17th Century Europe.

Oddly enough, the "socialism-is-dead" theme is today found in the writings of such prominent American neo-conservatives as Irving Kristol, George Gilder, and many others. It is also echoed in Europe in the writings of such eminent philosophers as Leszek Kolakowski of Poland and Paul Johnson of England. A caustic critique of such insouciant views has recently been expressed by Harper's contributing editor Tom Bethell, in his "What a Fool Believes," in *The American Spectator*.[1]

There is another reason why Marxism-Leninism is not taken seriously in the United States. For all of its powerful aspects as an operational weapon, it

[1] April 1985, pp.9–11.

has been rationally rejected in all of its parts. Since it has been so long at the service of the *nomenklatura* of the Soviet Union, who employ it as a weapon against us, the unrelenting incantation of its dogmas has dulled our interest in it. The effect of this ceaseless bombardment has been to turn our attention from it, if only to preserve our sanity; overexposure to it can have exactly the same dulling effect as it has upon those who are condemned to live under Soviet rule. Life, with its wonders, is too short to take Marxist-Leninist ideology seriously as an "objective" fact of our existence. Thus, the suggestion that there actually are those who do take it seriously is not taken seriously. One is reminded of the historical fact that almost no one in the United States in the 1930s took Hitler's ideology, laid out in *Mein Kampf*, seriously either. The unexpurgated version of that volume never appeared in English translation until 1939, when it was published in New York by Houghton-Mifflin. But by then, the hour was late. The writings of the Ayatollah Khomeni, widely disseminated in Farsi in the 1970s, did not appear in English until 1980 and, in fact, I doubt that many Americans have bothered to consult them. And, of course, one might wonder how many intelligent Westerners have ever seen, much less read, Kadaffi's official Green Book, another tract of our times. Such is the regnant power of our own Western, liberal system of beliefs that we relegate these foolishnesses to trash bins, if ever they come our way.

Such is our confidence in our own successful political system that we encounter a puzzling phenomenon: those who regard such strange beliefs as something to be taken seriously are all too often scoffed off the reservation. To take these beliefs seriously as fundamental threats to ourselves, is to risk being regarded as paranoid. The long plague upon anticommunism (now known as anti-anti-communism) is an important fact of contemporary Western intellectual life. The relationship between confidence and complacency is always ambiguous, but never more so than today.

And then there are those who fear that a concern about Marxism-Leninism will lead to a perverse, emulative mirror-imaging. To take it seriously, many argue, would be also to advocate a negative and repugnant ideology, subversive of our liberal democratic institutions. An early victim of this criticism was Whitaker Chambers; a more recent one, Solzhenitzyn; a most recent one, Sakharov. Yet, these individuals stand in a long tradition; one need only recall from the early war years the powerful warnings of Hermann Rauschning, the Nazi defector, who, in his *Revolution of Nihilism*[2] described the inner nature of national socialism.

Thus, the difficult, paradoxical challenge is how to take dangerous ideas seriously without taking them seriously.\Westerners are too often outraged

[2] Herman Rauschning, *The Revolution of Nihilism; Warning to the West* (New York: Alliance Book Corp., Longmans, Green & Co., 1939).

by the excesses of inhumane regimes without bothering to explore the ideas which give rise to them in the first place. Such organizations as Amnesty International, it seems to me, illustrate the point: by focussing exclusively upon inhumanities *per se*, they cover their eyes to the differing worlds of political ideas which inspire them. Thus, they indiscriminately lump together those whose inhumanities are of an age-old nature, with those whose inhumanities are consequences of all-too-contemporary ideologies. One cannot understand our times without admitting that Pol Pot, whose Khmer Rouge in 1975 exterminated perhaps twenty percent of the Cambodian population, is a child of our times, a former Sorbonne student and not an atavistic throwback to an older barbaric era.

And our thought about terrorism is often similarly flawed. Many tend to address the problem of meeting terrorism tactically, in concrete situations, while ignoring its deeper ideational origins. Also, Americans particularly tend to accept the benign view that revolutionary developments in Central America, for example, spring somehow from our own failure to treat with the "indigenous" roots of revolt and rebellion, ignoring the specifically modern ideas which inform and control them these movements.

II

For purposes of clarity, I will treat the central topic of this paper in two of its principal manifestations. First, in what ways does Marxism-Leninism inform the specific military-combative aspect of our chief adversaries, contributing to their strategic and tactical dispositions toward us and toward others of their avowed enemies? Second, in what ways does Marxism-Leninism as philosophy and action-strategy affect our strategic defense policies in areas other than that of our direct confrontation with the Soviet Union? While the first of these questions is certainly the more important one, I think its broad outlines are such that I need only sketch them.

In the "good old days," as far as the United States is or was concerned, this particular challenge was not very important.[3] Until World War II, whatever could be said of the Soviet Union as a power, it certainly was not more than a huge regional power. Its military capacities were deployed toward geographic areas immediately adjacent to it. This is not to denigrate that power; before 1939, the U.S.S.R. already occupied most of what the British geopolitician Halford Mackinder referred to as the "Heartland." It loomed over Europe; it had great capacities. But, at that time, few aside from Stalin's immediate neighbors, and the inhabitants of the Soviet Union, had

[3] For a discussion of this, see Reinhold Niebuhr's famous work, *The Irony of American History* (New York: Charles Scribner & Sons, 1962). For a more recent study, see Michael Howard's *War and the Liberal Conscience* (New Brunswick, NJ: Rutgers University Press, 1978).

much reason to fear it as a military power. By 1938, in fact, the general tendency in the West (and in Nazi Germany as well) was to denigrate Soviet military capacities. The fear of the Soviet Union in the West was not so much fear of its military capabilities (who, in the 1930's stayed up nights fearing that Soviet tanks would smash westward to the English Channel?) as of its looming presence as an ideological force with strong allies in the Communist parties in the West. That is not to say that this fear was unjustified. The United States at that time had perhaps the least to fear from this power. Russia was very far away and Communism had little appeal in the U.S., even in the Depression; the Soviet armed forces, even in the eyes of U.S. military observers, were not highly regarded. (In early 1941, when Operation Barbarossa broke forth, U.S. military experts gave the Red Army only a few weeks before it would break under the weight of the German *Reichswehr*.)

Much has changed since those times. But there is an important thread of continuity of a political-military nature which links those times to ours in a very important fashion. Then and now the Soviet Union was and is informed in its fundamental strategic view of the world by doctrines derived from Lenin. These Leninist tenets permeate their strategic planning.

Soviet views about the relationship between war and politics were and still are a radical readaptation of the views of Karl Von Clausewitz (1780–1831), the great Prussian strategic thinker. It was Clausewitz who coined the aphorism that war is a continuation of politics by an admixture of other means. It was Lenin who reversed the dictum: politics is a continuation of war by an admixture of other means. In the Soviet view then and now, in strategic matters both in times of fighting and nonfighting, the Soviet Union is always necessarily at war; politics is not just a *particular* aspect of the general art of warfare – politics *is* war. Therefore, the formal distinction usually drawn by Western nations between times of war and times of peace is – in Soviet eyes – not a valid one.[4]

Politics is a friend-foe relationship. This idea, not novel in world history, is nevertheless diametrically at odds with Western views which regard peace not just as the absence of fighting but as a time when the friend-foe relationship should have no meaning. In this regard, the Marxist-Leninist view of contemporary world history as class conflict on a global scale takes on particular meaning. Even in the so-called phase of detente of the 1970s, the Soviets never abandoned this framework.

The Clausewitz/Lenin view, imbedded in Soviet doctrine, necessarily and at all times provides a strategic starting point for an analysis and

---

[4] Lenin once remarked to an associate that "political tactics and military tactics represent that which Germans call *Grenzgebiet* [adjoining areas], urging party workers to study Clausewitz concerning this principle.

understanding of international relations. Realists in the West – a minority at odds with the dominant, liberal view of world politics – have depicted international relations as a balance of power. This view, too, is competitive and rivalrous. But such a world view differs fundamentally from the Leninist one: the realists' "balance" is inherently nonideological, arising from tensions among the interests and security concerns of individual nations, concerns which are essentially the same for all nations. The Leninist equivalent of the balance of power is a doctrine called the "correlation of forces" *(sootnoshenie sil)*, a standard by which the Soviet Union at all times measures its own forces and those of its allies against its necessary and inevitable ideological enemies – the capitalist world and the *chief* capitalist enemy, the United States. This view is indeed a far cry from original Marxist, pre-Leninist views of politics, which saw the contemporary class struggle as inherently a passing aspect of the inner polities of advanced industrial states. It is now largely forgotten that Marx and Engels' emphasis on class conflict did not lead them to employ it (as Lenin later did) as a theory of international politics and war. Lenin transposed the conflict into encounters among states; contemporary Soviet theory continues this tradition. But as Engels wrote, a century ago:

> The entire danger of a world war will vanish on the day when a change of affairs in Russia will permit the Russian people to put an end to its tsars' traditional policy of conquest and attend to its own vital interests, . . . instead of to fantasies of world conquest.[5]

The world view of the correlation of forces translates international conflict into a dichotomy between the Soviet Union (and its proxies and satellites) and the West. Further, and most importantly, this world view, in the eyes of many Western observers, is one in which the communist/Leninist element, for all practical purposes, is now virtually indistinguishable from that of the Soviet state and from that of Russian imperialism, a phenomenon which long antedates the Bolshevik Revolution.

This view, though it is advocated by some Western observers, must be severely qualified in order to have any credibility. If we observe all of those communist states which are communist "in their own right," and not simply Soviet satrapies such as the Eastern European countries, we note the ubiquitous manifestations of the Clausewitz-Leninist view. If war and politics are indistinguishable, then it follows that the Marxist-Leninist state at all times must be thoroughly militarized, vigilant, and prepared with huge forces-in-being prepared for combat both at home and abroad.

---

[5] Quoted in Richard Pipes' *Survival Is Not Enough* (New York: Simon and Schuster, 1984), p.207.

Thus, wherever one looks in the world today for great military garrison states, one looks almost exclusively at the communist world. For instance, the armed forces of North Korea, considered as men-under-arms, exceed those of the United States of America; the Cuban army is the largest in Latin America; the army of Communist Vietnam exceeds the U.S. Army in numbers by nearly half a million; the army of Nicaragua under the Sandinistas is larger than those of all its neighbors combined, and is four times the number of Canadian soldiers.[6] The plans of the Communist New Jewel Movement in Grenada, before that regime collapsed, were to mobilize as much as 25 percent of the Grenadian population. And, of course, this is before we begin to count noses of the Red Army in the Soviet Union, the forces of the other Warsaw Pact nations, and the People's Liberation Army of China.

III

We should disabuse ourselves of the notion that Marxism-Leninism represents a threat to us only because it is wedded to Soviet and Soviet/Russian imperial propensities: the threat is more serious than that. As a world view and an operational code, it is now accepted by all major Communist states and by many other states in the pro-Soviet parts of the Third World. In these states, military power at all times is Janus-headed: the enemy is both within and without; military and paramilitary forces are guardians of the state against external enemies and their own populations.

At the beginning of the long contest between the communist world and ours in the 1940s, the West, and America in particular, was able to maintain its overall strategic preeminence by virtue of its commanding lead in high technology and fire power. In the early years of the Cold War, for instance, the Soviet capacity to project military power was strictly limited to regions immediately adjacent to it in Europe and the Far East. The United States could and did accept numerical inferiority in conventional forces because of this fact. The United States and its NATO allies, in designing their European theater forces, adopted what might be called a "capital intensive" system of forces-in-being, juxtaposed to a Soviet "labor intensive" force. This led the West to introduce nuclear forces into Europe at a time when the Soviets were not yet able to reciprocate in kind. In Korea, we saw (as we later would see in Vietnam) a war in which the Communist side deployed huge forces of combat soldiers, while the other side deployed significantly smaller numbers with greater fire power and more sophisticated technology. In both wars, the Communists accepted gigantic battlefield losses in manpower, far greater than did its adversaries.

---

[6] See The International Institute for Strategic Studies, *The Military Balance 1984–1985* (London, 1984).

I mention these historical facts in order to point out that this original capital-intensive versus labor-intensive opposition in part made it possible for the United States and its allies to avoid "mirror imaging" their opponents by drafting huge armies. But as time has gone by, the Soviets and their allies have rectified their side of the balance. In all or nearly all categories of sophisticated weaponry, they are now keen rivals of the West, and the Soviets can project their forces in distant parts of the globe where their presence was scarcely felt before. The overall comparability of the U.S. and the U.S.S.R. in nuclear weaponry is now too familiar to warrant extended attention. The increasing dependence of the U.S. on ever more sophisticated and costly weaponry as a means of recovering its once unparalleled technological advantage has created severe logistical problems.[7] For example, the length of time required in 1980 from order to delivery of highly sophisticated U.S. fighter planes was almost exactly the length of time between Pearl Harbor and VJ-Day. The Soviet Union, with its enormous military forces, is now *both* capital and labor intensive.

IV

As these observations suggest, the strategic implications of Marxist-Leninist ideology for established Communist states differs from its original role as a *movement* ideology. When it is institutionalized, the movement ideology becomes a weapon administered by the state to mobilize and control its people and to expand the range of the movement-state's power into other regions.

This matter of internal control is of seminal importance in any Communist State, and the military forces are a principle vehicle by which this control is cemented. Obviously, the armed forces provide a powerful weapon to directly control the population. They also serve as a means of indoctrinating youth into the proper ideological conformity, i.e., a means of transforming consciousness. Yet, the matter goes far beyond this into the doctrinal necessity to regard all forms of social, artistic, and economic activity as combat. As the bishops of Nicaragua observed, in a pastoral letter of 29 August 1983, the Sandinista's then proposed universal conscription law:

> . . . is strongly politicized in its fundamental points, it has a partisan character and it follows the general lines of all totalitarian legislation . . . . The Military Service does not only 'promote the learning of the most advanced military techniques' (Consideration VII), but also 'will form in our youth the sense of *revolutionary* discipline and

---

[7] It is not known whether this situation has improved. See, for instance, my chapter in Chalmers Johnson, *The Industrial Policy Debate* (San Francisco: Institute for Contemporary Studies, 1984), pp.204–205.

morality.' That is, the Army is converted into an obligatory center of political indoctrination in favor of the Sandinista Party. . . . To force the citizens to join an 'Army-Political Party' without being in agreement with the ideology of said political party, is an act against the liberty of thought, of opinion, and of association. (Ref. Universal Declaration of the Rights of Man, arts. 18, 19 and 20.)[8]

Does the ideology of the military/revolutionary Communist state differ essentially from the "movement" ideology? Yes and no. It differs in that its function is transformed into that of consolidating a totalitarian regime and subjugating a captured society. But it resembles the "movement" ideology in that the state becomes the "movement" and the "movement" is henceforth at the disposal of those who intend to employ it for the further revolutionary transformation of those still beyond its reach. This expansionist propensity has always been the case with truly revolutionary regimes. The French soldiers under Bonaparte, sweeping across Europe, carried the Declaration of the Rights of Man in their knapsacks. Cuban mercenaries in Africa and the Middle East are presumably indoctrinated with the Communist version of revolutionary romanticism. It may be supposed, that the Grenadian conscripts of Maurice Bishop would have been enlisted for a similar role in the English-speaking areas of the Caribbean and Africa, as proxies of the Cubans and the Soviet Union.

It seems to me that the problem which the United States now faces in Central and South America and the Caribbean has been misunderstood by many influential Western leaders and opinion-makers. Not so long ago, the point was made by some distinguished critics of Reagan Administration policy that the *tumultos* (uprisings) of that region were matters somehow separable from the rivalries of East-West relations. This group, including such figures as Cyrus Vance, Edmund Muskie, David Rockefeller, General David Jones, and Robert McNamara, stated:

> We all favor keeping Latin America and the Caribbean out of the East-West conflict to the greatest extent possible. It does not serve the purpose for the United States to oppose changes in the region simply because they diminish U.S. influence and hence are perceived as advantageous to Cuba and the Soviet Union, unless they are clearly related to basic security concerns. We believe that the United States can better achieve its long-term interest in regional stability, one shared by Latin Americans, by exercising measured restraint in the projection of its power.[9]

[8] "General Considerations of the Episcopal Conference of Nicaragua Concerning Military Service," Episcopal Conference of Nicaragua, 29 August 1983.

[9] *The Americas at the Crossroads*, Report of the Inter-American Dialogue, Woodrow Wilson Center for Scholars, April 1983, p.41. (Emphasis in the text.)

The sentiment expressed in this passage is shared by many well-meaning Westerners, but unfortunately the wish is rarely father to the reality. Often the wish is that reality correspond to policy, rather than the other way around. In my book, *The Grenada Papers*,[10] I document the extent to which that East-West conflict had permeated a tiny Caribbean island. Before the Bishop regime suddenly collapsed of internal contradictions, it had become a base for Soviet, Cuban, Bulgarian, East German, North Korean, Vietnamese, and other Marxist-Leninist forces. On a larger scale, Cuba and Nicaragua have become tools of Soviet imperialistic objectives, but of course we do not have the advantage of the full documentation of this as we do in the case of Grenada.

V

In the context of Western security concerns, the Grenada documents are chiefly of importance because, in microcosm, they provide evidence of a general pattern of Marxist-Leninist forces at work in our own hemisphere as both "movement" and state. A reader of these documents can not fail to be impressed by the extent to which these localized struggles in Nicaragua, Grenada, and El Salvador have been orchestrated and exploited by the Soviets to further their larger objectives. When, in March 1983, the Grenadian chief of staff met with the then Soviet chief of staff, Marshal Ogarkov, the latter remarked, *inter alia*, that over two decades ago, there was only Cuba in Latin America. [But] today there are Nicaragua, Grenada, and a serious battle is going on in El Salvador."

In Central America today, we encounter a conundrum: What is the nature of the relationship between the gigantic apparatus of Soviet-bloc state power, which sponsors these movements, and these intra-hemispheric movements themselves? Here we encounter two opposed interpretations. Both, I emphasize, contain important elements of truth.

One is that these Central American *tumultos* are essentially products of Soviet strategic nurturing and that they therefore should be viewed as extensions by proxy of Soviet power in the Western Hemisphere, or even (as in El Salvador) as proxies of proxies. Seen in their totality, then, these movements would comprise a geographic aspect of a larger "correlation of forces," a part of a whole. If, therefore, it is true, as Zbigniew Brzezinski said recently, that Soviet political-military strategy today concentrates not so much upon conquest of the West as upon its strategic destabilization and disruption, the specifically *military* implications of Central America (forward

---

[10] Paul Seabury and Walter McDougall, eds., *The Grenada Papers* (San Francisco: Institute for Contemporary Studies, 1983).

military, naval, and air bases) are of far less importance than the *political-military* ones.

In this respect, the transformation of the whole region of the Caribbean, Central America, and Mexico into a zone of hostile totalitarian regimes, or the degradation of the region into socio-political turmoil, would have equally damaging consequences for the overall strategic posture of the United States in the world. For more than a century and a half, since the Napoleonic Wars in fact, the United States has never been faced by powerful, hostile forces and states or social chaos in the Western Hemisphere. Were Marxist-Leninists to triumph in a series of victories in Central America, the symbolic importance surely would have profound effects in Mexico. The United States, faced by a large, hostile, or profoundly destabilized Mexico directly on its border, would be compelled to direct its attention away from other crucial regions of the world in order to face this ominous challenge on its doorstep.

It is here that a second interpretation of these hemispheric events must be carefully considered: that the events themselves are not so much strategic exports of the Soviet Union, as they are *indigenous* Marxist-Leninist developments. On this interpretation, these forces (which also include Maoists and Trotskyites among their ranks) arise spontaneously, having been inspired by strands of Marxist-Leninist thought which have existed in the Western Hemisphere for a very long time. This process does not necessarily require nor is it necessarily dominated by the experiences of Marxist-Leninist regimes elsewhere. One important inspiration to regional Marxism-Leninism arises from a hatred of Yankee North America born of an admixture of envy and contempt. In this regard, many Americans fail to realize that the chief intellectual center of Marxism-Leninism in the Western Hemisphere is not Havana, but Mexico City, and that idiosyncratic Latin characteristics of these revolutionary communist movements predates the Second World War. Until now, the governing party of Mexico (the PRI) has hosted and tolerated these forces inside its borders, warily professing its revolutionary credentials by evincing sympathy for revolutionary causes as long as the sites of battle are outside Mexico.

The PRI's self-proclaimed status as an authentic revolutionary political order, however, are now proving a somewhat mixed blessing. Its sympathy for "progressive forces" at work in areas adjacent to it, is increasingly mixed with fear that the success of those forces may spill over into Mexico itself. Its support and toleration of truly Marxist-Leninist forces abroad is a form of calculated appeasement. Given the grave social problems which Mexico now faces, one must assume that Mexican political stability is not to be taken for granted.

It would be dangerously wrong to regard the vitality of Marxism-Leninism in this region only as an extension of Soviet strategic operations. Leszek Kolakowski, the Polish intellectual who has pronounced Marxism-Leninism as "dead" in his country and in Eastern Europe as a whole, would be hard put to pronounce it dead in the Western Hemisphere. One interesting lesson to be drawn from the captured Grenada documents is that the leaders of the New Jewel Movement were not poseurs or apparatchicks) they were convinced true believers.

The common denominator of all Marxist-Leninist groups in Central America, as one observer pointed out, has been "their open, consistent, and deeply felt belief that the United States is their main enemy. . . . The realization that external support necessary to conquer power would come only from the U.S.S.R. and its satellites was the necessary corrollary of a rapidly spreading conviction . . . that victory required a regional and ultimately global perspective that put aside doctrinal differences."[11]

It would be myopic to reduce the importance of these regional Marxist-Leninist movements to a sterile debate as to whether they are primarily indigenous or primarily nurtured by Soviet strategy. The sources of hatred and animosity toward democracy, the free enterprise system, and the United States in particular, are not confined to these two sources. To refer once more to the Grenada documents, what is striking is the *range* of material and spiritual support which flowed into that tiny island, and the degree of affinity which the New Jewel Movement found with movements and radical states far removed from itself. This moral and material help came not only from Cuba and the Soviet Union and its satellites, but from such diverse places as North Korea, Vietnam, Libya (a principal supplier), Syria, Algeria, Iran and Iraq, the P.L.O., and other terrorist organizations.

VI

The curious relationship between "progressive" Marxist-Leninist revolutionary ideologues and atavistic non-Western religious fanatics needs to be explored. Another trend worthy of further examination is the role played by liberation theology in various parts of the Third World. There are paradoxes here: on the one hand, the "progressives" and the "atavists" are united in a common hatred of Western constitutionalism, democracy, and capitalism; yet from a strategic perspective the atavists are clearly dependent as proteges upon the power of their "modern" allies and sponsors. The hatred of Western culture surely will continue indefinitely, but its symbiotic alliance with Marxism-Leninism is a marriage of convenience. The marriage will

---

[11] Michael Radu, "Soviet Proxy Assets in Central America and the Caribbean," unpublished paper (Philadelphia: Foreign Policy Research Institute, 1984), p.8.

flourish as long as both continue to regard the West, and America in particular, as weak and/or irresolute.[12]

What is the significance of this world-wide network? It seems to me that its significance lies in a generalized hostility to the West. This hostility extends beyond the confines of Marxist-Leninist movements and states. All of these anti-Western movements think that they would benefit from the strategic weakening of the United States. The most effective means of paralyzing the United States as a global force is to confront it with insurmountable problems in its own backyard, thereby crippling its capacity to sustain its friends and allies elsewhere.

When the doctrine of containment was embraced by the United States in the early Cold War years, it focused upon containing the Soviet Union. There was no need then to deal with the strange network of Soviet surrogates which we now confront. In dealing with this burgeoning network as it affects the Western Hemisphere, we see that the multiplicity of forces arrayed against the United States in Central America have not been opposed by an equal, countervailing opposition. America's European allies are indifferent to her regional difficulties; the many friends of civic freedom throughout the world observe these events passively; and Americans are divided among themselves as to the severity of the danger and the manner in which it should be countered. Many people who hold no illusions about the implications of Marxist-Leninist incursions into the Western Hemisphere are nevertheless demoralized into inaction by the seeming "inevitability" of their success. There is no necessary reason why this should be so. For this reason, a primary future task of American foreign policy should be to forge coalitions of friendly and democratic forces which would join in containing and repulsing these incremental encroachments on the free world, whether they occur in Central America or elsewhere.

Political Science, University of California, Berkeley

---

[12] In attempting to understand this relationship, two major contemporary novelists (neither one a product of "advanced industrial societies") have given us stimulating insights into the problem: the Peruvian novelist Mario Vargas Llosa, in his *War of the End of the World*, (New York: Farrar Straus Giroux, 1984), and the Trinidad-born V.S. Naipaul, in his *Among the Believers: An Islamic Journey* (New York: Alfred A. Knopf, 1981).

Social Philosophy & Policy 3:1 Autumn 1985 ISSN 0265–0525 $2.00

TOCQUEVILLE ON WAR

Eliot A. Cohen

The title of this article has been chosen deliberately, for we find interesting parallels in the careers and outlooks of Alexis de Tocqueville and the great Prussian theorist of war, Carl von Clausewitz whose master work, *On War*, remains *sui generis*. They overlapped in time (Tocqueville lived from 1805 to 1859, Clausewitz from 1780 to 1831), but, more importantly, their major theoretical works dealt in large measure with the same problem – the democratic revolution and its impact on politics. As Clausewitz argued, the warfare of the new era was

> caused by the new political conditions which the French Revolution created both in France and in Europe as a whole, conditions that set in motion new means and new forces, and have thus made possible a degree of energy in war that otherwise would have been inconceivable.
>
> It follows that the transformation of the art of war resulted from the transformation of politics.[1]

There are intriguing personal parallels between the two men as well. Minor aristocrats in societies in the midst of transition, they had perhaps the best of all vantage points on the democratic revolution. Both men had theoretical interests yet also held posts of real responsibility; both had rather aloof personalities, and both failed to reach the summits of military leadership and politics respectively.[2] Both wrote works of extraordinary scope and durability, which were published not terribly far apart from one another (*Democracy in America* appeared between 1835–1840; Clausewitz's *On War* was published posthumously in 1832). Perhaps most interesting of all, the two have attracted and enthralled similar intellects. The most notable of these was Raymond Aron, the leading figure in the renewal of French

---

[1] Carl von Clausewitz, *On War*, trans. Michael Howard and Peter Paret (Princeton: Princeton University Press, 1976), p.610. I have benefited as well from Samuel P. Huntington, "Tocqueville's Armies and Ours," text of remarks delivered at the University of Chicago, 15 February 1985.

[2] See Raymond Aron, *Pensee la Guerre, Clausewitz*, 2 vols. (Paris: Gallimard, 1976), vol. 1, p.39 for a particularly acute comparison; also, see p.65. In addition, see Peter Paret, *Clausewitz and the State* (New York: Oxford University Press, 1976), pp.351–3.

interest in Tocqueville, who concluded his career with a massive two volume work on Clausewitz.

The teachings of the two men are, I would argue, complementary – at least from the point of view of a student of war. Clausewitz concentrated his study on the dynamics of war, on the nature of war itself, as shaped and directed by political conditions. Yet Clausewitz did not examine in detail (at least in his masterwork, *On War*) the relationship between domestic politics and war-making, though he surely acknowledged its importance.[3] Similarly, although much of Tocqueville's writing dealt with the problems of war and the preparation for it in democratic societies, he had a far less comprehensive view of it than did his Prussian counterpart. When put together, however, the two authors offer us a remarkably comprehensive picture of the problems faced by democratic states at war.

It should be remembered that Tocqueville, though without formal military experience, knew military men well and observed military institutions closely. As a member of the French Chamber of Deputies, he traveled several times on official business to Algeria, to report back on the conduct of the bloody conquest of that greatest of French colonies. He had among his fr nds and acquaintances prominent soldiers, including General Thomas b..geaud, the ruthless and brilliant conqueror of Algeria. He witnessed several episodes of street fighting (or urban warfare, as we now call it) in Paris, and in his memoirs commented coolly on both the tactics and social psychology of the fighting that he watched. During his brief tenure as Minister of Foreign Affairs, he made use of the threat of military force (mobilizing an army corps stationed on the border) to secure French interests in Italy. Throughout his life, as notes of his conversations and his minor writings attest, he was a keen military, sociological, and strategic observer, discoursing on the fortifications of Cherbourg, the strategic advantages of Mers el-Kebir as a naval base from which to control the Western Mediterranean, and analyzing the strengths and weaknesses of the long-service Russian army.[4]

We may take Tocqueville's observations on war in *Democracy in America*, like the rest of his teaching there, as bearing either on democratic societies and states generally, or on the United States in particular. Tocqueville

[3] See Book I, ch. 1, sec. 28. Clausewitz, *On War*, p.89.
[4] For a brief summary of Tocqueville's activities in Algeria see Andre Jardin, *Alexis de Tocqueville* (Paris: Hachette, 1984), pp.302–327. His report on Algeria can be found in Alexis de Tocqueville, *Oeuvres*, 9 vols., ed. Mary de Tocqueville (Paris: Michel Levy 1866), vol. 9, pp.423–438, 469–480. (Note: the more recent and complete edition of Tocqueville's works was not available to me in writing this article.) See also Melvin Richter, "Tocqueville on Algeria," *Review of Politics* vol. 25 (July 1963), pp.362–398. Finally, for a miscellany of Tocqueville's observations on these matters see M.C.M. Simpson, ed., *Correspondence and Conversation of Alexis de Tocqueville with Nassau William Senior*, 2 vols. (London: Henry S. King, 1872), vol. 1, pp.118, 225–243; vol. 2, pp.8–9, 93–103, 126, 179–183.

observed that the United States had little to fear from external enemies, and hence needed to pay little attention to military matters. As a result, in part, he spent much of his time dealing with the more general problem of the subordination of military organizations to civil authority, and devoted a disproportionate amount of space (at least for the contemporary observer of American military politics) to the prospects of *coups d'état* in democratic societies.[5] At least since the abortive mutinies of the Continental Army at the end of the American Revolution, however, overt intervention of the American Army in politics has been almost inconceivable.

These cautionary notes notwithstanding, the contemporary student of American military affairs finds a great deal to learn from Tocqueville's analysis of civil-military relations and his assessment of the peculiar strengths and weaknesses of democratic armed forces. This holds true not simply for those parts of *Democracy in America* which deal explicitly with war (Volume II, Part III, Chapters 22–26) but others as well, including several which shall be discussed below.

In what follows, I propose to examine two aspects of Tocqueville's thought on war: the relationship between armies and democratic societies in peace and war, and the problem of the role of the officer in democratic armies and democratic societies. In the first section, I will suggest that Tocqueville offers a depiction of the strengths and weaknesses of democracies in war which is born out, in large measure, by American experience in this century. In the second, I will argue that his teaching offers valuable insights into the longstanding and increasingly vexatious dispute about the ethos of the contemporary American officer corps. The article concludes with a broader discussion of the need to integrate Tocquevillean institutional analysis into a Clausewitzian discussion of military affairs.

ARMY AND SOCIETY

Tocqueville makes a sharp distinction between war and peace. The way in which he does so reveals an inherent difficulty in Clausewitz's analysis of war; Clausewitz holds that war is a mere continuation of political inter-course, with the addition of other means.[6] Clausewitz does not discount the role of democratic passion in war, but sees it as only one of three elements in shaping war, the other two being the skill and organization of the armed forces and the strategic acumen of the government. It is quite clear, in Clausewitz's analysis, that the rational aspect of war – i.e., governmental control – must dominate the other two.

---

[5] Alexis de Tocqueville, *Democracy in America*, trans. George Lawrence (New York: Anchor Books, 1966), vol. 2, pt. 3, chs. 22–23, pp.645–654.
[6] Clausewitz, *On War*, bk. 1, ch. 1, p.87.

Tocqueville, however, starts with a discussion of the popular basis for war fighting, arguing that initially, at least, democracies fight wars at a serious disadvantage. He says this because he holds that the martial spirit is simply antithetical to the beliefs and aspirations of democratic man:

> The ever increasing number of men of property devoted to peace, the growth of personal property which war so rapidly devours, mildness of mores, gentleness of heart, that inclination to pity which equality inspires, that cold and calculating spirit which leaves little room for sensitivity to the poetic and violent emotions of wartime – all these causes act together to damp down warlike fervor.[7]

This is not to suggest that democratic man is incapable of military exploits – indeed, once war begins a democratic army makes the most formidable of opponents. According to Tocqueville:

> War, having destroyed every industry, in the end becomes itself the one great industry, and every eager and ambitious desire sprung from equality is focussed on it. For that reason those same democratic nations which are so hard to drag on to the battlefield sometimes perform prodigious feats once one has succeeded putting arms in their hands.[8]

Tocqueville, therefore, describes escalation in democratic warfare as a quantum leap, a radical transformation of popular attitudes towards warfare that requires some time and effort to achieve, but which produces an extraordinary explosion of violence. Clausewitz, by way of contrast, has a more complicated and gradualistic understanding of escalation, which involves incremental and reciprocal increases in animosity, political objectives, and the means used to conduct war. For him, the popular dimension of war constitutes but one factor pushing armed conflict to extremes.[9]

On balance, Tocqueville's account fits the United States more accurately than that of Clausewitz. Tocqueville's description surely fits the United States in this century's major wars, when a society that had proven reluctant to plunge into wars to preserve a balance of power in Europe finally entered such conflicts and turned the tide against a hitherto victorious coalition. In both cases, enormous reluctance to go to war for narrowly conceived political aims (preservation of the balance of power in Europe) eventually yielded to commitment to war with the most extreme objectives.

The practical implications for our own day are troubling, for it is in the

[7] Tocqueville, *Democracy in America*, vol. 2, pt. 3, ch. 22, p.646.
[8] *ibid.*, ch. 24, p.657.
[9] For Clausewitz's analysis of escalation, see *On War*, bk. 1, ch. 1, p.77.

nature of a Great Power that it finds itself compelled to fight wars for limited political objectives, and democracies find such wars intrinsically difficult (though by no means impossible) to conduct. Rather than grapple with this issue directly, however, American statesmen since 1945 (and particularly since the Vietnam war) have attempted to avoid the issue by pretending that such conflicts can be avoided.[10]

The characteristic democratic transition from pacifism in peacetime to extreme and effective bellicosity in war is all the more remarkable, in Tocqueville's view, because of the disrepair into which democratic armies commonly fall in peacetime. Neglected – if not, indeed, despised – by the bulk of the population, armies fail to attract the country's best young men: "The elite of the nation avoid a military career because it is not held in honor, and it is not held in honor because the elite of the nation do not take it up."[11] Nor is this simply true of the officer corps. The average enlisted man in democratic armies, according to Tocqueville, is someone who cannot make it in normal democratic society. In the United States, this presents few difficulties, for it needs (or rather, in Tocqueville's day, it needed) no large standing armies to protect its frontiers. For most countries, however, conscription is necessary, for democratic man, preoccupied as he is with individual prosperity, has neither the taste nor the aptitudes for voluntary military service. Moreover, universal military service answers the demand for the equality of sacrifice which egalitarian nations require.

Conscription, however, does not necessarily lead to the creation of democratic armies, since conscripts are simply unwilling, temporary, and on the whole powerless members (if also the majority of) military organizations. The officer corps, according to Tocqueville, may consist of either of two groups of men: would be aristocrats (who, by and large, come to adopt democratic characteristics) or comfortable time-servers, whose sole ambition is a placid existence. Democratic armies are plagued by competition for promotion, since anyone can aspire to officership, and since status varies simply according to rank. (This phenomenon can be observed today in the difference in attitude towards their careers of British and American officers, the former generally caring less about advancement, the latter operating under an "up-or-out" personnel system.) The result, according to Tocqueville, is a promotion system based exclusively on seniority, which has the result of providing democratic armies with tired and often incompetent

---

[10] See the exchange of speeches between Secretary of Defense Caspar Weinberger and Secretary of State George Shultz, *New York Times*, 29 November 1984 and 10 December 1984.

[11] Tocqueville, *Democracy in America*, vol. 2, pt. 3, ch. 22, p.648.

leadership in wartime. The results are not encouraging:

> because in democracies the richest, best-educated, and ablest citizens hardly ever adopt a military career, the army finally becomes a little nation apart, with a lower standard of intelligence and rougher habits than the nation at large.[12]

Tocqueville follows this analysis with a generally pessimistic assessment of the prospects for stable and decent civil-military relations.

One suspects, however, that Tocqueville's insight here applies above all to democratic societies which have yet to develop free institutions. His discussion of the origins of *coups d'état* among younger, disgruntled officers and NCO's corresponds well to what we know of coups in Latin America and Africa, for example. Yet his analysis of civil-military relations in a democracy with free institutions – the United States – runs counter to much of what we know, or at least think we know.

For example, the most prominent student of American civil-military relations, Samuel P. Huntington, has argued that the instinctive antipathy between liberal institutions and military organizagions actually produces the *best* state of civil-military relations. Soldiers rejected by society turn inward, developing professional characteristics which serve the country well in war.[13] Tocqueville (living, it must be confessed, at the beginning of the age of the professional soldier) does not discuss the nature of military professionalism: for him, as for others in the early nineteenth century, the models of military excellence were the armies of late revolutionary and Napoleonic France. Not until the German wars of unification (fought by Prussia with Denmark in 1864, Austria in 1866, and France in 1870) did it become clear that the age of the scientifically trained soldier had arrived.

Nonetheless, Tocqueville's analysis sheds a different light on the paradigm we use to understand military institutions. He was, after all, well aware of the existence and nature of professions (as demonstrated by his famous discussion of the role played by lawyers in American life), and he knew many well-educated and scientifically trained soldiers (it was, after all, in France that some of the Western world's first major military academies were established, among them the model for West Point). By analyzing the nature of modern officer corps through the prism of the dichotomy between democracy and aristocracy, he calls to our attention the survival of – indeed, the necessity for – aristocratic characteristics in all officer corps. This is a particularly important point, because most discussions of professionalism set

---

[12] *ibid.*

[13] See Samuel P. Huntington, *The Soldier and the State* (Cambridge: Harvard University Press, 1957), ch. 6, pp.143–162.

it against aristocratic (i.e., amateurish) domination of the officer corps.[14] Yet the manners and qualities of the good officer continue to have much in common with the aristocratic virtues, even though aristocratic birth has long since ceased to be associated with military service. I will return to this point further on.

Tocqueville describes a state of democratic civil-military relations in peacetime that produces an army of either dull and uncouth or unwilling and balky soldiers led by geriatric commanders and restlessly ambitious junior officers and sergeants. Needless to say, it is his view that such armies are far from formidable, for a number of reasons. Aged leadership is poor leadership (a view supported by most military history, for war is a young man's work). Just as bad, in Tocqueville's view, is the mentality foisted upon officers by a long period of democratic peace:

> Those of most ambition and resources leave the army; the others, finally adapting their tastes and desires to their humdrum lot, come in the end to look on a military career from a civilian point of view. What they value most is the comfort and security that goes with it. They base their vision of the future on the assurance of a small competence, and they ask no more than to be allowed to enjoy it in peace. So not only does a long peace fill democratic armies with aging officers, but it often gives even those who are still in the vigor of their years the instincts of old men.[15]

Tocqueville's diagnosis rings true today as well. Critics of the contemporary American military often attribute the same effects – careerism, managerialism, and other civilian attributes – to other causes such as changes in the technology of warfare, or to peculiarly inept leadership.[16] Tocqueville's analysis, however, suggests that the explanation lies deeper, that particularly in a country such as the United States, which has neither an aristocratic tradition nor a sense of immediate danger, it is virtually inevitable that its army will enter a war led by peacetime managers rather than military leaders. The experience of World War II, in which an extremely capable corps of relatively *junior* officers such as Eisenhower, Bradley, Collins, and others were swiftly promoted over the heads of peacetime generals (such as Ben Lear and Hugh Drum), indicates that this is indeed the case.

[14] See Franklin D. Margiotta, ed., *The Changing World of the American Military* (Boulder: Westview, 1978), pp.37–70.
[15] Tocqueville, *Democracy in America*, vol. 2, pt. 3, ch. 24, p.656.
[16] For a recent (and heated) example of this debate, see *Armed Forces Journal International* (September 1984), and the spate of letters and articles which followed this issue, which contained a discussion of the Army's personnel management system.

Implicit in Tocqueville's analysis of military institutions is the view that armies invariably reflect the societies from which they spring, a view echoed in many contemporary scholarly writings.[17] And not merely in scholarly writings, since it is a view often expressed by officers seeking to explain or defend the American armed forces' breakdown in morale in the early 1970s and its subsequent difficulties with the All-Volunteer Force. Thus, there is a paradox here (in Tocqueville's view), for an institution which mirrors society is also despised by it. Democratic armies suffer from general social disapprobation, which is natural because, as de Gaulle once remarked:

> The fact that men can devote their lives to preparing for crises which nobody wants, very naturally antagonizes the masses, the more so since the professionals, though they deplore the arbitrament of force from a purely human and speculative point of view, see in it an opportunity to make a career for themselves, and take, in the problems it presents, a technical interest which cannot fail to be unpopular with those who have nothing to gain personally from battle, murder, and sudden death.[18]

Moreover, the structure of military organizations is one quite different from that of larger democratic society, for it is based on rigid promotion on the basis of seniority. And yet, in the Tocquevillean view, the result is one in which the military ends by resembling the society from which it springs.

Tocqueville argues, however, that this pernicious resemblance in time of peace offers unique advantages in times of war. Once a democratic people have roused themselves, once (through conscription) the most active and talented members of society see that their main chance for glory and advancement comes through successful military service, the result is an unusually active and alert wartime officer corps. "Officers whose minds and bodies have grown old in peacetime are eliminated, retire, or die. In their place a multitude of young men, already toughened by war, press forward with ambitious hopes aflame."[19] Motivated by ambition, and taking advantage of the sudden vacancies which war creates, a new officer class emerges.

In addition, it appears that in wartime there is a special harmony between democratic mores and those required by war. Daring and innovation – characteristics present in the daily lives of peacable, acquisitive democratic man – are at a premium in war. Democratic armies – adaptable, inquisitive, changeable – learn quickly from their mistakes. General Erwin Rommel, for

---

[17] M.R.D. Foot, *Men in Uniform* (New York: Praeger, 1961), p.30.
[18] Charles de Gaulle, *The Edge of the Sword*, trans. Gerard Hopkins (London: Faber and Faber, 1960), p.67.
[19] Tocqueville, *Democracy in America*, vol. 2, pt. 3, ch. 24.

example, described the Americans as possessing, "an intellect directed to practical ends, initiative, and the urge for material wealth." He noted in his retrospective analysis of the North Africa campaign that the American troops, though initially inferior in skill to their British allies, learned much faster.

> What was astonishing was the speed with which the Americans adapted themselves to modern warfare. In this they were assisted by their extraordinary sense for the practical and material and by their complete lack of regard for tradition and worthless theories.[20]

Rommel's observation confirms that of Tocqueville, namely, that democratic armies end a war far more formidable than they begin it.

Tocqueville notes the evolution of new, democratic forms of discipline, which he sees as a remedy for the more natural and rigid discipline of an aristocratic army. Where the serf follows his noble officer because the former is accustomed to obey the latter in peacetime, democratic man has no particular customary obedience. The result, which often frustrates the leaders of democratic armies, is the failure of aristocratic forms of discipline, i.e., those based on formal gestures of deference and submission.

Tocqueville's insight on this point accounts for the fact, oft-noted by observers of democratic armies, that they attempt to instill far greater discipline of a formal kind than do their more traditional counterparts. Because the superiority of officers is seen to be artificial, it is at once resented by the men and (perversely, perhaps) reinforced by the system.[21]

Democratic armies have devised any number of solutions to this problem. One is that referred to above, the effort to create artificial barriers and distance, and thereby recreate the conditions of obedience that obtain in aristocratic armies. Another is that of allowing soldiers to exercise some democratic control over officer selection. In colonial times units often elected their leaders, a procedure often derided by historians and, indeed, by the aristocratic officers of that time. Yet many modern armies have returned to modified versions of the same procedure, for example, by making frequent use of peer evaluations to select officers.[22] In a larger sense, officers have realized since the late nineteenth century that discipline rests on silent forms

[20] Erwin Rommel, *The Rommel Papers*, trans. Paul Findlay (New York: Harcourt Brace, and Co., 1953), p.521.

[21] See Samuel A. Stouffer, *et al.*, *The American Soldier*, vol. 1, *Adjustment During Army Life* (Princeton: Princeton University Press, 1949), pp.362–429.

[22] As the author discovered by personal experience (1980–1983). Most armies, including the American, rely heavily on peer evaluations during officer training courses, and even (in some cases) for picking out promising enlisted men (communications with senior American and Israeli military officials, including commanders of basic training brigades). On the use of peer

of consent. General James G. Harbord, Chief of Staff to General John Pershing, commander of the American Expeditionary Force during World War I, wrote:

> Discipline and morale influence the inarticulate vote that is constantly taken by masses of men when the order comes to move forward – a variant of the crowd psychology that inclines it to follow a leader. But the Army does not move forward until the motion has carried.[23]

Tocqueville offers as a solution to the problem of consent the development of democratic discipline, which "ought not to try to cancel out the spontaneous exercise of the faculties," but rather should "aspire only to direct them." The result is a discipline "less precise but more impetuous and intelligent."[24] Here, too, Tocqueville anticipates the writings of early twentieth century soldiers, who saw in the evolution of discipline a response to the increasingly complex technology of war and the modern dispersal of soldiers on the battlefield. He foresees as well the looser discipline of the most egalitarian armies of the two World Wars, those of Australia and New Zealand.[25]

One of Tocqueville's most famous formulations is that of the doctrine of self-interest well-understood. He describes this as a semi-fiction which allows Americans to behave cooperatively, often selflessly, while convincing themselves that by so doing they are simply taking an intelligent view of their long-term self-interest. This curious mixture of self-deception and calculation moderates and disciplines the egoistic individualism which otherwise threatens the cohesion of civil society. Its power in modern America appears in military organizations as well as their civilian counterparts. When the military attempts to recruit soldiers by suggesting that thereby they will "be all you can be," and when young officers are instructed to teach their troops the self-interested benefits of cooperation, it would appear that this doctrine has become a military creed as well as a civil one. The notion that military virtue ultimately rests on self-interest pervades the theorizing of America's

---

evaluations, see Morris Janowitz, *Sociology and the Military Establishment*, 3rd ed. (Beverly Hills: Sage, 1974), pp.76–77. In the Swiss and Israeli armies officers are selected from the ranks, in part by use of peer evaluations. See Karl Haltiner and Ruth Meyer, "Aspects of the Relationship between Military and Society in Switzerland," *Armed Forces and Society*, vol. 6 (Fall 1979), pp.57–58.

[23] Quoted in S.L.A. Marshall, *Men Against Fire* (New York: William Morrow, 1947), p.106.

[24] Tocqueville, *Democracy in America*, vol. 2, pt. 3, ch. 25.

[25] For personal recollections, see Stephen Roskill, *The Art of Leadership* (Hamden, CT: Archon, 1965), pp. 69–70 and Lord Moran, *The Anatomy of Courage* (Boston: Houghton Mifflin, 1967), p. 166.

contemporary military leadership. The U.S. Army's leadership manual (FM 22–100), for example, expounds on Abraham Maslow's "progression of needs" as the authoritative guide to human behavior. In a scale of "motivators and dissatisfiers" it describes patriotism as the weakest of positive motivators, "self fulfillment" and "responsibility" as the strongest. Throughout, the manual emphasizes individual motivators, not collective ones. By implication, the key to leadership lies in an intelligent appeal to the educated and moderate egoism of one's soldiers.[26]

It must be admitted that at first there is something peculiar about such doctrines, particularly because they contradict our usual conception of battlefield heroism, the bravery which leads to the individual exploits of a Sergeant York, for example, and to which societies pay homage with medals and state funerals. Military organizations certainly value such feats, and seek to foster such behavior. It is nonetheless true, however, that the most successful armies are not those in which individual prowess, including reckless bravery, wins the highest acclaim, but those which inculcate cooperative behavior. The Greek conception of heroism was individual, witness the exploits of the heroes of the Iliad. The Roman code of discipline, however, punished crimes against one's comrades (e.g., falling asleep on guard duty) with death, but not so cowardice; similarly, Roman leaders gave the highest rewards not for individual acts of heroism but, rather for those of cooperation (e.g., saving the life of a fellow citizen).[27] And yet, as Tocqueville observes, Roman discipline, not Greek valor, conquered the world.

Since aristocratic or individualistic heroism lies beyond the reach of most men – including most soldiers – it is wise to ground courage on elements of reason: in particular, military organizations attempt to elecit desired behavior that is distinctly hazardous by playing on an individual's self-interest, broadly understood. As John Keegan has shrewdly observed, this often involves placing soldiers in positions where their self-interest directs them towards the preferred outcome.[28]

Tocqueville's description of the nonmilitary characteristics of democracy in general, and the United States in particular, also shed light on the American way of war. A good example of this is his discussion of "Why the Americans are More Concerned With the Applications Than With the Theory of Science," (Volume II, Part III, Ch.10, pp.459–463). Tocqueville describes the talent of Americans for technical innovation, as opposed to theoretical breakthroughs in science. The pattern of American technical innovation in war – a technological ascendancy upon which, perilously

[26] See department of the Army, *Military Leadership*, Field Manual 22–100 (Washington: Department of the Army, 1973), ch. 7, pp.7–1 – 7–5.
[27] Polybius, *The Rise of the Roman Empire*, trans. Ian Scott-Kilvert (Harmondsworth: Penguin, 1979), pp.318–338.
[28] John Keegan, *The Face of Battle* (New York: Viking, 1976), p.324.

perhaps, we now depend – had been established as early as the Civil War and was confirmed during World War II. The Americans surprised both enemy and ally not merely with such superweapons as the atomic bomb, but with a host of innovations (the bazooka, the proximity fuse, the jeep, the "Dakota" transport, the Norden bombsight, and even dehydrated rations), each a small improvement, but cumulatively quite devastating. This democratic ferment enabled the United States to overcome by mid-war the technological inferiority with which its forces entered the war, and replace it with a considerable margin of technological superiority.

Tocqueville's assessment of democratic civil-military relations in the United States is colored, it must be confessed, by the discrepancy between the United States of his day and the United States of ours. It seems reasonable to assume that the difficulties of a country with a tiny standing army and only marginal threats to its national security bear little relation to those of a Great Power in the twentieth century, a Great Power which finds itself engaged on several continents simultaneously. Yet there is one fundamental problem that Tocqueville addresses which remains with us today, and to which he speaks. It is to this subject that I now turn.

DEMOCRATIC OFFICERS AND DEMOCRATIC ARMIES

The dilemma to which Tocqueville alludes, but which is particularly acute in our day, is the tension between the nature of democratic society and that of military organization. Simply put, the difficulty lies in the dependence of military hierarchy on essentially aristocratic relations between officers and men and, above all, on an aristocratic sense of identity among the officer caste.

Modern armies continue to labor under the thrall of medieval European class struture, in which noble officers exercised command over peasant soldiers. Almost every attempt to escape this seemingly atavistic relationship has failed, most noticeably the attempt by revolutionary armies (including those of the Soviet Union and China) to abolish rank and external forms of deference such as saluting. Purely democratic selection of officers (i.e., *periodic* and *conditional* election solely by the men over whom an officer serves) has never survived a modern war, or even its early stages.[29]

---

[29] The transformation of the Civil War army is one case in point; the purge of the officer corps of the National Guard in 1940 is another. See Russell Weigley, *History of the United States Army* (New York: Macmillan, 1967), pp.229–230, 427–428. Informal election, however, continues on the battlefield. "In a battle crisis, a majority of Americans present will respond to any man who has the will and the brains to give them a clear, intelligent order. They will follow the lowest ranking man present if he obviously knows what he is doing and is morally the master of the situation, but they will not obey a chuckle-head if he has nothing in his favor but his rank."; S.L.A. Marshall, *The Armed Forces Officer* (Washington, DC: Department of Defense, 1975), p. 192.

In most armies and navies, including in large measure the American, officers form a caste: relationships within this group have a qualitatively different character from relationships between officers and men. Officers often eat separately (at least in garrison, where there is an officer's club or mess), and are expected to socialize apart from their men. Officers are held to peculiarly strict codes of honor; an officer will find his career ruined by the writing of one or two bad checks, a drunken driving violation, or even (in some cases) indiscreet sexual adventures. There is a double standard, openly acknowledged, and it does not work to the advantage of the officer.

There are perquisities, of course, most noticeably better pay, but above all formally expressed deference: salutes and the use of the word "sir" (itself a vaguely aristocratic term) in addressing a superior officer. In return, officers are expected to show conspicuous physical courage, to accept risks that their men will not or at least will not without seeing someone else go first.[30] At a certain level, it is acceptable for the average soldier to be a bit of a coward – officers and sergeants exist to supply the incentives (be they of fear or material inducement) to force him to his duty. Only an officer's sense of honor, however, keeps him at the front and, by and large, only shared risk can validate leadership.

The ideal relationship between officer and man is, in most armies, a paternalistic one. In the World War II German Army, for example, officers were encouraged to address their men as "Kinder," or "children," and this despite the fact that the officer was often considerably younger than the men he led. An officer's duties include a measure of solicitude for all aspects of his men's lives.[31] One of this century's most successful commander, Sir William Slim, put it to his young officers this way:

> I tell you, *as officers*, that you will not eat, sleep, smoke, sit down or lie down until your soldiers have had a chance to do these things. If you will hold to this, they will follow you to the ends of the earth. If you do not, I will *break you in front of your regiments*. (Emphasis in the original.)[32]

William L. Hauser, a former colonel in the U.S. Army, juxtaposed Slim's notion of leadership with that of Commander Lloyd Bucher of the ill-fated

[30] Keegan, *The Face of Battle*, pp.189–192. For a detailed comparison of officers and enlisted men, see Charles C. Moskos, *The American Enlisted Man* (New York: Russell Sage Foundation, 1970), pp.38–62.

[31] This is discussed (if not indeed hammered home) in Department of the Army, *Military Leadership*, ch. 2.

[32] William L. Hauser, "The Will To Fight," Sam C. Sarkesian, ed., *Combat Effectiveness: Cohesion, Stress, and the Volunteer Military* (Beverly Hills: Sage, 1980), p.193.

Pueblo, an American electronic-intelligence ship captured by the North Koreans during the Vietnam war. This contrast is quite revealing.

> As told in his memoirs, Bucher was opposed to the social separation of officers and men, perhaps as a product of his own penurious upbringing and resentment at the elitism of some of his Navy peers. In Hawaii, while the ill-fated *Pueblo* was being refitted for its reconnaissance mission off the North Korean coast, Bucher participated in drinking parties with his sailors. He explained without embarrassment that he regarded such camaraderie as beneficial to shipboard teamwork.
>
> The reckoning came when Bucher was deciding whether to try outrunning the enemy gunboats firing on his ship. When the helmsman refused to obey his orders to increase speed, Bucher apparently realized (although he does not spell it out) that he lacked the moral authority to demand resistance unto death. He then himself emotionally collapsed into submission to the enemy. This harsh judgment of his behavior on the quarterdeck of the *Pueblo* takes nothing away from his subsequent record of courage as a prisoner. He was personally a brave man, but nonetheless a victim of his own previous abdication of the leader's lonely role.[33]

The requirements of a mixture of solicitude and distance match, in fact, those of the true aristocrat, who at once cares for his social inferiors while maintaining a psychological distance from, indeed, superiority to them. What is described above as the ethic of the officer has outlasted the formal democratization of the officer corps in most countries. It has long been argued that professionalism is the antithesis of *ancien regime* style armies, and in some measure this is true: the professional's authority is legitimated by expertise, not birth or charisma. In this view, the emergence of modern professionalism, particularly in democratic armies, respresents a rejection of feudal relationships and organization. In fact, however, military professionalism represented a synthesis of aristocratic leadership and technical expertise. The reforms of the pre-revolutionary French Army in the early 1780s for example – reforms which laid the tactical and doctrinal groundwork for the stunning victories of Napoleon – *increased* the proportion of aristocratic blood required for officership. Somewhat similar changes occurred in the Prussian Army after 1806, and in the British Army at the same time.[34] The melioration of discipline advocated by Tocqueville and

---

[33] *ibid.*

[34] In neither army did massive social reform (change in the composition of the officer corps) accompany tactical and organizational reform. See Eliot A. Cohen, *Citizens and Soldiers* (Ithaca: Cornell University Press, 1985), pp.50–55.

discussed above was in fact first implemented by officers in aristocratic armies, specifically those of France and Great Britain.

The aristocratic pattern of military organization has, if anything, been enhanced by the development of professional noncommissioned officer corps, the sergeant class which provides the backbone of most European armies. This creates in most armies yet another caste, with its own peculiar perquisites and requirements. While there is movement between castes (upward, that is, for, as in the aristocratic world, it is virtually unthinkable that a noble could become a peasant) they remain well-defined.

Few armies have been run along democratic or even quasi-democratic lines (using the word in the Tocquevillean sense). The Romans, to be sure, drew no sharp distinction between the officer class and the noncommissioned officers, mixing the two in one group (the centurions), who, like their common soldier counterparts, lived under one rigorous code of discipline. And indeed, an alternative means of constructing an officer class along what a sociologist of American class structure, Digby Baltzell, calls "democratic elitist" as opposed to aristocratic lines, does exist. The officer corps of the Israeli army combines an informality of relations between officers and men (including use of first names) with military efficiency. Israel, however, is a special case.[35] In its small size and the gravity of the threats it faces, it resembles nothing so much as the Athenian democracy of ancient Greece. Israel's military system is that of a militia, which embraces virtually the whole able-bodied male population (and a large portion of the younger female population as well). Service in it is virtually synonymous with citizenship. Such a system, appealing as it is to democratic states, does not generally meet their strategic (as opposed to their ideological) needs. In the case of the United States, for example, a true militia system would provide at once too large and too inefficient a force for the military commitments it must meet. It must rely, therefore, on armed forces led by a cadre of career officers, with ranks filled either by volunteers or conscripts, and thus it faces the problems described here.

In most modern armies, even officers who do not come from military families, or from a traditional aristocracy, must adapt to the aristocratic mores of an officer class, and it is here that Tocqueville again offers us instructive insights. The glue of an officer corps is its sense of honor. This is so for a number of reasons: the crudest (but perhaps the most important) is that men are held to battle either through fear or the inspiration of their officers; but officers (who often must act independently) need other motivations to keep the battleline steady.[36] Even today, young American officers are constantly reminded that their standards of integrity and

[35] Yigal Allon, *The Making of Israel's Army* (New York: Universe Books, 1970), pp.249–269.
[36] Keegan, *The Face of Battle*.

selflessness must be higher than those of their men and, indeed, of society at large, which brings us to Tocqueville's discussion of the problem of honor.

Tocqueville's discussion of the subject appears in Volume II, Part III of *Democracy in America*, and he begins by distinguishing between honor and "simple notions of right and wrong." Honor is by far the more potent force:

> Honor, in times of the zenith of its power, directs men's wills more than their beliefs, and even when its orders are obeyed without hesitation or complaint, they still feel, by some dim yet powerful instinct, that there exists some more general ancient, and holy law which they sometimes disobey, though they still acknowledge it.[37]

The form of honor with which modern societies are most familiar is aristocratic honor, which is primarily martial and holds military values (daring and fidelity particularly) above all others. American notions of honor are different. Tocqueville says:

> The American will describe as noble and estimable ambition that which our medieval ancestors would have called base cupidity. He would consider as blind and barbarous frenzy that ardor for conquest and warlike spirit which led the latter every day into new battles.[38]

Yet, not only is the sense of honor different in democratic societies, it is weaker than in previous times, and progressively deteriorating. The reason for this is that a notion of honor answers the need of particular groups, and since the nature of democracy is to level man down and to atomize society, honor serves no particular purpose. As proof of this observation, one can offer a contemporary *instrumental* defense of the American officer's code of honor:

> That is why there is such extreme emphasis on the imperative of personal honor in the military officer: not only the future of our arms but the well-being of our people depend upon a constant reaffirmation and strengthening of public faith in the virtue and trustworthiness of the officer body. Should that faith flag and finally fail, the citizenry would be reluctant to commit its young people to any military endeavor, however grave the emergency.[39]

---

[37] Tocqueville, *Democracy in America*, vol. 2, pt. 3, ch. 18, p.616.
[38] *ibid.*, p.626.
[39] Marshall, *Armed Forces Officer*, p.1.

Although Tocqueville does not spell this out, the implications for standing armies in democratic societies is obvious. Their officer corps will, over time, find themselves caught by pressures to conform to the standards of civil society: should they yield, they will diminish the competence and distinctiveness of their organizations; should they resist, they risk isolation. The result of the latter is either ostracism and ridicule, or interference in the intimate workings of the military.[40]

These pressures have operated on the American military, particularly since the end of World War II, when it finally assumed an importance (and indeed, a sheer size) unprecedented in American history. In a variety of ways – through the increased use of women, the virtual abolition of traditional barracks life, and the development of educational norms comparable to those of the business world – the American military finds itself uncertain of its exceptionalism. Indeed, the reaction in some quarters is simply to deny the uniqueness of the military function and social structure. The result has been a lingering and as yet unresolved crisis of identity and self-confidence in the American officer corps.[41]

TOCQUEVILLE AND THE STUDY OF WAR

The foregoing suggests only some of the avenues of inquiry that open to us when we adopt the Tocquevillean approach to the study of war. Indeed, it is this article's main purpose to suggest that we undertake such a study, beginning with a consideration of Tocqueville's writings on the subject of war. Many commentators have remarked on the curious paucity of critical studies of Tocqueville as a political philosopher; there are to my knowledge virtually none on Tocqueville as a military thinker.

This is not to suggest that a Tocquevillean approach by itself is adequate, for it is not. Tocqueville did not occupy himself with questions of strategy – the application of force for political ends – although he was familiar with them. His main works dealt primarily with domestic politics, with questions of foreign policy merely hovering on the periphery of his investigations. In this regard Tocqueville was not unusual, for most students of military affairs, historians and political scientists, statesmen and military leaders, concentrate on either one or the other aspect of war: strategy or military institutions.

The study of military politics properly consists of at least three subfields: strategy, institutions, and civil-military relations. All three are interrelated,

---

[40] I differ from Huntington in describing the military ethos as aristocratic, where he calls it conservative. The implied tensions between officer and society are, if anything, stronger in the former view. See Moskos, *American Enlisted Man*, pp.8–9, for a discussion of the Doolittle Board reforms, which addressed the caste issue directly.

[41] See Margiotta, *Changing World*.

and history suggests that some of the worst mistakes in the conduct of war emerge from the concoction of a strategy that is out of harmony with institutions and civil-military relations, or from military institutions and patterns of civil-military relations inimical to the sound conduct of war.[42]

An example of the former is the Dardanelles campaign of 1915–1916 conducted by Britain against Turkey. Strategically it made excellent sense, for it offered the opportunity to knock out in quick succession the two major allies (Turkey and Austria-Hungary) of Britain's enemy Germany, to influence several as yet uncommitted states (Rumania and Bulgaria), and to restore communications with Russia. Yet the campaign failed because military institutions had not adapted to the demands of amphibious warfare, and because the central defense organization could not allocate military resources to support the campaign in a speedy and sensible manner. Moreover, the unresolved strategic differences between soldiers and statesmen – in fact, their profound mutual suspicion – precluded the effective implementation of an intelligent strategy.[43]

A more recent example of the second problem – flawed military institutions which obstruct the creation of sensible strategy in the first place – is that of the American effort in Vietnam. A pattern of civil-military relations at once too permissive (in the ground war in South Vietnam) and too restrictive (in the air war over North Vietnam) of military action precluded the formulation of a coherent, let alone an effective strategy. The result was divided command. The commanding general in Vietnam was not the central figure in formulating strategy, since the air war was conducted by an admiral in the Pacific and diplomatic relations by the U.S. ambassador to Vietnam. No single official, civilian or military, held overall responsibility for defeating the Communist insurgency and building the South Vietnamese Army.[44]

The peculiar subdivisions of the strategic studies community in the United States (it is split along disciplinary as well as ideological lines) have prevented this kind of holistic approach to military questions, and it is here that a synthesis of Clausewitz and Tocqueville would aid Americans most. A Tocquevillean analysis of American military dilemmas would point us in directions rather different from those of the current American military debate. The United States today is an overstretched global power, which finds its commitments gradually slipping beyond its capability to meet them.

[42] I make this point in a minor way with reference to the Israeli campaign in Lebanon in 1982: Eliot A. Cohen, "Peace for Galilee: Success or Failure?" *Commentary*, vol. 78 (November 1984), pp.24–30.

[43] The best book on the Dardanelles is still Robert Rhodes James, *Gallipoli* (London: Batsford, 1965).

[44] For a recent inside account of the difficulties of strategy-making in Vietnam, see General Bruce Palmer, Jr., *The 25–Year War: America's Military Role in Vietnam* (Lexington: University Press of Kentucky, 1984).

Military reformers within government and outside it search for ways of reestablishing a balance, by suggesting that we devise new doctrines (e.g. maneuver, as opposed to attrition, warefare), developing new weaponry (so-called emerging technologies), or reforming the Joint Chiefs of Staff system.[45]

A Tocquevillean perspective on such matters would lead us down different and more productive paths. Rather than search for central strategic direction through changes in the titles or formal lines of command, for example, a Tocquevillean analyst might consider such institutional reforms as changes in the war college system to foster the creation of a more coherent strategic culture. Rather than search for technological or narrow organizational solutions to the problems posed by limited wars such as Vietnam, he might suggest that we first must understand the difficult questions of civil-military relations they present, and consider ways (e.g., special recruitment policies, attention to the morale problem at home) to ameliorate the difficulties created by wars of this type in the past. In short, a Tocquevillean or, more accurately, a Tocquevillean-Clausewitzian approach would help us understand that questions of civil-military relations, strategy, and institutional impetus are inextricably linked, that institutional pressures may cause strategic difficulties, and vice versa.

Tocqueville thought the Americans peculiarly fortunate in their freedom from worry over their national security, fortunate because the aptitudes and abilities of democracy are peculiarly unsuited for the conduct of strategy and foreign policy more generally. Yet the world which he knew has changed. American liberty is no longer challenged simply by domestic or internal threats, but by external ones, and for better or ill democracy must work within its limitations to meet and overcome them. Tocqueville saw in the peculiar mores and construction of America's civil institutions (jury trial and the New England town meeting, for example) bulwarks of American freedom, freedom threatened by majoritarian tyranny and the bureaucratic, schoolmaster state. American military reformers must set themselves the task of devising institutional remedies to external threats, threats which are no less pressing, and no less ominous.

Political Science, Harvard University

---

[45] For a good introduction to the military reform debate, see Asa Clark, *et al.*, *The Defense Reform Debate* (Baltimore: Johns Hopkins, 1984).